*Dedicated to
Tony Storey, Headmaster of The Hayfield School,
Doncaster.
For me, he sets the standard by which
headteachers are judged.*

ACKNOWLEDGEMENTS

I should like to thank Richard 'Fairy' Fairclough for suggesting the title; my ever-patient editor and dear friend Jenny Dereham for her continued encouragement and advice; and my wife and family for their forbearance.

'A Parent's Prayer' on page 421 is taken from *The Day Our Teacher Went Batty* (Puffin 2002).

So There!

Our English teacher, Mr Smart,
Says writing English is an art,
That we should always take great care
When spelling words like *wear* and *where*,
Witch and *which* and *fair* and *fare*,
Key and *quay* and *air* and *heir*,
Whet and *wet* and *flair* and *flare*,
Wring and *ring* and *stair* and *stare*,
Him and *hymn* and *their* and *there*,
Whine and *wine* and *pear* and *pare*,
Check and *cheque* and *tare* and *tear*,
Crews and *cruise* and *hare* and *hair*,
Meet and *meat* and *bear* and *bare*,
Knot and *not* and *layer* and *lair*,
Loot and *lute* and *mayor* and *mare*.

Well, frankly, sir, I just don't care!
So there!

CHAPTER ONE

I stared with disbelief at the object in the display cabinet. It took pride of place amidst the shells, pebbles, fronds of dried seaweed, pieces of coloured glass, bits of driftwood and other detritus collected from the beach.

'What do you think?' asked the nun with a great smile on her round, innocent face.

'It's . . . er . . . well . . . er . . . interesting,' was all I could manage to splutter out.

I was at Our Lady of Lourdes Roman Catholic Primary School, the second week of the new school term, to inspect the English teaching. I had been a school inspector now in the great county of Yorkshire for three years and each week brought something new and unexpected. And I was certainly not expecting what I saw in the display cabinet that cold September morning.

'You see,' explained Sister Marie-Thérèse, the headmistress, 'I like to mount a colourful display in the first week.'

'I'm sorry?' I said, my eyes still glued to a certain object.

'Mount a display,' she said, 'to make the entrance hall that little bit brighter and more cheerful. This year, I have decided it would be about the seashore. At the end of last term we took the junior children, Mrs McPhee and I, on a school trip to the East Coast. We visited Whitby, climbed all the steps up to the abbey, called in at the Captain Cook Museum and had some lovely long walks along the beach. I asked the children to pick

1

up anything of interest which they found on the seashore—shells and pebbles, of course, but also any unusual or interesting items which might have been washed up. No old bottles, though, I had to put my foot down about bottles.'

'I see,' I said, still staring incredulously at the object resting in the centre of the display cabinet.

'And they came back with so many fascinating things.'

'So I see,' I murmured.

'You'd be surprised what gets washed up on a beach.'

No I wouldn't, I thought to myself.

'We've got all manner of different shells and strangely shaped pebbles, polished glass and some amazingly coloured seaweed. Mrs McPhee found some pieces of jet on the beach. It's fossilised Monkey Puzzle Tree, you know. It's quite rare, I'm told. They still make jewellery out of jet. Not that I wear jewellery, of course!' I continued to stare at the display as the nun chattered away. Words failed me. 'It was all the rage in Victorian times.'

'I'm sorry?'

'Jet. I think Queen Victoria took to wearing it after the death of Prince Albert and it started a trend. Of course, it's not so popular today. Oh, and one child found some fossils near the cliffs and another a dried starfish and there's a little seahorse there, see. All sorts of flotsam and jetsam that was washed ashore. Such intriguing bits and bobs. So we have a nice little collection to stimulate the children's discussion and their writing.'

'Sister,' I said, 'about the flotsam and jetsam, the . . . er . . . bits and bobs.'

'And do you know what that is?' she said

pointing to the centre of the display.

'What?' I asked, with a sinking heart.

'That little shiny orange pebble, at the front.'

I sighed with relief. 'No, I'm afraid, I don't.'

'That's amber. Sometimes little pieces of amber are washed up on the beach but only along certain parts of the coast and it's very difficult to find. It's fossilised resin from trees, you know, millions of years old and quite valuable, I believe. It starts off in the Baltic and is washed across the ocean and ends up on the East Coast. That's used for jewellery too,' the nun burbled on. 'Sometimes you find little insects fossilised inside. Mrs McPhee—she's my deputy by the way—met a delightful man on the beach, used to be the curator at the museum at York, I believe, who lived just along the coast at Runswick Bay, and he showed her—'

'Sister,' I began.

'Yes, Mr Phinn?' She looked directly at me, smiling.

'About the display.'

'Yes?' She stared up with a wide and innocent expression.

'Well, Sister, there is—' I opened my mouth to continue but lost courage. 'Oh, nothing.'

Someone was going to have to tell her, I thought, but it certainly wasn't going to be me.

'Last week,' she babbled on, 'the older children wrote some delightful little poems and descriptions, which I've mounted on the wall around the display. Don't you think it looks wonderful?'

'Yes, indeed, wonderful,' I murmured, my eyes still riveted on the offending object in the cabinet.

'I want the school to look really nice for when

3

the bishop visits on Monday.'

'The bishop's coming on Monday?' I asked in a doom-laden voice.

'Yes, he's coming to talk to the children about their First Holy Communion. Last year he brought his crosier to show them. One child wrote to him afterwards: "Thank you for coming to see us, Bishop Michael. I now know just what a real crook looks like." We did laugh, Mrs McPhee and me.'

Just then a small boy approached the headmistress and tugged on her cloak. At last the nun stopped her babbling, and bent down to hear what the child wanted to tell her. I grabbed at my chance to get help.

'Sister,' I said quickly, 'I've forgotten to sign in. I'll go and do it now.'

'Oh, don't worry about that now, Mr Phinn,' said the nun. 'You can do it at morning break.'

'No, no, I had better do it now,' I insisted. 'I'll just pop into the office.'

Without waiting for a reply, I shot across the hall and into the school office, making the school secretary jump with surprise.

'Quick!' I hissed. 'Can you come with me?'

'Pardon?' she replied.

'Can you come with me now, it's urgent!'

'I'm in the middle of checking the dinner money,' she told me. 'It's extremely inconvenient.'

'It really is *very* important,' I told her.

'But I'm half way through—'

'Please,' I begged.

'Oh very well,' she said, shaking her head, 'but I don't know what can be so urgent.'

'You'll see in a minute,' I said, and popped my head out of the office to see where Sister

4

Marie-Thérèse was. Fortunately the headmistress had moved down the corridor with the small boy who was showing her a picture on the wall.

'Look,' I whispered, pointing to the manifestation in the display cabinet.

There was a sharp intake of breath. 'Oh dear,' groaned the school secretary, raising her hand to her neck and wincing visibly.

'Do you see what I mean?'

'I do,' she mumbled. 'However did *that* get in there?'

'I suppose Sister must have put it in, without realising what it is. Perhaps you ought to tell her.'

'Tell her?' she hissed.

'What it is.'

'Me?' she exclaimed. 'Why me? You're the English inspector, you're the one who's supposed to be good with words.'

'No, no, I couldn't possibly do it. It would be much better coming from you.'

'Mr Phinn,' she said, looking me straight in the eyes, 'I am prepared to do most things as a school secretary but explaining to a nun what a condom is, is not one of them.'

'Well, I certainly can't,' I said.

'And what are you two talking about?' came a cheerful voice from behind us.

The school secretary and I swung round together to find Sister Marie-Thérèse, with that sweet innocent expression on her round face.

'We were just looking at your lovely display, Sister,' I replied feebly.

'I'm very pleased with it,' trilled the nun. 'I am sure Bishop Michael will get quite a surprise when he comes on Monday.'

'I bet he will,' I said *sotto voce*.

'It's very nice, Sister,' said the school secretary, giving a watery smile. There was a nervous red rash creeping up her neck. Then she turned to me and gave me a conspiratorial look. 'I'll see to it,' she whispered. 'Just keep her occupied.'

'Perhaps we should make a start, Sister,' I said pleasantly.

'Yes, yes, of course, Mr Phinn,' said the nun. 'The children are all very excited about meeting you.'

I followed the headmistress as she headed for the junior department with a veritable spring in her step. When I glanced back, I saw the school secretary still staring at the display cabinet like a hungry cat watching a tank full of goldfish.

At the end of the corridor was a large plaster statue of Our Lady of Lourdes. She had a pale, gentle face with downcast eyes, a golden halo, and her hands were pressed together in prayer. In the long blue veil and white cloak and with an innocent expression, the figure did not look dissimilar to Sister Marie-Thérèse. I was brought up short and gasped out loud. On a plinth, beneath the statue, was the instruction:

As you pass Our Lady,
Say an ejaculatory prayer.

'Whatever is an ejaculatory prayer, Sister?' I asked the nun, who had turned back to me when she heard my gasp.

'"Our Lady of Lourdes pray for us."'

'I'm sorry?'

'That's an ejaculatory prayer, Mr Phinn,' said

6

the nun. 'Just a small appeal for Our Lady to watch over us and keep us safe.'

'I see,' I said, my mind whirling back to the object in the display cabinet.

The junior classroom was warm and welcoming. The children, aged between nine and eleven, looked up eagerly as we entered.

'Good morning, children,' said the headmistress with jovial earnestness.

'Good morning, Sister Marie-Thérèse. Good morning, everybody,' chorused the children.

'Have they been good, Mrs McPhee?' the nun asked the teacher.

'Need you ask, Sister?' replied her colleague, scanning the sea of faces before her, with an expression which defied contradiction.

Mrs McPhee was a plump woman with a thick fuzz of white hair and the pale eyes of a piranha. She wore a tight-fitting, wheat-coloured turtleneck sweater, heavy brown tweed pleated skirt, thick woollen stockings the colour of mud and substantial brogues. Around her neck hung a single rope of large blue beads. I could tell she was the 'I-stand-no-nonsense' sort of teacher.

'This is my indispensable deputy headteacher, Mr Phinn,' said the nun, giving her colleague the fullest and most charming of smiles. 'She's worth her weight in gold.'

'Oh, Sister, really!' said Mrs McPhee, laughing in an enthusiastic, horsy sort of way.

'Now, children,' said the headmistress, 'I told you that we would be having a very special visitor this morning and here he is. Mr Phinn is a school inspector, here to look at all the lovely work you have been doing.' The nun turned in my direction,

7

rested a small hand on my arm and said, in a lower voice, 'This group, Mr Phinn, is one of the junior classes. There's quite a range of age and ability, as you will see. The children have been busy composing prayers and when Bishop Michael comes on Monday, we shall have a very special assembly when some of them will read out their efforts.'

'That sounds splendid,' I said, wondering what sort of mood the bishop would be in if he had seen what I had seen in the display in the entrance hall.

'Now, Mr Phinn,' continued Sister, 'would you like to have a little look around the classroom, perhaps listen to some of the children read and examine the work they have been doing and then—'

'There's not much written work in their books,' interrupted Mrs McPhee in one of those deep, loud voices possessed by market traders. 'But you will not be expecting to see a lot, will you, Mr Phinn, this being the start of term?' She gave me a look which said: 'Disagree with me, if you dare!'

'No,' I assured her. 'I shall not be expecting to see a lot.'

'Well, that's just as well,' said Mrs McPhee, her face relaxing, 'because they haven't done much yet—just the prayers they are working on.'

'I'll leave you to it then,' simpered Sister. 'I have paperwork to attend to.'

As she headed for the door, the headmistress stopped in her tracks and peered out of the window. I followed her gaze to see the school secretary creeping past in the direction of the dustbins. She was wearing bright yellow rubber gloves and a pained expression and she was carrying something, at arm's length, on a shovel.

'Whatever is Mrs Sanders up to?' said Sister to Mrs McPhee. 'Perhaps the school cat has . . .' and she mouthed 'mouse' to her colleague before leaving the room.

The first pupil I approached was very keen to tell me about the books he liked to read. He was a small boy with shiny blond hair, clear blue eyes and a face full of freckles. He told me his name was Alexander.

'I expect all your pals call you Alex,' I said to him.

'No they don't, actually,' he told me seriously. 'They call me Alexander. I don't like my name shortened.'

'No,' I said smiling, 'neither do I.' Connie, the caretaker at the Staff Development Centre, sometimes referred to me as 'Gerv'. It sounded like a brand of cheap petrol. 'And how are you today, Alexander?' I asked.

'Well, I'm not a hundred per cent,' he told me. 'But I don't like to miss school.'

'And what is your reading book about?'

'Dinosaurs. I'm really into dinosaurs,' the boy explained solemnly.

'Are you?'

'Oh yes. They're incredible creatures. I know quite a lot about dinosaurs. Do you know much about dinosaurs, Mr Phinn?'

'No, not a lot.'

'Do you know which was the longest?' asked the boy, looking me confidently in the eye.

'I'm not entirely sure,' I said and I wasn't. 'Is it the brontosaurus?'

'No. It's the diplodocus. As long as two double-decker buses, end to end. Do you know which was

9

the biggest?'

'Was *that* the brontosaurus?'

'Wrong again. It was the brachiosaurus. It was taller than two giraffes and as heavy as eight full-grown elephants. Mind-blowing isn't it? They weighed about thirty tonnes. Do you know which was the smallest?'

'I've no idea,' I told him.

'Compsognathus. It was about the size of a chicken. You'll not know which was the fastest, then?'

'No, I'm afraid not.'

'Gallimimus,' said the boy. 'It was a bit like an ostrich and could run over thirty miles an hour.'

'Really. I do know which was the fiercest, though,' I said.

'Which one?' The boy looked up at me intently with the clear blue eyes.

'The tyrannosaurus rex.'

The boy smiled and shook his head. 'Wrong again, I'm afraid. It was the deinonychus. It had huge slashing claws on each back foot and a set of killer teeth.' He made a gnashing movement, then clacked his teeth together to emphasise his point. 'They hunted in packs. Its name means "terrible claw". A lot of people think the tyrannosaurus rex was the fiercest,' he said leaning back in his chair, 'but they're wrong.'

'Which was the last dinosaur to live on Earth?' I asked him. I was genuinely interested. Very often the questions I asked pupils were pseudo questions. I already knew the answers and was merely seeing if the children did. It was very refreshing to ask questions for which I did not know the answers.

'Now that's a tricky one, Mr Phinn.' He sucked

in his breath and thought for a moment. 'Most people would say it was the triceratops, but we can't be sure. They lived about sixty-five million years ago, give or take a million. Shall I read you a bit from my book?'

'Yes, I think that's a very good idea,' I said.

So the boy read with great gusto from a thick tome. He stopped at intervals to tell me additional fascinating facts about the great creatures and to point out interesting features in the pictures.

'You're a very good reader as well as being so knowledgeable, Alexander,' I told him.

'Yes, I know,' he said in a matter-of-fact voice. 'And you're a very good listener.'

I smiled and shook my head. I have met many a precocious child in my time but Alexander took the biscuit. 'And when you leave school, I expect you want to work in the Natural History Museum in London, don't you, and be the world expert on dinosaurs?'

'Oh no, Mr Phinn, I want to be a solicitor, like my father. There's not much of a future in dinosaurs.'

The next child, although younger than Alexander, was a large girl with saucer eyes and thick black hair tied in great bunches. Her thumb was stuck in her mouth. I had intended asking her to read me a few sentences from her book but this turned out to be not much more than a picture book. Clearly she had some special needs and experienced difficulty with her reading. The page she was looking at depicted a large black horse galloping across a river. Beneath it was written: 'The horse is in the water.' When I asked her what it said, she looked at me for a moment, regarded me as if I were simple-minded, removed the thumb and informed me bluntly, 'It sez: "T'nag's in t'beck!"'

While I was listening to another child read, I heard Mrs McPhee's threateningly low voice somewhere behind us.

'No, Alexander, I said a prayer.'

'But, miss, I want to write about my holidays,' appealed the child.

'Well, you are not going to,' said the teacher sharply. 'You are to write a prayer like everyone else and that is that.'

'But, Mrs McPhee,' persisted the child, 'I really don't want to write a prayer.'

'Alexander,' snapped the teacher, 'everyone is writing a prayer. We have looked at prayers, listened to prayers and read prayers. I have spent a full lesson telling you how to write a prayer. We are not writing about your holidays. When the bishop comes in on Monday and we are in assembly reading out our prayers starting "Thank you, God"—it would sound rather strange your reading about your holidays, "Last summer we went to Blackpool", wouldn't it?'

'Actually, we didn't go to Blackpool, miss,' the child told her. 'We went in a *gite* in France.'

'I'm not in the slightest bit interested where you went, Alexander,' interrupted the teacher sharply. 'Now get on with your prayer. Chop! Chop!'

'But, miss—' began the boy, in a wheedling tone of voice.

Mrs McPhee drew a deep exasperated breath. 'No buts, Alexander, off you go. "Thank you, God!"'

But the child wouldn't let it lie. 'You see, Mrs

12

McPhee, I don't know whether I believe in God.'

'Not believe in God!' exclaimed the teacher, heaving her ample bosom, her pale eyes now ablaze.

'I think I believe in the "Big Bang" theory like my father,' said the child, quite undaunted by the teacher's dramatic display of outrage.

'Alexander Maxwell-Smith,' said Mrs McPhee, slowly and in a hushed and slightly sinister voice, 'if you do not start your prayer "Thank you, God" in the next few seconds, there *will* be a "Big Bang!"'

I turned round to look at Alexander. The boy, shoulders drooping and with a weary expression on his small face, slouched in his chair, sighed and took up his pen. Mrs McPhee gave me an exasperated look and shook her head. 'Not believe in God, indeed,' she mouthed.

A little while later, having heard more children read and looked at some of the prayers, I arrived back at Alexander's desk. His prayer was written in large neat handwriting. 'Thank you, God,' it started. Good, I thought, he had decided to do as he was told. Then I read on: 'Thank you, God, for my holidays. This year we stayed in a gite in Vence (that's in the south of France) and had a most enjoyable time.' He had followed this with an account of his holiday which sounded anything but 'most enjoyable'. His mother, he wrote, had got sunburnt and looked like a cooked lobster, his father had been ill for three days with his head down the lav, his brother had fallen over and sprained his wrist and his little sister had got lost and they had all ended up at the police station. His eventful account concluded with: 'But in spite of all the problems, I had a good time and thank you

13

God, for my holidays. Amen.'

I left before the 'Big Bang' which would surely occur when his teacher read Alexander's prayer, and headed for the infant department. I had a vision of the boy garrotted by the blue beads or suffocated in the heaving bosom of the formidable Mrs McPhee. Passing through the entrance hall, I stopped by the display and, much to my relief, saw it was bereft of the offending article.

In the next class, I discovered Miss Reece, a young woman with sandy-coloured hair tied back in a pony tail and wearing a bright yellow mohair jumper and pale cream slacks. She sat with the children clustered around her and was reading them a story from a large coloured picture book which was displayed on an easel beside her. One small girl sat on her knee. I crept to the back of the classroom, perched on a small melamine chair and listened.

'I can see the little lamb bleating in the meadow,' read the teacher slowly and dramatically. She pointed at the picture. 'Can you see the little lamb, children? Isn't he lovely and woolly?' The children nodded vigorously. Miss Reece continued, 'I can see the little calf mooing for his mother.'

'He's black and white, miss,' volunteered the child sitting on the teacher's knee.

'He is, isn't he, Chloë.' The teacher read on. 'I can see the little foal frisking in the field. "Frisking" is an unusual word, isn't it, children?'

'It means kicking up its legs, Miss Reece,' called out a child sitting cross-legged in front of her.

'Well done, Martin. It does mean that.'

Another child raised a hand. 'Miss! Miss!' she cried.

14

'In a moment, Caitlin. We will be able to talk about the animals when I've finished reading the book.'

'He's sweet, isn't he, miss?' said the little girl sitting on the teacher's knee.

'He is very sweet, Chloë,' agreed the teacher, 'but just listen, dear, there's a good girl, otherwise we will never get to the end.' She turned the page. 'I can see the little piglet grunting in the grass.'

A small boy, with a shock of red hair and a runny nose, who was sitting directly in front of me, began snorting and grunting like a pig.

'We don't need the animal noises, John-Paul, thank you very much,' said the teacher with a slight edge to her voice. 'Just look at the pictures and listen to the words.' She turned the page.

'Miss! Miss!' cried little Caitlin again.

'What did I say, Caitlin?' asked the teacher. 'Just be patient, you can tell me in a minute.' She read on. 'I can see the little chicks chirping in the farmyard.' The small child sitting on the teacher's knee leaned forward and looked intently at the picture of the bright yellow chicks in the picture. 'They look as if they have just hatched out of their eggs, don't they, children?' said the teacher. 'All soft and fluffy and golden.'

Chloë looked at the picture and then at the teacher and then back at the picture. After a moment she began stroking the teacher's bright yellow mohair jumper.

'Do you know, miss,' she said in that loud, confident voice only possessed by young children, 'you look as if you've just been laid.'

Miss Reece turned crimson and I nearly fell off the chair, laughing.

'Miss! Miss!' Caitlin's voice now sounded desperate.

'What is it?' asked the teacher, attempting to gain her composure.

'Miss,' moaned the child, 'I've been sick in my jumper. I've been trying to tell you.'

I watched Miss Reece with great admiration as she produced a black bin-liner from her desk drawer, stripped the child of her jumper like a poacher skinning a rabbit and deposited the soiled article of clothing inside without so much as an iota of vomit touching anything or anybody. The teacher then expertly tied a tight knot in the bin liner and dropped it next to her desk. 'We'll let your mummy take that home after school, shall we, Caitlin?' she said pleasantly. Miss Reece then took the child's hand and asked me, 'Will you be all right on your own for a few minutes, Mr Phinn? I'm just going to take Caitlin to the school office. Sometimes one child being sick starts all the others off. There are plenty of bin liners in my top drawer, if you need them.'

Later that morning, while the children were busy writing short poems and descriptions about the animals, I listened to a series of very competent little readers who had a great deal to say for themselves. One little girl, with apple-red cheeks, was particularly chatty.

'Are you a good speller, Mr Phinn?' she asked.

'I am a very, very good speller,' I teased. 'I can spell any word.'

'Any word?' she gasped.

'Any word at all. I'm the world's best speller. Would you like to tell me a word and I will spell it for you?'

16

'Yes, but you're a grown-up,' she said, folding her small arms across her chest. 'Grown-ups can spell words.' She thought for a moment. 'Can you spell my name?'

'Of course, I can,' I replied, but knew that this might prove tricky. I have met children with a range of unusual, not to say bizarre names, as well as names which were not spelt as they sound. There was Kristofer, Curston, Mykell, Charleen, Kaylee, Heyleigh, Kylee, Barby, Blasé (pronounced Blaze), Gooey (spelt Guy) and a child called Portia but spelt Porsche for, as the teacher explained to me with a wry smile, the girl's father had always wanted a Porsche car. In one school there were two sets of twins from the same family, aged ten and eleven respectively, named after great tragic heroines: Cleopatra and Cassandra, Desdemona and Dido. Then there were the brother and sister, Sam and Ella which, when said at speed, sounded like food poisoning.

'My name is Roisin,' said the little girl bringing me back to the present. 'It's Irish. It means "little rose".'

How very apt, I thought, looking at the rosy cheeks. I spelled it correctly and pulled a smug expression.

'And my brother's name's Niall.'

I got that one right, as well.

'My sisters are called Siobhaun and Nuala.'

I was doing really well now and obviously impressing my little interrogator who wasn't to know about my Irish background.

'And there's my brother, Rory and remember, Mr Phinn, he has eight letters in his name. And my cousin, Orlah, who has nine in hers.'

17

I buried my head in my hands in mock helplessness and heard the child giggle uncontrollably. Then Roisin spelt the names for me, speaking the letters loudly and slowly as if I was hard of hearing.

'R-u-a-r-a-i-d-h and O-r-f-h-l-a-i-t-h,' she told me. 'Easy-peasy!'

*   *   *

I stood with Sister Marie-Thérèse in the entrance hall at the end of the morning.

'Well thank you, Sister,' I said. 'I shall send in my report in a few days' time, but everything appears to be fine. The children read extremely well, the writing is above average, the atmosphere in the school is positive and the teaching very good.' I looked in the direction of the display cabinet. 'And the display . . . is wonderful.'

'"How beautiful upon the mountains are the feet of him who bringeth good tidings,"' said the nun.

My attention, however, had been caught by the school secretary standing in the doorway of the office. She gave me a vigorous thumbs-up sign.

'I'm sorry, what did you say, Sister?'

'Isaiah, Mr Phinn.'

'Who?'

'From the Bible. Isaiah,' said the nun. '"How beautiful upon the mountains are the feet of him who bringeth good tidings."'

'Yes, of course, Sister.'

'Now, that's most odd,' said the headmistress, resting a small hand on my arm. 'I think I am either going mad or we have a ghost.'

'A ghost?' I repeated.

'Well, I'm sure I put a little coloured balloon which one of the children found on the beach in Whitby in my display and it's just disappeared into thin air.'

'A balloon?' I sounded like an echo.

'Don't you recall seeing a pink balloon in my display this morning?' asked the nun with a puzzled expression.

'No, Sister,' I said firmly, 'there was no balloon in your display. I would have remembered. No, no, there was definitely no balloon.'

CHAPTER TWO

I was still smiling later that afternoon as I began to draft the report on Our Lady of Lourdes. The office was unusually peaceful for that time of day, for my three colleagues, with whom I shared the cramped and cluttered room, had not yet returned from their school visits. I was grateful for a bit of peace and quiet. There would be precious little of it when Sidney and David arrived.

Sidney Clamp, the larger-than-life inspector for Creative and Visual Arts, and David Pritchard, the Mathematics, PE and Games inspector who could talk for Wales (and frequently did), were witty, warm, clever and generous people but it was quite impossible to concentrate on anything if they were together in the office. They had worked together for many years and were good friends, but when they started bouncing insults off each other, scoring points, bemoaning, arguing, philosophising and regaling anyone within earshot with anecdotes and opinions, nothing could be done. Sidney and David were like a comedy duo.

The final member of our team, who put us to shame with her razor-sharp intelligence, superhuman efficiency and the tidiness of her desk, was Dr Geraldine Mullarkey, in charge of Science and Technology. Gerry liked to keep herself to herself and spent as little time as possible in the office. She was a single parent with a young child and tended to hide herself away at the Staff Development Centre at lunchtimes to write her reports and letters, and catch up with all the other paper work at home in the evenings. Down the corridor was our team leader, Dr Harold Yeats, the Senior Inspector, and next to his room was the small office where Julie, our secretary, presided.

I turned back to my report and read my first sentence: 'The school is a bright, welcoming and cheerful building, enhanced by interesting and colourful displays.' Immediately my mind went back to the morning's drama and I wondered again just what Bishop Michael would have said and done if he had caught sight of the condom nestling amongst the display which Sister Marie-Thérèse most surely would have shown him as she had me. It would probably have set his mitre askew. I threw back my head and began to laugh out loud.

A voice interrupted my reverie. 'Someone's in a good mood.'

Julie tottered in, cradling a large mug of coffee in her hands. I watched her as she carefully set down the mug in front of me and then perched on the end of my desk. She looked as if she was off to a disco in her bright red top, incredibly short,

20

tight-fitting black skirt, long, dangling metallic earrings and the ridiculously high-heeled patent leather shoes she was so fond of wearing. Julie, with her bubbly blonde hair, cheerful good humour and incessant chatter, was guaranteed to brighten up the dullest of days.

She had left school at sixteen with few qualifications and had secured a position in the post room at County Hall doing general and largely undemanding jobs: franking letters, filing, photocopying, taking messages. Then, when a flu epidemic had hit County Hall and half the ancillary staff had been off ill, Julie had been dragooned in temporarily to man the telephones and take on some extra duties. That was when she had come to the attention of Harold Yeats. Harold had been greatly impressed by the young woman's verve, energy and cheerful good nature, and by her willingness to tackle whatever came her way. She was funny, forthright and strong-minded. Just the sort of person, Harold had thought, to cope with the school inspectors who were reputedly not the easiest of people with whom to work. This was a couple of years before I had come to County Hall and the inspectors' secretary at the time, I had been told, was the rather serious and nervous Miss—'a martyr to my joints'—Pruitt. She was due to retire (and not before time from what my colleagues in the office had said) and Harold had persuaded Dr Gore, the Chief Education Officer, to assign Julie to our office as the clerical assistant to learn the ropes. Julie had enrolled on a secretarial course, surprised everyone, including herself, by achieving high grades and when Miss Pruitt had retired she had stepped into her shoes,

21

metaphorically speaking, of course. There was no possibility whatsoever of Julie ever wearing a pair of Miss P's sensible court shoes. She was much more at home in her red stilettos.

Not only was Julie cheerful, hard working and efficient, she was also extremely loyal and highly discreet. Nothing she read in the school reports she had to type, or anything she heard confided over the telephone, ever went outside the office. Her telephone manner sometimes left a little to be desired—she could be as blunt as a sledgehammer but we all thought the world of Julie and valued the work she did.

'So come on, then,' she said now, resting her hands behind her on the desk and leaning back like a model posing for a photograph. 'What's tickled you?'

When I had told her the saga of the nun and the condom she looked at me quizzically. She clearly did not feel it was quite as funny as I. 'You would have thought, in this day and age, she'd have known what a condom was.'

'Julie, she's a *nun*, for goodness sake!' I exclaimed. 'When would a nun come across a condom?'

'I thought everybody knew what one was. You can't get away from them. I mean, my little nephew, Kenny, is only nine and he knows what one is. I overheard him and his friend last week in the garden. The other little boy was telling our Kenny that he'd found a condom on the patio. Our Kenny asked him what a "patio" was. I suppose it's all this sex education at school. We were never told anything.' She stood up and straightened her skirt. 'We were very naïve.' That, I thought to myself, was a trifle difficult to believe. 'We had to find out the facts of life in the corner of the playground and then most of what we learnt wasn't true. We thought you got babies through kissing. What are you staring at?'

'Nothing,' I chuckled. 'You see, Julie, nuns are very innocent and unworldly. They're not like other people.'

'Well, that Sister Brendan at St Bartholomew's is about as innocent and unworldly as Al Capone. I bet *she* knows what a condom is.'

'Yes, I think Sister Brendan would, but she's a rather different kettle of fish. She's worked in the slums of South America and the inner cities and has seen more of life than most of us. I have an idea the nun at Our Lady of Lourdes has spent all of her childhood in rural Ireland and all her adult life in a convent, so she is still one of life's innocents. Her lack of worldly knowledge is quite endearing.'

'I once went as a nun to a fancy dress party,' Julie told me. 'But that long habit got in the way.'

'Got in the way of what?' I asked, dreading what she might answer.

'My dancing. I had to take it off in the end. It was really hot as well and made me itch.'

'Well, I suppose Sister Marie-Thérèse has got used to it by now,' I said. 'And I shouldn't imagine she will be doing much dancing.'

'I couldn't be a nun,' said Julie, examining her long nails.

'No,' I replied, looking at the vision in red and black, 'you couldn't. Well, not in that outfit anyway.'

'What's wrong with this outfit?'

'Oh nothing. It looks . . . er . . . very becoming.'

'It's my power-dressing combination, if you must know. Red and black are strong primary colours, you see. I've just read this magazine article all about it. The clothes you wear say a lot about you and the different colours give off different messages. Red warns of potential danger. Black means strength. It says to people: "Don't you mess with me, mate, or you'll get a smack in the face." If you want to appear really nice, you wear pastel colours, light browns and greens and pale yellows. I've not got any outfits like that.'

Such an assertion really didn't hold water when one thought of the impregnable Mrs McPhee in her tight-fitting wheat-coloured turtleneck sweater, heavy brown skirt, dark woollen stockings and substantial shoes.

'So, why do you want to be power-dressed this afternoon?' I asked. 'Is there something special on?'

'Yes, there is, as a matter of fact. I need to be assertive when I meet Lady Macbeth shortly.'

'Mrs Savage,' I sighed.

'The very same.'

Mrs Brenda Savage, Personal Assistant to Dr Gore, was the bane of Julie's, the inspectors' and most other people's lives. She was a strikingly elegant looking woman of an indeterminate age but could be extremely prickly and unpredictable, and had her long nails in every pie around. We all felt she had been promoted way beyond her intelligence and capabilities. Mrs Savage had a fearsome reputation, an acerbic manner, and could curdle milk with one of her sour stares.

'Why are you seeing Mrs Savage?' I asked.

24

'We've got a meeting on "Health and Safety in the Workplace" and she's been put in charge. Goodness knows why. She's a danger to everyone's health, the stress she causes. Anyway, no sooner has she been given the job, but she's produced this set of wretched guidelines and all the office and ancillary staff are going to have to sit and listen to her giving us one of her endless lectures. She's only been on a one-day course, for goodness sake, and now she thinks she knows everything there is to know about health and safety in the workplace. It'll be the school inspectors' turn next, so you can take that cheesy smile off your face. She sounds like Mussolini in knickers when she gets started, sticking out her chin, stabbing the air with those sharp witch's nails and laying down the law. Anyway, I must be off. The meeting will have started. I'm going to make a dramatic entrance and I'm determined to be really assertive. She's not treating me like something she's discovered on the sole of her designer shoes.'

'I'm surprised you're not in combat trousers and army boots,' I told her, still smiling. 'You sound more aggressive than assertive.'

'Well, that woman brings out the worst in me, she really does,' said Julie. 'When you've finished that report, pop it on my desk and I'll get on with it tomorrow. Oh, and you've had a lot of telephone calls, and I mean a lot. All the details are on the pad in my office. Mostly from people you know but there was a call from a really loud man, nearly deafened me shouting down the phone, wanting to speak to you urgently but he wouldn't leave his name or number. Said he'd call back. See you tomorrow.' With that Julie tottered for the door.

25

I returned to the report. 'The school is a bright, welcoming and cheerful building, enhanced by interesting and colourful displays,' I re-read but got no further. The sound of argumentative voices wafting up from the bottom of the stairs signalled the imminent arrival of two of my colleagues. I threw down my pen.

A moment later Sidney breezed in followed by David. You would be hard pressed to find two people so entirely different in appearance: the one a burly, bearded figure with a thick head of woolly hair, rather like a friendly old lion, the other a small, dark-complexioned man with a close-shaven face and black eyebrows which seemed to fly outwards like wings. As usual, they were in the middle of an animated discussion.

'I might have predicted that you would take a contrary view,' Sidney was saying irritably. He dropped his briefcase on the nearest desk, flopped in a chair and leaned back. 'Good afternoon, Gervase. David is being perverse again.'

'Good afternoon,' I said.

'Yes, good afternoon, Gervase,' said David, hanging up his coat. 'I am not taking a contrary view, Sidney. I have a great deal of sympathy with what you say. I am merely attempting to put things into some sort of perspective.'

'About what?' I asked.

'About art, what else?' sighed David, settling behind his desk. He turned his attention to me. 'He's miffed because the headmaster of West Challerton High School has decided to reduce the amount of time on the curriculum for creative and visual arts.'

'I hardly think "miffed" is the most appropriate

26

description,' said Sidney angrily. '"Irate", "incensed", "enraged", "furious", might be more fitting to describe how I feel, but hardly "miffed".' Sidney swivelled around in his chair to face me. 'I arrived at West Challerton to find that insufferable new headmaster Mr double-barrelled Smith outrageously rude and dismissive. He kept me waiting for half an hour and then said he could only spare me a few minutes. I then discover, when I speak to the head of the Art and Design Department, that Mr double-barrelled Smith has castrated creative and visual arts to give more time to mathematics and science!'

'He's a great one for changes is Mr Pennington-Smith,' I said. I recalled when the man in question had become headmaster the previous year. One of his first innovations had been to produce a showy school brochure packed with glossy colour photographs, ambitious aims and long lists of examination successes and sporting achievements. His predecessor, Mr Blunt ('Blunt by name and blunt by nature') had not been one for anything fancy but he ran a very good school. A great many changes took place at West Challerton when Mr Pennington-Smith arrived and few had been for the better.

'The man is a philistine and a poltroon,' said Sidney. His voice was now squeaky and petulant, like a child who is suddenly forbidden an ice-cream. 'He is the Dr Goebbels of the educational world.'

'What's Dr Goebbels got to do with it?' asked David.

'It was Goebbels who said: "When I hear the word culture, I reach for my gun." If I had had a

27

gun I would have reached for it when he dropped the bombshell. The headmaster of West Challerton High School is the self-opinionated, prosaic and cultureless Dr Goebbels of the educational world, and the savaging of the creative and visual arts is quite frankly scandalous.'

'I take it you had a run in with Mr Pennington-Smith?' I observed.

'Something of an understatement, Gervase,' Sidney told me angrily. 'As I said, I visited West Challerton this afternoon on a routine visit to look at the Art and Design Department to find the headmaster had "realigned his priorities", as he put it, for this academic year. I felt like "realigning *his* priorities", I can tell you! No consultation with the head of department or myself. He just made "an executive decision" as he termed it. When I demanded to see him at the end of the afternoon, do you know what he said?'

'No,' I replied, 'but I can hazard a guess.'

'He said he had no time to discuss it with me and, in any case, it had been decided. None of the more able pupils would be studying art in the future and the rest, the less academic, would only have two periods a week. Two periods, I ask you! He then had the brass neck to tell me that, in his considered opinion, art decorated the margins of the more serious business of study, that it was not a proper academic discipline anyway and that it had very little relevance in the modern world of science and technology. I'm just bereft of words. Speechless.'

'Well, there's a first!' remarked David, removing his spectacles and polishing them with the end of his tie.

28

'Don't you think you are rather over-reacting, Sidney?' I said. 'You make it sound as if Armageddon is on us.'

Sidney slammed his fist on his desk. 'No, I am *not* over-reacting, as you put it. How would you feel if English were described as "decorating the margins of the more serious business of study" and reduced to a mere two periods a week?'

'But English, like mathematics, is a core subject,' I said. 'There is a difference.'

'So English and maths are more important? Well, I can see I'm to get precious little support from my colleagues,' blustered Sidney, rising from his chair. 'We will see what Harold has to say about it.'

'Leave the poor man alone,' said David. 'You know how busy he is at the moment.'

'Not at all!' said Sidney, heading for the door. 'I shall have a few well-chosen words to say to Harold, I can tell you.'

'And what will they be?' I asked.

'I don't know. I haven't chosen them yet,' replied Sidney, making a grand exit.

'You get worse, Sidney,' I shouted after him.

With Sidney's dramatic departure, peace descended on the office. When the clock on the County Hall tower struck six o'clock, I surveyed my empty desk with great satisfaction. The report on Our Lady of Lourdes School was finished and ready for Julie to type up, the batch of letters I had received that day had all been answered, the questionnaire from the Ministry of Education on boys' under-achievement in English had been completed and I had even made a good start at planning next month's English course. I had

29

managed to deal with all the telephone messages save for the one from the very loud individual who wished to speak to me urgently but who had not left a number. I sat back in my chair and sighed with contentment. Life was good.

'You appear remarkably pleased with yourself,' said David, looking up and staring over the top of his spectacles. 'You look like the Cheshire cat that has got the cream.'

'Well, I *am* pretty pleased with myself, if truth be told,' I replied. 'This term has started off really well. The school visits have gone smoothly and I have all my paperwork under control.'

'Well, long may it continue,' said David, 'but be warned. In my experience, there is always something or somebody who manages to spoil one's equilibrium when things seem to be going really well. Everything appears to be perfect and then disaster! You are cycling along a country lane on a bright summer's day without a care in the world. The birds are singing, the sun is shining, the fresh wind is blowing through your hair and suddenly somebody pushes a thundering great stick through your spokes and you're over the handlebars and flat on your face.'

This was one of David's favourite aphorisms. 'Ah, well,' I said smiling, 'I think it is highly remote that anyone will push a stick though my spokes at the moment. Only one more school visit this week, and then a conference on Friday.'

'And where are you tomorrow?' asked David.

'King Henry's College,' I replied. 'It's just a routine visit. I should have been before now really but from what I've read about the school, things in the English department seem to be fine.'

'Ah, your first introduction to the Admiral.'

'Who?'

'Mr Nelson, the headmaster. Known as the Admiral. You know, Horatio Nelson.'

'Do I detect a certain ominous tone to your voice?' I asked.

'Not at all,' said David. 'The headmaster of King Henry's is an amiable enough sort of chap, easy going, a little complacent perhaps. But try and get him to make a decision, give an opinion or take a stand on anything and you will wait until the proverbial cows come home. He's the sort of person who nails his colours firmly to the fence. He's all for a quiet life is Mr Nelson and, like his namesake, is a great one for turning a blind eye when it suits him.'

'Well, I can't say he was over-keen on my visiting, that's for sure,' I said. 'He didn't sound particularly easy going and complacent to me. I wrote informing him that I would be spending a day with the English department and he tried his hardest to put me off. I can't think why because, as I explained to him, it's just a routine visit, not part of a full inspection. From the details I asked him to send, the English department seems to be in a healthy state. The examination results are good and—'

'So they should be,' interrupted David. 'It's a highly selective school. You have to have a PhD to pass the entrance examination at King Henry's. If the teachers cannot get good results from that calibre of student, they might as well pack their bags and go home. And speaking of going home, it's about time we made tracks. I really don't want to be here when Sidney returns. I couldn't bear

31

another diatribe about Mr Pennington-Smith and the state of the art at West Challerton High School.'

'He did rather over-react, don't you think?' I said. 'Rushing off to see Harold like that.'

'Ah well, to be fair,' said David, 'there was rather more to it than just having the art reduced. Evidently Pennington-Smith refused to discuss the situation and when Sidney said he would make a return visit to inspect the department in a couple of weeks' time, he told him it was pointless and he need not bother. He virtually ordered him off the premises. I'm afraid that that particular headmaster has to learn that he cannot just suddenly change the curriculum on a whim. Every student is entitled to a broad and balanced range of subjects. What's more, he can't prevent school inspectors from visiting his school. The law says we have rights of entry. I think Sidney is hoping Harold will convey this fact to Mr Pennington-Smith in no uncertain terms.'

'Do you think he will?' I asked.

'I'm sure he will,' said David. 'As you know, when Harold is roused it is not a pleasant sight.'

'I feel a bit guilty now, for being in such a good mood,' I said. 'I wasn't the most sympathetic of listeners.'

'Oh, Sidney will get over it. He does tend to make a drama out of things. I wonder where on earth he has got to? He has been gone for over two hours.'

'Probably stormed off in a huff,' I suggested.

'Poor Sidney,' said David, screwing the top back on his pen. 'He does get into a state but it soon blows over. Well, I'm off home and if I don't see you tomorrow, Gervase, enjoy your weekend with that lovely wife of yours. How is Christine incidentally?'

'She's fine,' I told him.

'You are a very lucky man, Gervase,' said David, rising from his chair and stretching.

'Yes, I know,' I replied.

As I drove home, I pondered on David's words. Yes, I was indeed a very lucky man. The Easter before, on a bright, cloudless spring morning, I had married the most beautiful, talented and gentle woman in the world, Miss Christine Bentley, headteacher of Winnery Nook Nursery and Infant School. I had met her a few weeks after starting in my post as county English inspector and for me it had been love at first sight. We had honeymooned in the Lake District and had returned to our dreamy Peewit Cottage in the village of Hawksrill in the Dales. The dream cottage, in fact, had woodworm, dry rot, rising damp, cracked walls, broken guttering and nearly every conceivable problem but we had fallen in love with the magnificent views and after spending most of our spare time renovating and refurbishing, it was beginning to take shape.

At the end of the previous summer term Christine had told me the most wonderful news— that I was to be a father the following spring. So everything in the world seemed right: home, family, friends and job. I was cycling along that country lane of David's on a bright summer's day without a care in the world. The birds were singing, the sun was shining, the fresh wind was blowing through my hair and nothing and nobody could possibly spoil the sense of elation I felt.

Little did I know that there was someone lurking in the bushes ready to push the thundering great stick through my spokes.

CHAPTER THREE

The frosted glass at the reception desk at King Henry's College slid back sharply and I was confronted by a tall, thin, hawk-faced school secretary with small, cold blue eyes behind unfashionable horn-rimmed spectacles. She gave me a stony stare. The feeling of pleasant anticipation I had felt as I had strolled up the long drive to the imposing school building immediately dissipated.

'Would you mind not tapping on the glass,' she told me in a superior voice. 'There is a buzzer, you know.'

'Where?' I enquired innocently, giving her an exaggerated smile and looking into the pale blue eyes.

She poked her head through the hatch like a tortoise emerging from its shell, and tutted noisily. 'The buzzer is under those registers, which should not have been left there,' she announced, giving me an accusatory glare as though I were the culprit. She snatched up the registers and pulled them through the window and into the office. There was a great in-drawing of breath. 'The number of times I tell the students not to leave the registers there,' she said to no one in particular. 'I might just as well talk to myself for all the notice they take.'

I continued to smile and await the apology but it

soon became apparent that none would be forthcoming.

'Now,' she said, 'may I help you?' Her face remained dramatically tight-lipped and stern, and her voice retained its weary condescension.

'I hope so,' I said pleasantly. 'I have an appointment.'

'With whom?'

'The headmaster.'

She began flicking through a large black book. 'At what time?'

'At a quarter to nine.'

She glanced up at the clock on the office wall. 'You're rather early.'

'I often am.'

She continued to turn the pages. 'And you are?'

I passed through the brown envelope that I had received from the school the week before. It was addressed to: 'Mr Gervase R. Phiss, Inspector of Schools, The Inspectors' Division, Education Office, County Hall, Fettlesham, Yorkshire.' Had my welcome been rather warmer, I would have pointed out that the name was Phinn and not Phiss, but after the reception I had just received, I did not feel quite so charitable, so I said nothing.

Having scrutinised the envelope, the secretary's manner changed instantly. 'Oh, oh, yes, the school inspector.' She allowed herself a small, thin-lipped smile. 'I'm so sorry, I thought you were a parent or a book salesman. It's always very hectic here. I never seem to have a minute to myself. It's like Euston Station at rush hour. Do please take a seat in the waiting-room, Mr Phiss. I shall inform Mr Nelson that you have arrived.'

In the small room a rather harassed-looking

woman with wispy greying hair sat straight-backed with her hands clasped tightly together on her lap. With her was an equally harassed-looking boy of about eleven. They both shifted uneasily on their chairs. The boy, who had a pale face, looked up when he saw me approaching and began twiddling his hair nervously.

The woman stood and extended a hand. 'Mr Nelson?'

'No, no,' I replied, 'I'm not the headmaster. I'm just a visitor.'

'Oh, I'm sorry, I thought you were Mr Nelson.' She sat down and swept away a stray strand of hair from her face. 'Nerve-racking, isn't it?' she said.

'What is?' I asked, sitting next to her.

'Meeting the headmaster. I know I shouldn't get into this state but I always have had a dread of headteachers' offices. It brings back unhappy memories.' I smiled. 'We've an appointment at nine. It's John's first day, you see.' She turned to the boy and gave a weak smile. 'He should have started with all the other boys last week but he's just got over glandular fever. He's a bit nervous, so I thought I'd come along with him.' A boy of eleven is quite capable of making his own way to school, I thought to myself, but I said nothing. 'He's worried that all the other boys will have made friends by now and he'll be left out.' She lowered her voice. 'And he's a bit on the sensitive side.'

'Oh, I wouldn't worry too much,' I assured the boy. 'You'll soon settle in and make friends.'

'I do hope so.' The woman sounded unconvinced. 'He's got asthma, as well, you know.'

'Really?'

'I wanted to see the headmaster, to tell him.

36

He's not the most confident child.' The boy continued to twiddle his hair. 'He's an only one. My husband thinks I'm a bit over-protective, to be honest.' Her husband was right. 'We arrived early just to be on the safe side. You see, we had to catch two buses. I thought I'd come with him on his first day. Show him how to get here and make sure he's all right.'

'You'll be fine, John,' I told the boy.

The boy pulled a tragic face but remained resolutely silent.

His mother prodded him. 'Sit up, John, and stop fiddling with your hair, for goodness sake. If you do that in front of Mr Nelson, he won't be very impressed.' She turned her attention back to me. 'Of course, he did very well to get in at King Henry's. Very good results. Excellent sporting facilities. Music's very good too. There's a waiting list as long as my arm for places.' She began wringing her hands. 'Yes, it's a very good school.' The boy looked up glumly. 'There were only three in his primary school who passed the entrance examination, you know.'

'Good,' I said to the boy. 'Well done.'

The boy continued to stare into the middle distance, a glum expression on his face.

'He had a private tutor,' his mother told me. 'Cost an arm and a leg, but you do the best you can, don't you?'

'Are you looking forward to starting, John?' I asked the boy.

'It's the best school in the area,' the woman told me proudly before the boy could reply.

I would reserve my judgement on that one, I thought to myself. If the icy reception was anything to go by, things did not bode well.

I had visited many schools during the relatively short time I had been a school inspector and was always intrigued and often amused by the reception I received. On some occasions I would be welcomed like a long lost relative, all smiles and handshakes, at other times it was as if the Gestapo had turned up. On one occasion I was mistaken for a Mr Davies. The headteacher had been devastated to learn that I was a school inspector, there to look at lessons and not the plumber to fix the smell in the boys' lavatories. Usually the school secretary greeted me with courtesy and good humour. It was rare, however, to be addressed with such polar hostility as I had been that morning. The cold blue eyes of the school secretary at King Henry's could freeze soup in kitchen pans.

The woman in question appeared before me. Her manner was distinctly different now. 'Mr Phiss,' she said, allowing herself another thin-lipped smile, 'the headmaster will see you, if you would care to follow me.' She ignored the woman and her son who looked up expectantly on her arrival.

'Good luck,' I said to the boy, getting to my feet.

'Say thank you to the man,' prompted his mother.

He stared up morosely and shrugged.

The secretary strode ahead of me, her heels clicking on the hard floor. There was the same smell in the air I recalled from my school days: stale cabbage, disinfectant and floor polish. There was the same long, cold corridor I remembered too, the wooden block floor, the high ceilings, the quadrangle, the heavy oak doors to the classrooms.

It was like going back in time.

At the school secretary's approach the hubbub of noise in the corridors subsided and the pupils opened their crowded ranks to allow her to sweep through.

'It's a most unusual name, Phiss,' she said over her shoulder.

'Yes,' I replied.

'Is it foreign?'

'Actually—' I began, about to enlighten her.

'I can't say I've ever heard the name Phiss before,' she continued. 'We have a boy here called Phipps, a Phillips, and another called Phillpots. Oh yes, and there's a Phillimore, but I have never heard the name Phiss.'

'It's French Huguenot,' I told her, keeping a straight face.

'Really?'

'My ancestors came over with the weavers in the seventeenth century after severe persecution at the hands of Henry of Navarre. My mother's still not quite got over it.'

'Oh, I am sorry,' she said, in a matter-of-fact voice.

'Actually, it's not pronounced Phiss.'

'Is it not?'

'No,' I said mischievously, 'it has a silent "aitch".'

We arrived at the headmaster's study. Mr Nelson rose from his desk to greet me.

'Headmaster,' said the school secretary, her face as solemn as ever. 'This is the inspector of schools, Mr . . . er . . . Pice.'

Mr Nelson was a gaunt, middle-aged man with grizzled grey hair and a pained expression. A black academic gown, with long dangling sleeves,

39

enveloped his lean frame, giving him the appearance of a giant spider. Through small, rimless spectacles he surveyed me critically like a doctor might a patient, before extending a long, cold hand.

'Mr . . . er . . .' he began.

'Phinn,' I said. 'There was a misspelling on your letter.'

'You might have said!' snapped the school secretary, her face white with displeasure and a fierce light in the small blue eyes.

'Thank you, Mrs Winterton,' said Mr Nelson with elaborate courtesy. The school secretary had not remained for his instruction to depart and was already heading for the door at high speed, tut-tutting as she went.

When she had gone the headmaster sat down, tapped his long fingers edgily on the desk and confided in a low voice, 'Mrs Winterton can be a trifle sharp at times, but she is quite indispensable. Worth her weight in the proverbial.'

More like a pain in the proverbial, I thought to myself. 'I'm sure she is,' I replied. 'I did try and tell her that there was a misprint on the letter.' The headmaster stared at me blankly. ' "Phiss" instead of "Phinn",' I elaborated.

'Quite. I have mentioned about her typing,' said the headmaster, 'but she can be very touchy.'

'Yes, I'm sure she can.'

'Well, Mr Phinn, do take a seat.' He indicated an uncomfortable-looking, ladderback chair placed to the front of his desk. 'So, you are to spend a day in the school inspecting the English Department?'

'Yes, that's right,' I replied.

The headmaster raised his head slowly, rubbed

his chin and sighed. He resembled a wounded admiral watching the return of his defeated fleet. 'Not the best time, I have to say, the beginning of term, for a school inspection, when things are especially busy. I did point this out in my reply to you when you informed me of this proposed visitation. No, not the best time at all. The new school year has barely started, teachers are just becoming acquainted with their classes, getting to grips with the timetables, sorting out their rooms, *et cetera*. Indeed, I have an exceptionally busy day ahead of me with a Management meeting and then the Governors' Finance Sub-committee and numerous other pressing commitments. This morning I have to see several parents, including one who is contesting our decision not to accept his son at the school. All very trying. As you will no doubt be aware, we are very heavily oversubscribed here at King Henry's. And it's such a tedious and time-consuming business this interviewing, and is not without its stresses.' He paused. 'But, of course, the Education Department, in its infinite wisdom, does insist on these appeals being heard.' I felt it politic not to enter this particular debate and remained silent. 'So, as I said, Mr Phinn, your visit has come at a most inconvenient time.'

I looked directly at him and he returned my gaze. 'I should imagine there is never a convenient time for a school inspection, Mr Nelson,' I told him amiably. 'As I explained in my letter, however, I do have a very busy programme of visits to schools this term and I must start somewhere. King Henry's is high on my list.'

'High on your list,' repeated the headmaster, twisting his mouth to one side and cocking his head. 'My goodness! That does sound ominous.'

'Not at all,' I assured him, 'it's just a short day's visit to look at the English teaching in the school. According to my records, it's been quite some time since you have had an inspector in the English Department. Indeed, I have not been in the school before and I have been working for the Education Department for three years. I thought it high time that I paid you a visit. As you are aware, the last inspection was carried out by my predecessor, Mrs Young, shortly before I started.' He looked at me sceptically. 'It is quite routine. I am sure everything will be fine.'

Mr Nelson took a slow, deep breath. His face was noble in its pallor. 'I did say in my letter to you, Mr Phinn, that I would have preferred a more suitable time.' He sat in thoughtful silence for a moment, drumming his long fingers on the desk top, no doubt awaiting a response. Perhaps he expected me to agree with him, arrange a visit for a future date and depart forthwith. When I remained firmly tight-lipped, he nodded and continued, his voice hardening a fraction. 'Well, if you *are* to join us for the day, I am sure you will find things in order. As you will have surmised from the details you asked me to send to you, our examination results are outstanding.'

They were certainly good, I thought, but not outstanding. The girls' high school achieved much better results. Anyway, King Henry's was a grammar school for which only the brightest pupils in the area were selected by examination and personal interview. As David had rightly pointed out to me, the school should indeed attain good results.

'And I have to say,' continued the headmaster, 'Mr Frobisher, the head of the English Faculty, is not entirely enthusiastic about the visit. You will find him a somewhat formal and traditional teacher, one of the "old school", and he does have his share of—' There was a sharp knock on the door, interrupting the flow. 'Ah, that must be him now. I asked him to join us before lessons commence. Come!'

Mr Frobisher bore an unnerving resemblance to the headmaster. He was also a lean, sallow-complexioned man with heavy-lidded eyes and a pained expression. The only difference was the hair. Whereas Mr Nelson's was grizzled, Mr Frobisher's hair was straight and black and carefully parted down one side. He too wore rimless spectacles and a capacious black gown.

'Good morning,' he intoned, giving me a calculating stare.

Oh dear, oh dear, I thought to myself, another chilly reception. I took a deep breath, stood and smiled. 'Good morning.'

'This is Mr Phinn,' the headmaster told him. 'The school inspector.'

'I thought it was Mr Fish.'

'There was a misprint on the letter,' explained the headmaster. 'Mrs Winterton again, I'm afraid.'

'Oh,' said the head of English. 'Well, I have to say, today is a very inopportune time for your visit, Mr Phinn.'

'The headmaster *has* pointed this out to me, Mr Frobisher,' I explained, not wishing to rehearse the whole conversation again. 'I appreciate that the beginning of term is not the best of times, but I do have a heavy schedule of visits over the next few weeks.' Before he could answer I looked theatrically at my watch and continued. 'I see the lessons are about to begin. Perhaps we should make a start?'

My attempt to change the subject fell on stony ground for Mr Frobisher continued regardless. 'The beginning of term is always rather fraught and Thursday is always an inconvenient day for me for I am on corridor patrol at morning and afternoon breaks, I supervise a detention at lunch-time and I am on bus duty after school.' He looked at me as if anticipating a reply. 'So—'

I stood firm. 'I would still like to stay,' I told him. 'Perhaps we could make a start?'

'Very well,' said Mr Frobisher loftily, glancing in the direction of the headmaster, as if to enlist his support, before turning his attention back to me. 'I trust you received the various details you requested—examination results, schemes of work, syllabuses, staffing complement, *et cetera*. I hope the programme I have devised for you to follow is acceptable.' He did not await an answer. 'I think you are to start with Mr Poppleton, the second-in-charge of the department, and his fifth year form.'

'I did receive them, thank you, Mr Frobisher,' I replied amicably, 'but I have planned a programme for the day. I do prefer to work from one of my own.'

'One of your own?' he repeated, bristling like an angry cat. 'You mean you roam freely between classes?'

'Yes, that is the usual practice. I try to visit all the teachers and see as wide a range of lessons as possible, taking the opportunity of talking to the students and looking at their work.'

'Well, it seems quite irregular to me. Do you mean the teachers will not know when you are visiting their lessons to observe them?' He turned again to face the headmaster, obviously hoping this time he would come to his defence. When this was not forthcoming, he swivelled back to face me.

'I generally start with the head of department,' I said. 'I noticed you did not include yourself on the programme you sent me, Mr Frobisher.'

'Surely, you do not wish to see *me* teach?' He looked appalled. 'I am the head of faculty.'

'Yes, I am aware of that,' I said pleasantly.

The headmaster sighed wearily. 'I really must ask you gentlemen to excuse me. I have a waiting-room full of expectant parents to see me. Mr Frobisher, if you wouldn't mind showing our visitor where the English rooms are. I look forward to seeing you at the end of the day, Mr Phinn, for you to share your deliberations with us. And now if you wouldn't mind.'

*   *   *

Mr Frobisher's classroom had an uninterrupted view over the playing fields. It was a spacious and very warm room with a highly polished floor of patterned wooden blocks, long elegant sash windows and a high ceiling with ornamental plaster coving. At the front of the room, on a dais, was a sturdy teacher's desk made of pine and a high-backed chair, while at the side was a bookcase containing neatly stacked books and folders, a set of dictionaries and some reference texts. Save for a few dog-eared and faded posters concerned with the rules of grammar, the walls were bare. The students' desks were of the small, lidded variety with holes for inkwells, entirely unsuitable for large adolescent boys.

The class of thirty or so fourth-year students, some in smart blazers, a couple in white shirts, stood when we entered.

'Sit down,' ordered the teacher, sweeping to his desk, gown a-fluttering. He surveyed the class before him and his eyes settled on two gangly boys at the back. 'I was not aware, Lister, that I had given permission for the removal of blazers.'

'It's really hot in here, sir,' replied the boy.

'Neither did I request a weather forecast. You know the school rules as well as I. Put on your blazer and that goes for you too, Wilsdon.'

'Can I open a window then, sir?' persisted the boy.

'You *can* indeed open a window, Lister, but whether or not you *may* is an entirely different matter.'

'What, sir?'

'I said you *can* open a window. Obviously my lesson on the auxiliary verb last term has had very little impact.' He picked up a stick of chalk and wrote the word CAN in capitals on the board. 'The word "can" is an auxiliary verb expressing an ability or knowledge of how to do something as in the sentence, "I can throw this chalk."' He twirled the chalk around between finger and thumb and smiled at his own witticism. 'The verb "may" is also an auxiliary verb expressing the possibility or the permission to do something as in the sentence, "You may open the window."'

'So, can I open it then, sir?' asked the boy, looking puzzled.

'No, you *may* not!' snapped the teacher. 'Now, it will not have escaped your notice that we have with us a visitor today. Mr Phinn is from the Education Office and he will be joining our lesson.' He gestured to an empty chair at the side of the room.

'Good morning,' I said cheerfully, as I headed for the chair.

'Good morning, sir,' chorused the boys.

'I was not impressed, not impressed at all with your homework this week,' said Mr Frobisher, reaching for the neat pile of exercise books on his desk. 'There was a great deal of inaccurate, untidy and slip-shod writing. And in some books we seem to have had an epidemic of the greengrocer's disease. Apostrophes everywhere.' He flicked open a book. 'I do not know how many times I have told you that, in general, in the singular the apostrophe appears before the letter *s*, and in the plural after the letter s when the plural ends in the letter *s* and before the letter *s* when the plural does not end in the letter *s*. It is quite simple.'

The pupils obviously did not agree since they were staring at him, entirely perplexed.

'Rutter, here,' and Mr Frobisher held up an exercise book, 'scatters apostrophes across the page like peppercorns. I don't know about you, Mr Phinn,' said the teacher, turning his attention to me, 'but I find it so irritating to see the flagrant misuse of the English language wherever I go. One passes the local fruiterer who sells "bananas" and "potatoes", or the supermarket promising "hundreds of products" at half price, all with redundant apostrophes before the *s*.' As he spoke, Mr Frobisher wrote the erroneous words on the board:

47

banana's
potatoe's
100's of products

'I had a political leaflet through my door only last week,' he continued, 'which wrote about raising standards in education, but that also, incredibly, contained superfluous punctuation. There were phrases like "the local MPs are concerned" and "the Government are keeping to its manifesto", the latter containing not only the errant apostrophe but a blatant misapplication of the verb.' Onto the board went:

the local MP's
to it's manifesto

The teacher now picked up a red chalk from his desk and with flamboyant strokes crossed out the offending apostrophes on the board.

He turned his attention back to the class. 'Some people think that every time there is a letter *s* at the end of a word there needs to be an apostrophe.' He faced the students who stared at him with expressionless faces. 'As you have heard me say on countless occasions, defective punctuation leads to confusion. So, the only use of the apostrophe is to denote possession or omission. Now—'

'Excuse me, sir.' The speaker was a gangly boy with lanky brown hair and angry acne across his forehead and cheeks. 'What about in this sentence: "The word 'Mississippi' contains four *i*'s and four *s*'s but only two *p*'s." Surely apostrophes are needed here, otherwise the reader will be left very confused.'

Mr Frobisher removed his glasses and stared heavenwards. 'Yes indeed, Smith,' he replied. 'Whether the apostrophe should be used to denote

48

the plural of a word that does not ordinarily make a plural depends on whether the plural is easily recognisable as such. Unless the reader needs assistance in understanding, which is the case with your example, one should not use the apostrophe. Now, we must get—'

'But didn't you just say, sir, that the apostrophe is only used to denote possession or omission?' enquired the boy in an overly polite tone of voice.

The teacher sighed. I could see he wished he had never entered this minefield. 'Yes, I did, but this is an exception. It is clearly justifiable with single letters as in your Mississippi sentence, or in mine, "Well-behaved, polite and attentive students watch their p's and q's." Does that clarify the matter for you?'

'Oh yes, sir,' replied the boy, smiling. 'Thank you, sir.'

'Now—' began the teacher again, replacing his spectacles and fixing the boy with a rattlesnake look.

'Excuse me, sir.'

'Yes, Smith, what is it now?' sighed the teacher.

'In the sentence that you quoted, "The Government is keeping to its manifesto", you said there is no apostrophe in the word "its".'

'That is correct,' said Mr Frobisher, taking off his glasses again and pointing with them to the board. 'All pronouns dispense with the apostrophe in their possessive case—hers, yours, theirs, ours and its. It's with an apostrophe is not the possessive of "it" but a contraction of "it is". The apostrophe is performing its normal duty of showing that a letter has been omitted. You shouldn't need to think twice about those any more. Now—'

'What about the pronoun "one" then, sir?' said the boy. 'Surely an apostrophe is needed in the sentence: "One is taking one's time in explaining oneself."'

The teacher eyed the boy momentarily, wondering if he were being impertinent. 'That is the one exception,' he finally replied in a dismissive manner.

'It is all very confusing, sir,' sighed the boy, leaning back on his chair. 'There seem so many exceptions to the rule.'

'It is a quite simple concept, Smith—that is if you listen and learn the rules.'

'Do you not think, sir, that the apostrophe has just about had its day?'

'No, I do not!'

'And that the greengrocer perhaps deliberately misuses the apostrophe to draw attention to his fruit and vegetables.'

'No, I do not! It is just plain ignorance.'

'I don't suppose that in the great scheme of things, it's that important,' said the boy, turning to address the class as a whole. 'I don't imagine that people buy less of the greengrocer's produce because he decides to insert an apostrophe here and there. I should think it's the quality of his fruit and vegetables and the prices that count with his customers.'

'It is important to me, Smith!' snapped the teacher. 'And it is also important to those who mark your examination papers.'

'But is it not the case, sir,' continued the boy, 'that many institutions, like Barclays Bank, for example, have dropped the apostrophe and this has not led to wholesale confusion?'

50

'Well if Barclays Bank has, Smith,' the teacher told him in a disparaging voice, which expressed both impatience and anger, 'then it is wrong.'

'And is it not the case, sir,' continued the boy, staring the teacher full in the face, not insolently nor with the trace of a smile, but with an intense gaze, 'that in Shakespeare's time it was quite common to find plural nouns with apostrophes?'

'Smith,' said the teacher, his forehead now unpleasantly shining, 'much as I would like to debate the rights and wrongs of using the apostrophe, we do have to press on.'

This remarkable exchange, something which I had rarely observed in a classroom before, was like a battle of wits between a clever barrister and a vulnerable defendant, the student pursuing the teacher like a terrier with a rat, but doing so in the most courteous of ways. Mr Frobisher was clearly disconcerted by the boy's constant interruptions and his earlier self-assurance seemed to be disappearing fast. He turned and vigorously cleared the board of the list of criminal apostrophes.

'Excuse me, sir,' began the boy again. Some of his classmates sniggered quietly.

'Smith,' said the teacher, attempting to control his displeasure, 'you are becoming wearisome in the extreme. Enough is enough. Now, I shall write on the board some sentences in which the apostrophes have been omitted. In your exercise books I would like you to copy out the sentences and—'

'Tell you where to stick them,' said Smith, just loud enough for me to hear.

However, Mr Frobisher also heard. 'I think a

quiet word with you is in order, Smith,' said the teacher. 'See me at lunchtime.'

While the class completed the exercise, I took the opportunity to walk round the desks, and look at some of the work. In due course, I reached the young man who had pressed the teacher with so many challenging questions. It soon became my turn to be interrogated.

'May I look at your book?' I asked pleasantly.

'Who exactly are you?' he said, looking me straight in the eyes.

'A school inspector.'

'Really?'

'Yes.'

'And what is it that you do exactly?'

'Watch lessons, examine books, talk to pupils, study examination results,' I explained.

'Bit of a cushy number that, isn't it?'

'Some would say so.'

'And how long are you here for?'

'Just the day.'

'You'll not see much in a day.'

'You'd be surprised.'

'And presumably you write a report at the end of your visit?'

'Yes, I do.'

'And what will be in your report of this lesson?' he asked bluntly.

Now it was my turn to be in the witness box and face the tricky questions. 'I haven't quite decided yet.'

'But you must have formed some impression.'

'It is usually me who asks the questions, you know.'

The boy was not going to let me off the hook so

lightly. 'But surely in a good school,' he said, 'the pupils are encouraged to ask questions, are they not?'

'They are,' I replied, 'but with some questions it would be inappropriate for me to answer.'

'Sounds a bit of a cop-out to me.'

'So, may I look at your book?'

He would not be distracted. 'I reckon you are here to discover whether the standard of education is satisfactory or not, that the lessons are up to scratch. Is that right?'

'Yes, that is part of my job.'

'And that being the case, surely it is we, the clients, who would be most interested to know.'

'My report is given to the headmaster. I never discuss particular lessons or individual teachers with students.'

'So much for freedom of information,' he said.

I changed the subject. 'Do you like English?'

'I like the language. I can't say that I like the lessons.' He waited for a response. 'I'm afraid I can't get too excited about where to put the apostrophe, can you? In fact, I couldn't really care less. It seems to me to be a very outdated concept and wants scrapping. It is such a deeply uninteresting topic, don't you think? When Shakespeare or Dickens or Jane Austen or Emily Brontë put pen to paper, I am sure that the last thing on their minds was where to stick their apostrophes.'

'Your book, please,' I said.

He slid his open book casually across the desk for me to examine. The book contained work of quite exceptional quality.

'I am sure you do not need me to tell you that

this work is excellent,' I told him.

'No, I don't really.' I could see that dealing with this young man was no easy matter. He smiled. 'What I mean is, I don't need you to tell me, but it is always nice to be told.'

'And what do you hope to study at university?' I asked.

'What makes you think I wish to go to university?' he asked.

'I assume you will be.'

'Maybe I will,' he said.

'And if you do, will you study English?'

'Law,' he replied. 'Like my father.'

I closed his book and passed it back to him. It was then that I saw the name on the cover: Hugo Maxwell-Smith. 'Do you have any brothers or sisters?' I asked.

'Yes, a younger brother and sister. My brother isn't at this school yet.'

'Ah, so that would be Alexander, a pupil at Our Lady of Lourdes?'

That did surprise the young man, but he didn't have a chance to question me because the bell signalling the end of the lesson rang shrilly.

'When you have handed your books in,' said Mr Frobisher, 'you can go.'

'You *may* go,' murmured Hugo Maxwell-Smith, rising from his seat and giving me the fullest and most charming of smiles.

54

CHAPTER FOUR

For the second period of the day, I joined a gentle-mannered if somewhat nervous young teacher called Mr Adams. The lesson had been well planned, the teaching was competent and focused and the work the students undertook was interesting and appropriate. It was a vast improvement on the last lesson that I had observed.

The students, aged twelve and put into groups of four, were asked to discuss a newspaper article with a number of question prompts provided by the teacher. They then had the task of writing a letter in response, rebutting some of the criticisms and setting out their own views. The article bemoaned the youth of today as largely rude and selfish, with little perseverance or inclination for hard work. According to the writer, young people had far too much money at their disposal, spent many a wasted hour glued in front of the television set, lacked respect for their elders and had parents and teachers who did not exercise sufficient discipline. It harked back to a 'golden age' when smiling bobbies walked the beat, pavements were litter-free and there were no teenage muggers, football hooligans or lager louts. Such was the enthusiasm of the pupils to contribute their views that I found little opportunity of asking any questions, so moved from group to group merely listening to the animated debate.

Just before the bell signalled morning break, I did manage to ask one of the students a question.

'Would you agree that the differences between the younger and older generations today are greater than they were when your parents were young?'

The boy thought for a moment, chewing the end of his pencil and nodding his head up and down slowly. 'Now, that really is a very interesting question,' he said, 'but I have no idea of the answer.'

At the morning break I went in search of Mr Poppleton who, I was informed by a helpful pupil, taught in a temporary classroom. I discovered an ugly shed balanced on six raised concrete blocks behind the main school building. The exterior of this mournful structure resembled a POW hut: wooden walls the colour of the slime which forms on stagnant ponds, grey asphalt roof, small square windows and a set of dirty brown steps leading up to a plywood door. It was a far cry from Mr Frobisher's elegant room. As I headed for the hut, the door opened and there appeared, like an actor stepping onto the stage, a small, spherical individual with a smile visible from fifty yards.

Mr Poppleton could have walked straight out of the pages of a Dickens' novel. His cheeks were as wrinkled as an over-ripe russet apple and his nose, of a most distinctive claret colour, was as round and heavy as a turnip. Fluffy outcrops of unnaturally bright gingery-red hair sprouted from around his impressive ears. Mr Poppleton was dressed in a loud checked suit (which was a size too small for him), a rust-coloured waistcoat (which had seen better days) and an enormous spotted bow tie. He sported a diamond ring on one fat little finger and a heavy silver chain stretched across his stomach. Mr Poppleton looked more like a circus

56

performer or a music hall comedian than an English master in a prestigious boys' school.

'Mr Poppleton?' I inquired, approaching the rotund little figure who remained standing by the classroom door, like a huge egg on legs.

'Indeed, it is I,' he said, beaming. 'Vernon Poppleton at your service. And you must be the expected Inspector Fish.'

'Phinn,' I said. 'It was a misprint.'

'What was a misprint?'

'My name.'

'You were a misprint? How very unfortunate.'

'On the letter.'

'Which letter?'

'I received a letter from the school,' I explained, 'with the name of "Gervase Phiss" instead of "Gervase Phinn" on the envelope.'

Mr Poppleton raised a ginger eyebrow. 'Ah, the inimitable Mrs Winterton,' he said knowingly. 'She is not the most proficient of typists but few would hazard to tell her as much. I recall once she sent a letter out to parents from "The Deadmaster".' Then he added in an undertone, 'Not entirely inappropriate if you have met our esteemed leader. I mustn't be unkind, but dear Mr Nelson does have the touch of death about him. He's a physicist, you know. On another occasion, when the pipes burst in the outside toilets and the floors were awash, a notice appeared from Mrs Winterton instructing students "not to slide on the frozen water unless passed by the headmaster". This time, she did, at least, manage to spell the word "passed" correctly but her instruction was still rather unfortunate in its phrasing, don't you think?'

'Well, it is easily done,' I said, smiling.

57

'Indeed it is,' he agreed. 'Language is a tricky and troublesome thing or, as Homer once observed, "as twisty as a snake". That is why one shouldn't be pedantic when the young make mistakes. There, for the grace of God, *et cetera*.'

Obviously this opinion carried little weight with his head of department, I thought to myself, casting my mind back to the first lesson.

Mr Poppleton produced a small silver heart-shaped box from a waistcoat pocket, flipped open the top and took a generous pinch of snuff which he sniffed up his nostril with a flourish.

'Dirty habit, I know,' he told me, before a tumultuous sneeze.

I climbed up the steps and, when he had returned the silver snuff box to his pocket and sneezed again, loud enough to wake the dead, I shook the soft, fleshy hand which was extended. 'Once, when I was left to my own devices,' I told him, 'and had to type a letter to a school, I wrote, "Dear Headamster". Fortunately, the person in question had a sense of humour and replied, "Dear Gerbil".'

'Ho, ho,' he chuckled, 'very droll! Would that our esteemed leader had been endowed with a sense of humour. He seems to carry the troubles of the world on his shoulders. Mr Nelson is most industrious and well meaning but he is a man of very serious, sober and sombre disposition. I suppose one has to be like that to ascend to the dizzy heights of headship. I don't suppose I should be telling a school inspector such things, should I?' He looked about him absent-mindedly. 'I do think it is an attribute of considerable importance in teaching, don't you think?'

'What is?' I asked.

'Why, a sense of humour. Sadly, education for some is such a deadly serious business, and yet young people are naturally very funny and do enjoy sharing a joke or listening to an amusing story. Humour, in my opinion, is highly related to learning and adds inestimably to our quality of life.' Obviously this opinion, too, carried little weight with his head of department. 'I do apologise for pontificating on the steps like a preacher of old. Do come along in, Mr Phinn. My little kingdom is not the most tasteful, architecturally speaking, but it is home and I can make as much noise as I like without disturbing others. Of course, it heats up like the Gobi Desert in summer and cools down like the polar ice cap in winter so I sincerely hope you are going to be warm enough. I am thermally insulated and, as you may observe, wear a suit like a shag-pile carpet. I get my suits from Fritters of Fettlesham.'

I had to smile. I had a suit, not dissimilar, from that ancient emporium, bought in the January sales at an incredibly knock-down price. It was a sort of mustardy-brown with a dog-tooth pattern in dark red; it had unfashionable wide curved lapels and large leather buttons. I had joined the interview panel at a grammar school in a cramped room as hot as a sauna. The heavy suit had stuck to my body and I had nearly fainted with the heat. I vowed never to wear the wretched garment again. In fact, I didn't have a chance since Christine had given the jacket to a local farmer for his sheepdog to lie on, and had cut up the trousers for polishing cloths.

As I followed him into the room, Mr Poppleton

remarked, 'I was under the impression that you were to join me for the first lesson.'

'Yes, but as I explained to Mr Frobisher,' I told him, 'I prefer to work to my own programme.'

'And wander whither and whence you wish.'

'Indeed. In fact, I joined the head of department and the fourth form for the first period,' I said.

'Ho, ho!' chortled Mr Poppleton, again raising a ginger eyebrow. 'He would not have been best pleased with that little ploy.'

'No, I don't think he was,' I said.

'I should imagine you put the very fear of the Almighty into him. I know that when we had a visitation a few years back from an HMI called Ball—a very singular man, as I remember—he did not endear himself to Mr Frobisher. Actually, Mr Ball and I got on rather well. In his report he described me as "a successful deviant". I took it as a compliment.'

'I'm sure it was intended to be so,' I told him.

'However, you are now here to watch me and it is my turn to feel the frenzied flutter of fright. The first period, which I was told you would be observing, was rigorously planned, carefully prepared and enthusiastically taught and, though I say so myself, it was quite a *tour de force*. This next lesson will, I fear, be rather lacklustre by comparison.'

'I'm not really interested, Mr Poppleton,' I told him, 'in carefully planned lessons or rehearsed performances. The reason I don't tell teachers when I am visiting their classrooms is to try and ensure that nothing special is prepared. I just want to see a typical lesson.'

'You certainly won't find my lessons typical,

Mr Phinn,' replied the teacher with mock horror. 'Every lesson of mine is a unique experience. Now, this morning, my "little ones"—these are the first-year pupils who have just joined us from the junior and preparatory schools—are completing a poem. I do hope you like poetry.'

'Yes, I do,' I replied. 'Actually, it's an essential component of the English curriculum.'

'That sounds dreadfully pompous,' he observed.

'I didn't mean it to sound like that,' I replied quickly. 'I just meant it was important to teach.'

'I fear that Mr Nelson would take issue with you on that one. He has a much more utilitarian view of language.' Then, as if hurling an insult, he said, 'He's a scientist, you know.'

'Yes, you did say.'

'Well, I am so glad you enjoy poetry,' continued Mr Poppleton. 'I am always deeply suspicious of those who do not enjoy it. Poetry is not merely "an essential component of the English curriculum", as you put it, poetry, in a sense, defines the world, it deals with the deepest emotions, it is language at its most precise, creative and vivid, don't you think?'

'Yes, indeed,' I replied.

'I was a student at University College, Oxford, you know, and every day I would pass the marble sculpture of Shelley reclining naked on his plinth. I am a great fan of Shelley. The sculpture was destined for the Protestant Cemetery in Rome but it was too big so they gave it to his old college. Mind you, he very nearly got me rusticated, did Shelley.'

'I'm sorry?'

'Sent down. One night, a little worse for drink, I

61

scrambled over the iron grill protecting the mausoleum and painted part of dear old Shelley a delightful shade of red.' I was about to respond but was not quite fast enough. 'And do you write poetry yourself, Mr Phinn?'

'Yes, I do.'

'Splendid,' he said. 'Perhaps you might share one of your poems with us.'

'I think not,' I said.

'Pity. Well, do feel free to look around.'

Mr Poppleton's room was as colourful, unusual and overpowering as the man himself. Every conceivable wall space was covered with posters, prints, portraits, paintings, photographs, articles, letters and pupils' work. It was a riot of shape and colour. From the ceiling dangled multicoloured mobiles—squares, circles, diamonds, triangles—with a few verses written on each. The windowsills were crammed with plants, some of which had given up the ghost weeks ago, feathers in jars, clay figures, carved boxes, animal skulls, fragments of pottery and glass and all manner of strange objects and artefacts. Dominating the room was an ancient oak desk of considerable proportions and remarkable ugliness with heavy brass fittings and numerous drawers. The top was entirely covered with a clutter of dog-eared folders and files, exercise books, teaching texts, thick dictionaries and numerous books of poems. Facing the monstrosity were rows of tables and hard-backed chairs for the pupils.

As the teacher busied himself rummaging through the volumes on the desk, I made my way to a shabby but comfortable-looking armchair positioned in the corner of the room. I presumed this was for me to sit in and observe the lesson. To the accompaniment of creaking wood and twanging springs, I lowered myself charily into its sagging seat, creating a small cloud of dust in the process.

Presently the pupils entered the room, went quietly to their desks and placed their bags and satchels beside them on the floor and stood facing the front.

'Good morning, boys!' trumpeted Mr Poppleton, with a theatrical wave of his hand.

'Good morning, sir,' they replied.

'You sound positively funereal this morning,' said the teacher. 'A reprise, please, with a great deal more gusto. Good morning, boys!'

The response was much louder and more good-humoured.

'Much better. Do sit down, please.'

By the door stood the boy I had met with his mother earlier that morning. He stared with wide disbelieving eyes and an open mouth at the small fat figure before him. He looked like a child who had just had his lollipop snatched from his sticky little hand.

'Ah,' said Mr Poppleton, displaying a set of impressive teeth. 'A new boy. And what is your name, young man?'

'John B . . . B . . . Brown, sir,' stuttered the boy, twiddling his hair nervously.

'John Brown, eh? A name in a million. Well, John Brown, you are very welcome, but you are late, nine days late to be precise.'

'I w . . . w . . . was ill, sir,' replied the boy. 'I had gl . . . glandular fever.'

'How very inconvenient for you, and not a little painful, I should imagine. Well, you are here now,

John Brown, and glad we are to have you with us.' He gestured to an empty seat. 'Take a pew and Simon Morgan, who will be your neighbour from now on, will explain all there is to know about KHC. I will be with you in a moment to tell you what work we are undertaking. Now, boys,' said the teacher, addressing the entire class, 'we have another new face in the classroom this morning. The gentleman in the corner is Mr Phinn, a school inspector, here to see how well we are doing. I hope he leaves us with a good impression, boys. Do you think he will?'

'Yes, sir,' they replied.

'Shall we say a hearty good morning to Mr Phinn?'

'Good morning, Mr Phinn,' chorused the class.

'Good morning,' I replied, sinking lower in the armchair.

'Now, you know what you have to do, boys,' continued Mr Poppleton. 'Today I would like you to continue with the poems you started last lesson. Mr Phinn is an *aficionado* of poetry, as I am, and might care to tour the classroom, talk with you about your poems and read some of them.'

So while Mr Poppleton furnished the new boy with the necessary books and equipment and explained the work he was to complete, I levered myself out of the armchair to look at the pupils' books. The boys were keen to show me what they had written and talk about their work.

'When we arrived,' said the first pupil I spoke to, 'we had to write a short autobiography so "Poppo"—I mean, Mr Poppleton—could learn a bit about us.' He opened his book to reveal a neat and informative account of his short life, together with illustrations and photographs. The work had been carefully and constructively marked in pencil. At the bottom was a long useful comment from the teacher with ideas for improvement.

'And how do you like English?' I asked.

'It's great. At prep school, I didn't enjoy it much. We did lots of boring exercises and copying but here it's really good. Mr Poppleton's a bit out of the ordinary but he's a really good teacher.' The boy thought for a moment before adding, 'He didn't tell me to say that, you know.'

'I'm sure he didn't,' I said, smiling. 'So what is your poem about?'

'We've been asked to write about somebody who is very special in our lives. It could be a parent or a friend, a brother or sister. I chose my Gran.'

'Why your Gran?'

'Well, grandparents are different from parents, aren't they? They're more fun, they don't tell you off as much as parents and they give you money. Do you want to read my poem?'

'Why don't you read it to me,' I said.

The boy turned a page, took a breath and read :

I like my Gran.
She's round and wrinkly and powdery
And smells of flowers and soap.
She's as comfy as a cushion to sit on.
When my mum shouts at me,
I go to my Gran,
And she says, 'Never you mind, love,
Your mum was like that when she was your age,
A real grumpybum!

Beneath the poem was a small sketch in black

ink of a smiling old lady with sparkling eyes and curly hair. There were tiny dots scattered on her upper lip.

'She has a lot of spots, your Gran,' I observed.

'No, they're not spots, Mr Phinn,' the boy told me. 'She's got a moustache.'

The next pupil, a bright-eyed Indian boy with a ready smile, shook my hand formally. 'Good morning, Mr Phinn,' he said. 'My name is Kirit Patel.'

'I'm pleased to meet you, Kirit,' I replied.

I talked to the boy for a while about his reading interests, tested him on some spellings and his knowledge of grammar and punctuation and was most impressed.

'May I look at your poem?' I asked finally.

'Of course,' he said, opening his book and then waiting expectantly for me to comment. His poem, entitled 'Shruti', was about his mischievous younger sister and was delightfully descriptive and amusing.

'Is it all right, sir?' he asked eventually.

'It's splendid,' I said.

'I've tried to put in some colourful words,' he told me seriously. 'I think it makes it more interesting, don't you? And there's some alliteration—that's when words in a sentence begin with the same letter. Mr Poppleton is very keen on alliteration.'

'Yes, I know,' I said, grinning.

I eventually found my way to the back corner desk where a small boy was putting the final touches to a poem about his father.

'Finished,' he said, with a sigh of satisfaction.

'May I look?' I asked.

He passed across his book, carefully backed in shiny brown paper and with his name, 'Russell Davis, Class 1A', written in large, neat letters on the front. I read the first few pages of his book—the potted autobiography. It was an immensely poignant account about his young life. He informed the reader in a matter-of-fact way that he was an only child and lived with his father in a 'pretty ordinary' redbrick terraced house close to the town centre. There was a small bedroom where he slept, a larger one for his father, a kitchen and living room, and a back yard with a shed where he kept his bicycle. There was not a great deal of money and they rarely went on holiday. Then his description became much more thoughtful and personal. His mother, he wrote, had left when he was small and he saw her infrequently. He saw nothing of his maternal grandparents. He felt sad about this and found it difficult to understand. However, he said he was happy living with a father who was as much a friend as a parent. The poem which followed was about a father whom he described as 'an ordinary-looking sort of man, a bit bald and overweight, the kind of man who wears shiny trousers, baggy cardigans and old slippers', but it went on to tell how special he was and how much he loved him.

'Your autobiography is a very honest account, Russell,' I told him. 'Do you not mind sharing such personal details with other people?'

'Why should I, sir?' he replied. 'It's the truth. I'm not ashamed of it. My father says it is always best to be honest.'

'He sounds a remarkable man, your father.'

'He is, sir. He works hard, he takes me to the

cinema, football matches, once we went to the theatre. We like to go for long walks and we talk about things a lot. We can talk about anything. He's just . . . well, special, you know.'

'And what quality do you admire most in this very special father of yours?' I asked.

The boy thought for a moment, staring at his book and biting his bottom lip. Then he looked up and into my eyes. 'When *he* makes a mistake, my father says he's sorry. Grown-ups don't tend to do that. If my father gets it wrong, he says so. He says it's not being weak to admit you don't always get things right or that you don't know something.'

I thought of the strident newspaper article the previous class had been asked to consider. The tub-thumping journalist who had little good to say about the younger generation ought to meet this polite, mature for his age, young student. There are many, many children who come from loving homes and are in the hands of hard-working and dedicated teachers but they are not the ones who appear on the front pages of newspapers. Boys like Russell do not make news.

'Sir?' The boy's voice broke into my thoughts.

'Oh, I'm sorry!' I exclaimed. 'I was miles away. I was just thinking about what you said. Well, Russell, I hope that if I have a son, he will speak about me in the same way as you speak about your father.'

'That's really up to you, isn't it, sir?' replied the boy, smiling broadly.

'Yes, I suppose it is,' I said.

When the bell sounded, the boys packed their bags, stood behind their desks and waited to be dismissed.

'Please complete your poem for homework,' the teacher told the class, 'learn the spellings I gave you yesterday and remember half an hour's reading every night. I tell them frequently, Mr Phinn, that they cannot become great writers unless they are great readers, for on the back of reading is writing. Good advice, eh?'

'Yes, indeed,' I said.

'Good morning, boys,' trumpeted Mr Poppleton.

'Good morning, sir, good morning, Mr Phinn,' they answered and filed out of the room.

'You have some talented pupils, Mr Poppleton,' I told him as we headed across the school yard. 'The work I have seen this morning was of an extremely high standard.'

'Yes, they are very good, but you would expect no less in a selective school. And I cannot really take credit for the standard of their work. The boys have only been at the school for less than two weeks and therefore any talent they have or good work they produce is down to their previous schools.'

'Yes, of course,' I said.

'Pupils of this calibre are sometimes a little daunting, I have to say,' he continued, 'but I have always been of the opinion that teachers should show children the ropes and not be at all surprised if they manage to climb higher than they. I'm sure somebody famous said that. Indeed some, like Kirit and Russell, will be making ropes of their own before long. Now, Mr Phinn, would you care to partake of a pre-prandial cup of tea prior to braving the school dining room and a plate of Mrs Payne's chicken nuggets and chips? Had Napoleon used Mrs Payne's chicken nuggets in his cannons at Waterloo instead of balls, the unfortunate emperor would, without a doubt, have won the day. They are like grapeshot, but few would hazard to tell her so.'

'That's kind, Mr Poppleton, but I want to look in at the library and see what is the extent and range of the stock. I need to report on the available resources, as well as on the teaching.'

'Ho, ho,' he chuckled. 'I shall await your observations on our college library with great interest.'

We had now arrived at the bicycle sheds where a knot of boys were in loud and intense discussion about a particularly impressive-looking machine with a shiny black frame and silver handlebars.

'What have we here?' asked Mr Poppleton. 'A little *conversazione*?'

'Oh no, sir,' said one of the boys, patting the bicycle they were discussing. 'It's a Raleigh Mustang.'

With a resounding laugh, the amazing Mr Poppleton scurried off in the direction of the school dining room for his chicken nuggets.

CHAPTER FIVE

As soon as I entered through the heavy doors of the school library, I knew exactly what Mr Poppleton meant by his enigmatic observation. It was a cold, gloomy room with wall-to-wall shelving in dark oak. There was not a student in sight, which was hardly surprising given the temperature and the inhospitable atmosphere. As I had told

Mr Poppleton, I always tried to find the time to check the school library even if it meant I had to do it during lunch—not that I had much appetite for chicken nuggets. I had come across some weird and wonderful titles in my time, most of which should have been thrown out onto the bonfire years ago. I made a habit of jotting down some of the worst into a notebook. They often came in handy when I was invited to give after-dinner talks.

I scanned the dull green and grey covers of the books on the shelves, and knew immediately I would be able to add to my collection: *Travels in Southern Rhodesia*, *Harmless Scientific Experiments for Boys* (I had once found the equivalent book for girls), *The Stately Houses of Scotland* (five volumes), *The Collected Sermons of Bishop Francis Feasby*. I prised a dusty volume entitled *Britannia's Empire* from the shelf. I opened the book at random and read: 'Pygmies are savage little black men but all loyal subjects of George V.'

The library of King Henry's College appeared not to have been updated for many years. I found *Scouts in Bondage* by Henry Prout, *The Skull of Swift* by Sir Shane Leslie, *Exhibition Poultry* by George R. Scott, *The Walking Stick Method of Self Defence* by an Officer of the Indian Army, *Leadership Secrets of Attila the Hun* by Wess Roberts PhD and, perhaps most bizarre of all, *Flashes from the Welsh Pulpit* by the Rev G. Davies. These were for the collector of the weird and wonderful but not of any interest to teenagers. I looked in vain for the bright glossy-backed paperbacks and sports magazines that appeal to adolescent boys but found none. I discovered a selection of more modern books in the fiction

71

section but the non-fiction stock was lamentably out-of-date and inappropriate.

I sat at a solid square table so typical of those found in old-fashioned libraries and began writing up some comments and recommendations about the lessons I had seen that morning, but found my mind kept wandering back to the conversation with young Russell. What would my sons or daughters say of me when they were teenagers, I thought. Would I be so loved and respected like Russell's father? Would I be as special to them as his father clearly was to him? I had been inspired in Mr Poppleton's classroom, by the man himself, by his infectious enthusiasm and by the poems the pupils had written. I pushed the notes away and began to scribble a poem of my own, dedicated to someone very special to me—my unborn child.

Always believe in yourself.
Promise always to be compassionate.
Appreciate that you make mistakes,
Recognise that I do, too.
Entrust me with—

I suddenly sensed a presence and, looking up, found a gangly boy with lanky brown hair and angry acne across his forehead and cheeks peering over my shoulder. It was Master Hugo Maxwell-Smith.

'Writing up your report?' he asked, eyeing the papers in front of me.

I quickly covered the poem. 'Yes, I am.'

'Should make interesting reading.'

I changed the subject. 'Is the library well used?' I asked, looking around the empty room. It was, of course, an inane question to ask.

'No, sir,' replied the boy simply. 'As you can see, there's nobody here except you and me. I hope your report will include some mention of the library. It needs a complete overhaul.'

'Yes, it will. So why are *you* here?' I asked.

'Doing a little research on the apostrophe, actually,' he replied.

'Really? I gathered it wasn't one of your favourite topics.'

'It isn't,' replied the boy, 'but I have been checking up on the rules.' No doubt to challenge poor Mr Frobisher again, I thought. 'It is interesting that the great writers didn't think much of the apostrophe. George Bernard Shaw, for example. The playwright, you know.'

'Yes, I do know,' I said.

'I found the following during the morning break,' he said, consulting a notepad. 'He says that he never used the apostrophe in any of his writing unless the omission would suggest another word. This is what he said. "There is not the faintest reason for persisting in the ugly and silly trick of peppering pages with these uncouth bacilli." That's what he wrote back in 1902. I couldn't have put it better myself. I thought Mr Frobisher might find that interesting.'

Infuriating, more like, I thought to myself.

'Well, I'll let you get back to your report,' he said, before disappearing behind a bookshelf.

*   *   *

The first lesson of the afternoon was with Mrs Todd, a former English mistress who had recently retired from the local comprehensive school but

73

who had been prevailed upon to return to the classroom to cover for a teacher who was away ill. She was a diminutive woman, smartly dressed in an expensive dark blue suit, a cream blouse and small black lace-up boots. She had neatly permed, tinted hair and an assortment of gold jewellery. There was not the slightest possibility of chalk dust coming into contact with Mrs Todd, I thought to myself.

The lesson, in which she revised some rules of spelling with a group of fifteen-year-olds, was lively and interesting. She was clearly a very knowledgeable teacher and she maintained order with a quiet self-assurance and good humour. I was interested to observe how she dealt with a confident, somewhat spotty-faced young man, in appearance and manner not unlike the rather unnerving Maxwell-Smith of Mr Frobisher's class. The boy was at pains to demonstrate what he thought was his strong command of the English spelling system. He raised his hand on a number of occasions to challenge the teacher but she retained her affable manner and composure. I am sure that the secret of dealing with such smart-Alecs is to keep calm and not let their clever comments affect you. Mrs Todd was consummate in dealing with such students.

Having completed her revision of the general rules, she wrote a list of awkwardly spelt words on the board, some correctly spelt, others not. Then, banning the use of all dictionaries, she told the students to write down in their exercise books the incorrect words correctly spelt. When they had completed the exercise, she wrote the correct spellings against the incorrect words, and asked each student to say how many he had amended correctly.

'But, Mrs Todd,' said the spotty boy when he discovered he was not as good as he thought, 'I'm certain "Inoculate" is spelt with two *n*'s. "I-n-n-o-c-u-l-a-t-e".'

'No, Michael, with just the one,' replied the teacher.

'Oh, I thought it was with two,' he said frowning. '*I've* always spelt it with two.'

'Have you really? Well, you were wrong to do so, I'm afraid,' replied the teacher pleasantly.

'"Innocuous" has two *n*'s,' he said.

'That is correct,' said Mrs Todd amiably. 'But "inoculate" has only the one.'

'Well, I'm pretty certain "desiccate" has two *s*'s,' he persisted and reached for his pocket dictionary.

'There are few certainties in life, Michael, but one of them is that "desiccate" has just the one *s*. The next time you are making a cake, have a look on the packet and you will see "desiccated coconut".'

The picture of the serious-faced but spotty young man baking a cake brought a smile to my lips. 'It's rather like the word which means "obstinate",' said the teacher, throwing me a knowing look. 'It is often thought that the word "asinine" has two *s*'s, too.'

The boy, having looked up the words in the dictionary and discovered that the teacher was, in fact, perfectly correct, remained in brooding silence for the rest of the lesson.

'You know, Mr Phinn,' Mrs Todd told me later, 'adolescence is a strange time in one's life, isn't it? All those changes. Some young people become so shy and self-conscious that to get them to talk is like getting blood out of a stone. Others, like Michael, do so enjoy showing off a little, and like to kick against authority. I have found that the very bright student can be as troublesome and challenging as the lazy and disaffected one. We have quite a few like Michael in the school. They just want to be noticed, be a little individual, flex their muscles. It's all part of growing up. I should know, I have four sons.'

'What a houseful you must have had,' I observed.

'Yes, indeed! And they all went on what felt like twenty-six-year long courses at university: medicine, architecture, French, fine art. That's why I need to do a bit of supply work, to put some money back into the bank account. It was an expensive business bringing up children.'

'You must be very proud of them,' I said.

'I am. Have you children, Mr Phinn?'

'No, not yet,' I replied. 'One on the way though.'

'Well, I expect your child will have all the advantages of life, as I hope my boys have had. Some children get so little support and encouragement at home, precious little love and attention. I used to work in an inner city school and, my goodness, some of those young people had desperate lives.'

'Did your boys come to King Henry's?' I asked.

'Good gracious, no!' she exclaimed. 'They attended St Ignatius, the Catholic Grammar. They would not have liked it here and, quite frankly, I don't intend to stay here for much longer. I've been asked to cover a maternity leave later this term at a girls' high school—The Lady Cavendish High

School for Girls. Sounds frightfully posh, doesn't it? Do you know the school at all?'

'I do,' I replied. 'It's an excellent school and the head of the English Department is one of the best teachers I have observed.'

Mrs Todd thought for a moment, as if considering whether or not to speak. 'This might sound a little unprofessional, Mr Phinn,' she said finally, 'but I do find the head of the English department at this school a very difficult man to relate to and his manner with the students is, at times, unfortunate.'

'I see.' I quickly changed the subject. I certainly did not wish to discuss Mr Frobisher with a member of his department. That *would* have been unprofessional. 'Michael seems quite a clever boy, doesn't he?'

'He is,' she agreed. 'Although he can be a little too clever for his own good. He's a very bright young man and he knows it. He just needs to exercise a little humility now and again. But I can handle Michael.'

'Yes, you certainly can,' I agreed. I had no doubt about that.

*　　　*　　　*

The last lesson of the day was with the sixth form and a newly qualified teacher. I arrived at the rather noisy classroom to find twenty or so students, all of whom I noted were in shirtsleeves, sitting around tables in animated discussion.

'Is there a teacher here?' I asked one young man sitting near the door, raising my voice above the hubbub.

'I'm the teacher,' he replied, giving me a broad smile. 'Simon Purdey.'

'Oh, I'm sorry, Mr Purdey,' I said, 'I thought you were one of the students.'

'Well, there are only a few years between us and I have been told that I look young for my age. You must be Mr Fish, the inspector.'

'Phinn,' I corrected.

'Oh, I did wonder when we were told it was Fish. Sounded a bit suspicious.'

'What are the students doing this afternoon?' I inquired.

'We're studying *Hamlet* as our "A" level text and I've asked the students to read through Act 1 and re-write it in a different genre: as a modern radio play, the opening chapter of a detective novel, a horror story, thriller, romance, monologue, documentary drama, that sort of thing. Each group has a different genre to consider.'

'Sounds interesting,' I said.

'Well, I thought it would get them straight into the play and also be a bit of fun before we start the more serious business of looking at the actual text. I think it's a better way than wading drearily through Shakespeare as I did at school. Do you know, we were made to write out passages of Shakespeare as a punishment? Would you credit that? The greatest words in the English language and they were set as a punishment! I only really came to appreciate Shakespeare when I was in the sixth form and a new teacher arrived. She just turned me on.'

'Yes,' I said. 'I had a remarkable English teacher in the sixth form, too.'

'Anyway,' continued the young man, 'I thought

that by writing the opening of the play in another form, the students would have to read the first act carefully and critically and then transpose it, making decisions about what to include and what to omit. Later we will look at the actual text itself and act it out. Do you want to see how far they have got?'

'Yes, I would,' I replied.

As I watched the series of highly original openings being acted out in front of the rest of the class, I recalled my sixth-form years when I too studied Shakespeare's most famous play. I was taught by a Miss Wainwright, a small, softly spoken woman who invariably wore a pristine white blouse buttoned up at the neck and a long dark skirt. The small lace handkerchief that she secreted up her sleeve would be occasionally plucked out to dab her mouth. Save for the large cameo brooch placed at her throat, she wore no jewellery and there was no vestige of make-up. What was so memorable about this remarkable teacher was her eyes. They shone with intensity, especially when she was discussing her favourite subject, Shakespeare. She had taken us to see a production of *King Lear* at the Rotherham Civic Theatre. I realise now that the acting had been wooden and the costumes bizarre, but the beauty and poignancy of the language had come through. King Lear had entered with his dead daughter draped in his arms and he howling to the heavens: 'She is gone forever!' To my horror, Miss Wainwright—sitting one away from me in the row had begun to cry, and I soon followed suit. She had indeed been an amazing teacher.

Whenever I saw an outstanding English teacher,

I often thought of Miss Mary Wainwright and thanked God for the good fortune of having been taught by her. She brought Shakespeare to life, and developed in me a love of literature for which I shall be forever grateful.

My thoughts were interrupted when I heard my name mentioned by the teacher. 'And the last version is one that Mr Phinn, as a Yorkshireman, will appreciate. It's the Yorkshire version of *Hamlet*.'

Two boys, ambled towards each other at the front of the room, hands thrust deep in their pockets.

'Hey up, 'Amlet.'

'Hey up, 'Oratio, what's tha doin' 'ere?'

'Nowt much. 'Ow abaat thee then, 'Amlet? I 'ant seen thee for a bit.'

'Nay, I'm not that champion, 'Oratio, if t'truth be towld.'

'Whay, 'Amlet, what's oop?'

'Mi dad's deead, mi mam's married mi uncle and mi girl friend does nowt but nag, nag, nag. I tell thee 'Oratio, I'm weary wi' it.'

'Aye, tha's not far wrong theer, 'Amlet. She's gor a reight gob on 'er, that Hophilia. Teks after 'er owld man.'

'Anyroad, 'Oratio, what's tha doin' 'ere in Helsinor?'

'I've come for thee dad's funeral.'

'More like mi mam's wedding.'

'Aye, she dint let t'grass grow under 'er feet, did she?'

'I don't know what mi owld man 'ud mek of it, 'Oratio, I really don't.'

'Well, tha can ask 'im theeself, 'Amlet.'

' 'Ow's tha mean?'

' 'E's been walkin' on t'battlements every neet this week, a-mooanin' and a-grooanin' and purrin' t'wind up iverybody. We're sick to deeath on it, 'Amlet, we really are.'

'Ger on!'

'It's reight, 'Amlet. 'E won't shurrup. A-mooanin' and a-grooanin' an' a-clankin' abaat like there's no tomorra.'

'I wonder wor 'e wants?'

'Well, tha can ask 'im thaself, 'cos 'ere 'e comes now.'

A third boy entered. ' 'Ey up, our 'Amlet.'

' 'Ey up, dad. How's it gooin'?'

' 'Ow's it gooin'? How's it gooin'? What's tha mean, how's it gooin'? I'm deead, 'Amlet, and I'm not that chuffed abaat it.'

'Oh, aye, I forgot.'

'I was done in, 'Amlet, murdered, killed, slayed, bumped off, hassassinated.'

'Ee, that were a rotten trick.'

'Rotten trick! Rotten trick! It were bloody criminal, that's what it were.'

'Who did it, dad?'

'Mi kid brother.'

'Mi Uncle Claudius?'

'Aye, 'im what's nicked mi crown and married thee mam.'

'What's to do, then, dad?'

'What's tha mean, what's to do?'

'What's tha come back fer?'

'I wants thee to sooart thy uncle out, that's what I wants thee to do. I wants thee to do to 'im what 'e did to me, our 'Amlet. Now I 'ope tha's got t'gumption for it. Come on, 'Oratio, let's let t'lad get crackin'.'

As I watched and laughed along with the teacher and students, I thought of Mr Poppleton's words that young people are naturally very funny. He was right: humour is highly related to learning and adds inestimably to our quality of life. There are few things more pleasurable to hear in life than young people laughing unselfconsciously.

Following the performance, there was loud and spontaneous applause and cheering which died suddenly when the door opened and there stood Mr Frobisher, like 'The Ghost of Christmas Past'.

'There is a great deal of noise coming from this room,' he said. 'I could hear it at the end of the corridor.'

'We're studying *Hamlet*,' explained Mr Purdey, seemingly unperturbed by the interruption.

'Really? I wasn't aware, Mr Purdey, that *Hamlet* was quite so amusing.' Mr Frobisher then caught sight of me and gave a watery smile. 'Ah, Mr Phinn, I didn't see you sitting there. I was wondering where you had got to. I shall be on bus duty after school, so will join you and Mr Nelson at about half past four, if that is convenient.'

'Yes, that's fine,' I said.

He peered around the room. 'And you boys will be aware of the school rules on the wearing of blazers. Well, do carry on, Mr Purdey,' said the head of English, leaving the room.

*   *   *

'What a day,' said Mr Nelson, breathing out heavily. 'I've barely had chance to get a cup of tea, it's been so busy.'

I sat before the headmaster at the end of the school day, on the uncomfortable ladderback chair, thinking that a cup of tea would indeed be most acceptable. Clearly one was not forthcoming and, anyway, if it had been, the school secretary might well have added more than milk to it.

'Mr Frobisher will not be long,' said Mr Nelson. 'I suggest, to save your repeating yourself, we wait for him to join us.'

'Actually, Mr Nelson,' I replied, deciding to get the difficult bit over with as quickly as possible, 'I would prefer to have a private word with you before Mr Frobisher arrives.'

The headmaster turned to face me, his brow furrowing. 'Oh.'

'I think it might be better.'

'This sounds rather ominous, Mr Phinn,' he said. 'Do I take it you are not entirely satisfied with what you have seen today?'

'Not entirely,' I told him. 'On the whole, the lessons I observed were very good. Indeed, some were excellent. Generally, the teaching in the department is highly competent and at times most innovative and imaginative, but there is one exception, I am afraid to say.'

'Ah,' sighed the headteacher, 'Mr Poppleton. It has to be said, he is rather eccentric and individualistic, but he has been at the school for more years than I can remember and the boys do so enjoy his teaching. Indeed, his examination results are most creditable. I have mentioned the snuff—'

'It's not Mr Poppleton,' I interrupted. 'His lesson was excellent.'

'Is it Mr Purdey? Mr Adams? I am sure you are

83

aware that they have just started their teaching careers and it is to be expected that—'

'No, their lessons were fine.'

'Surely, it's not Mrs Todd. I am aware that she has not taught in a grammar school before, but she came highly recommended by the headteacher of the comprehensive where she taught and has had extensive teaching experience. Indeed—'

'Mr Nelson, it is none of these teachers,' I told him.

The headmaster began rubbing his temples. 'Then, by a process of elimination, it must be the head of department. You know, I had a feeling it would be Mr Frobisher.'

'It is Mr Frobisher,' I said.

'And you felt his lesson to be unsatisfactory?'

'I appreciate that Mr Frobisher has one particularly difficult boy in his class—'

'Ah, yes, Maxwell-Smith. He can indeed be a thorn in the side, that young man. His father is quite a handful too and often contacts the school with one complaint or another.'

'Yes, the boy was a difficult and very demanding student. I am aware that I have only observed the one lesson, but I did judge it to be less than satisfactory.'

'What was the lesson about?' asked the headmaster.

'It was an extremely dreary lesson on the use of the apostrophe.'

'I was under the impression, Mr Phinn,' said Mr Nelson, 'that the apostrophe *is* a dreary subject.'

'More importantly,' I said, 'Mr Frobisher has not the best relationship with the students and the work that I managed to see was extremely narrow in range.'

Mr Nelson thought for a moment before replying. 'Mr Frobisher, it has to be admitted, is not the most dynamic and enthusiastic of teachers and I have noticed that he found teaching rather more exacting last year but he is very loyal to the school, has not had a day's absence as long as I can remember and, with regard to his duties, is punctilious. But—'

'But as a teacher?' I inquired.

'He is, how does one put this, not as good as he was. In fact, he became rather disillusioned several years ago. He applied for deputy headships a number of times but was unsuccessful, despite his excellent academic qualifications. I imagine he thought he would end his career as a headmaster. He finds the students these days rather more outspoken and less attentive. He harks back to a golden age, I'm afraid, when pupils did what they were told without question, a time when there was the cane. Young people these days do tend to be more forthright and, of course, we have some very exigent students here. Maxwell-Smith is not alone. I realise Mr Frobisher is not the best teacher in the world, but he is sound enough, don't you think? Certainly his classrooms are quiet, the students always appear to be in a workmanlike atmosphere and he marks his books thoroughly. And he has only a couple more years to go. Of course, when he retires, it is my intention to appoint someone with greater energy and enthusiasm.' This monologue sounded to me as if the headmaster was trying to convince himself.

'As I said, I have only observed one lesson,' I

replied, 'and it would be unreasonable to judge a teacher on the evidence of one lesson but I am sufficiently concerned to make a return visit and spend more time in the department observing him.'

'I don't think that will be very well received,' sighed the headmaster. 'Your predecessor, Mrs Young, did spend some time a few years ago doing just that but with little effect.'

'I wasn't aware of that,' I said, sitting up on the hard wooden chair.

'I am sure her report will be filed at the Education Office. Did you not read through it prior to your visit?'

'No, I didn't,' I replied, feeling rather guilty.

'Well, Mrs Young felt very much the same way as you do. Following her visit, Mr Frobisher agreed to relinquish the sixth form teaching which he was finding the most irksome. He also attended one or two courses on the development of communication skills but it is very difficult to change the habits of a lifetime.'

'So, there have been reservations expressed about his competence before?' I asked.

'Well, yes, but I never considered them serious enough to institute any kind of disciplinary proceedings. Mr Ball, one of Her Majesty's Inspectors, who visited us some years ago, was not impressed but, as I said to him at the time, I've seen far worse teachers than Mr Frobisher in my career. It is true I have received one or two parental complaints about him but not enough to take things further. In any case, as you will be well aware, it is very difficult to do anything about a teacher in terms of disciplinary action unless he runs off with a sixth-form girl or steals the dinner money. I have, it is fair to say,' said Mr Nelson, staring out of the window like the great admiral himself looking for his lost fleet, 'tended to turn a bit of a blind eye. As I intimated, Mr Frobisher is near the end of his career. Is it really worth all the time and trouble, quite apart from the effect it will have upon the man himself and on the school, to pursue this further?'

'Children deserve the best, Mr Nelson,' I said.

At that very moment there was a rap on the door and the man himself entered. 'May I come in?' said Mr Frobisher.

CHAPTER SIX

That evening I arrived home to find a note from Christine. She had a governors' meeting after school that afternoon, followed by a parents' meeting in the evening, so would not be in until late. I was pleased in a way because I could settle down without any disturbance and try to put together the report on King Henry's—a report I knew would be the most difficult I had ever written. It was after ten o'clock when I finally put down my pen and placed the completed report in my briefcase, just at the very moment when Christine walked in.

'Hello,' she said brightly, coming over and pecking me on the cheek.

'How did it go?' I asked.

'Fine. I couldn't ask for better governors, and the parents' evening went like a dream. It's so good to have supportive colleagues and parents. It makes such a difference.'

'That's good,' I said.

'And did you have a good day?' she asked.

'How long have you got?'

'Oh dear,' she said, 'that bad? Do you want to talk about it?'

'No,' I said, 'not now, anyway. I'm bushed. I think I'll turn in.'

'Are you sure you don't want to talk about it?' Christine asked, slipping her arm through mine. 'We could have a glass of wine, snuggle up in front of the fire and you could tell me all about it.'

'Not now, love,' I replied. 'I've had a really tiring day. I'm sorry I'm such a misery. I'll snap out of it this weekend, I promise.'

The next day, on my way to a conference in York, I dropped the report off at the office for Julie to type. I spent the morning in lectures, the content of which, I fear, passed clean over my head, and the afternoon in discussion groups. I contributed nothing, sitting there in brooding silence. My mind was full of the events of the previous day at King Henry's College.

I arrived back at the office at the end of the afternoon to find Julie had typed out the report, placed a copy on my desk and sent another to Dr Gore's office. This would be despatched to the school. I read through what I had written. In the cold light of day, it sounded extremely critical.

At that moment Sidney and David breezed in. 'Friday!' exclaimed Sidney. 'Thank God it's Friday!'

'Do keep it down, Sidney,' said David. 'You know the psychologists on the bottom floor have complained about your booming voice and Gervase is trying to work. Hello, Gervase.'

'Hello,' I replied wearily.

'Oh dear,' said Sidney, dropping his briefcase on his desk with a thump and flopping into his chair. 'Our young colleague does look down in the dumps. Whatever's the matter?'

'I've got things on my mind,' I told him with the voice of a peevish child.

'We've all got things on our minds,' said Sidney unsympathetically, stretching back and observing the cracks on the ceiling.

'Well, you don't look as if you have,' I retorted. 'I've never seen you so cheerful.'

'That is because,' said David, 'Harold has laid down the law to the headmaster of West Challerton High School and Sidney is to make his triumphant return next week.'

'Yes, indeed,' chortled Sidney. 'Harold was quite superb. It was a bravura performance on the phone. I heard it all. He's going in with me next week to see Mr Pennington-Smith.'

'I'm glad somebody's happy,' I said.

'Gervase,' said David, peering over the top of his spectacles, 'if I had pulled an expression like that when I was a lad, my old Welsh grandmother would have told me I had a face like a smacked bottom.'

'Yes, for goodness sake, cheer up,' said Sidney, throwing a ball of screwed up paper in my direction. 'You are about as much fun as an incontinent trapeze artist. There's the weekend ahead of you. No more reports, school visits or paperwork, no shrill telephones ringing every five minutes. Above all, a blessed rest from the homely words of wisdom of David's old Welsh grandmother whom, if I could get hold of her, I would cheerfully throttle.'

'I don't feel like cheering up, Sidney,' I said. 'I've told you, I've got things on my mind.'

'What, pray,' asked Sidney, 'could a healthy young man like you, with a beautiful wife, a youngster on the way, a picture-postcard cottage in the Dales and a rewarding and relatively well-paid profession, have to worry about?'

'Yes, do tell us,' said David. 'You were in such high spirits a couple of days ago. Whatever's happened?'

'As Connie would say,' said Sidney, ' "A trouble shared is a trouble doubled." Do tell.'

Connie, the caretaker of the Staff Development Centre, was a mistress of malapropisms and *non sequiturs*.

So I told them about my visit to King Henry's College the previous day and the verbal report I had given after school.

'And how did the head of department react,' asked Sidney, sitting up, 'when you informed him that he was useless?'

'Sidney!' I snapped. 'I did not say he was useless. I said that his lesson was less than satisfactory.'

'It's much the same thing. You're just couching it in euphemistic language. "Less than satisfactory" means "unsatisfactory" which means "weak" or "poor", "below standard", "inadequate", "incompetent", ergo "useless". I recall once when I had a similar tricky situation—'

'Look, Sidney,' interrupted David, holding up a restraining hand, 'let the poor man finish. Now, Gervase, what happened when you told the head of English that his lesson wasn't up to much?'

'Less than satisfactory,' I corrected him.

'Yes, yes, less than satisfactory,' David repeated.

90

I related the whole dreadful episode: how Mr Frobisher had turned a ghastly white, shot bolt upright in his chair and had begun to tremble with anger; how he had told me that he had never had his professional competence challenged like that in all his forty years of teaching and that he intended to take matters further with his union representative.

'Then he upped and walked out,' I told my colleagues.

'High drama, indeed,' said Sidney.

'And what was old Horatio doing while all this was going on?' asked David.

'Who?'

'Nelson.'

'Turning a blind eye,' I said glumly. 'He never opened his mouth.'

'Typical,' said David. 'Anything for a quiet life. He is not a man of decisive action, Mr Nelson. It's a case of the captain having lost control of the ship at KHC or perhaps, more appropriately, the admiral having lost control of the fleet.'

'Well, to be frank, I think you could have handled it rather better,' said Sidney unhelpfully.

'Really?' I replied, with clear irritation in my voice. 'How?'

'By bottling out, like Sidney would have done,' murmured David.

'Not at all,' said Sidney. 'By employing greater tact and diplomacy.'

'Ha!' snorted David. '"Tact" and "diplomacy" are not words in your vocabulary.'

'Had it been me,' continued Sidney, 'I would have told the headmaster, prior to the head of English arriving on the scene, that I had an urgent

91

meeting after school so could not stay to discuss the day. I would have told him that I would be submitting a full and detailed written report of my visit and that I would make another appointment with the head of English, should he wish to discuss it. Of course, it would be very unlikely, given the circumstances, that this Mr Frobisher would wish to see me again. I should then have left the school before the arrival of the head of department. I really think it was neither the time nor place to give such critical feedback to the man, particularly in front of the headmaster.'

'That's only putting it off,' I replied.

'No, it isn't,' said Sidney, 'because, after sending the report, I would have placed the matter firmly in Harold's in-tray. Firstly, he has vast experience in coping with awkward issues and secondly, as the Senior Inspector, he is paid to deal with such difficult situations. Harold would then go into the school and talk with the headmaster and the head of English and I should be free to get on with my other work.'

'In other words,' said David smugly, 'you would bottle out and get somebody else to fire your bullets for you. That is so typical of you, Sidney!'

'Well, come on then, fount of all wisdom, what would you have done?' asked his colleague.

'Well,' said David, removing his spectacles, 'I do think it was perhaps a little unfortunate, Gervase, that you criticised the head of department in front of the headmaster. You might have guessed, from seeing him teach and his manner, that he would be a prickly customer. Had it been me, I should have arranged to see the head of English privately next week and held off writing the report. I would have

92

discussed the lesson with him in detail and given him the opportunity of responding. After all, it was just one lesson and it was with the older pupils who tend to be more difficult to handle. This lesson might not have been at all typical.'

'Then what?' I asked.

'I would have written the report, shown it to Harold and sought his advice. I would then have returned to the school to discuss it with the headmaster, arranging further visits to observe a series of lessons and to offer advice and support.'

'He wasn't the sort of man to readily accept any advice and support,' I said glumly. 'Anyway, it's easy with hindsight. It's too late to do any of that now. I've already sent the report in.'

'My goodness, how expeditious!' exclaimed Sidney.

'There are some people in life who like to get things done quickly,' David told him, staring at the pile of papers on Sidney's desk. 'Of course, there are others who do not.'

'I wanted it out of the way,' I said. 'I finished it last night and Julie typed it up and took it over to County Hall this morning.'

'Have you got a copy to hand?' asked David.

I reached over to my out-tray and passed the document across the desk. David read it without comment then passed it to Sidney who huffed and puffed and grimaced his way through it.

'You don't mince your words,' said Sidney. 'Talk about "going for the juggler", as Connie would say.'

'Well, I was irritated by the man,' I said defensively. 'He was quite offhand with me and his lesson was unsatisfactory. Furthermore, one of the English staff told me he was a difficult man to work with and wasn't good with the students.'

'A bit unprofessional that, Gervase, if I may say so,' said Sidney, 'discussing the head of department with a colleague. He might have an axe to grind.'

'It was a woman, actually, and I didn't discuss him with her. The information was volunteered. And she didn't have an axe to grind either. She was the supply teacher. I have strong reservations about Mr Frobisher and that is what I have put in my report.'

'But it was only one lesson,' said David quietly.

'I know.'

'And you speak in all these glowing terms about his colleagues,' said Sidney. 'He stands out like the proverbial wicked fairy at the christening. I mean, to be told everyone in your department is brilliant and you are useless could finish the poor old bloke off.'

'Sidney! How many more times! I did not say he was useless and if you had met him the last description you would use of the man is "poor old bloke".'

'Well, if I received a report like that,' said Sidney, 'I would contemplate throwing myself head first down a pothole in Grassington.'

'Why a pothole in Grassington?' asked David.

'You know what I mean,' replied Sidney. 'A report like that one would make me feel positively suicidal.'

I felt considerably worse now. Perhaps the report was, after all, too critical. 'Does it sound that bad?' I asked.

'I'm afraid it does,' said David. 'But all is not lost. The county mail into schools doesn't go out until next Tuesday afternoon. If you retrieve the report, moderate the tone a little, let Harold have a glance through it and get his advice on the matter, all is not lost. Of course, it will have to be Monday morning now. They will have all left by this time.'

'An excellent idea,' said Sidney, just as the clock on the County Hall clock struck six. 'And that's home-time, I think. Oh, and Julie said there was that loud man on the phone to speak to you again. I hope it isn't another problem, old boy.'

*　　　*　　　*

Christine had obviously taken considerable trouble to prepare a nice supper that evening but I just did not feel like eating. I poked the potatoes around the plate and made a half-hearted attempt to eat the meat.

'Don't you like it?' she asked. 'I thought fillet steak with garlic butter was one of your favourites.'

'It's fine,' I said, 'it's just that I'm not that hungry.'

'What's wrong?' she asked, sliding a hand across the table and taking mine. 'You were upset about something last night. What is it?'

'I think I really mishandled a situation in a school yesterday,' I told her gloomily. 'There was a head of department whom I criticised in front of the headmaster and he just stormed out of the room. I feel quite bad about it now.'

'I'm sure you're over-reacting,' said Christine. 'Did you have a word with Harold about it?'

'No, I should have done,' I replied. 'I did tell David and Sidney today and asked what they thought.'

'And?'

'Talk about Job's comforters. They think I could have handled it better.' I told her what they had said.

'This head of department, is he any good?'

'Well, the lesson I observed was certainly rather poor. It wasn't disastrous. The pupils weren't shouting and running about or anything like that, but he had quite an unpleasant manner with the students, the work in their books was narrow and he'd gone mad with the red pen. It looked as if someone had bled over the pages. And he was very brusque with me.'

'Were the pupils making much progress in their work, do you think?'

'No, not really.'

'Do you think they were enjoying the subject?'

'No, I don't think that they were.'

'How long has he been teaching, this head of department?' asked Christine.

'Nearly forty years.'

'Forty years? And nobody's ever said anything about him before?'

'Well, they have as a matter of fact. I believe an HMI, a man called Ball, was critical of him and I dug out the report that my predecessor, Mrs Young, had written about him.'

'And?'

'She was not that impressed and tried to get him on some courses but it doesn't seem to have done much good.'

'Well, things don't seem to have improved by the sound of it,' said Christine, 'and he's gone on teaching class after class, year after year. It seems to me that the headmaster has a lot to answer for and, for that matter, the inspectors who have seen him teach and not really taken any action.'

'It's not quite as easy as that, Christine,' I told her. 'As the headmaster was at pains to point out, and he's right, it's really hard to dismiss a teacher unless he steals the dinner money or runs off with a sixth-form girl. This man's lessons are not so bad as to lead to his being sacked. I mean, the students don't riot, he sets homework and marks their books.'

'Look, Gervase, you are always going on about children deserving the best that teachers can give, how they only have the one chance at education, that they need to be taught by enthusiastic, committed, good-humoured and hard-working people.'

Christine was throwing my own words back in my face. 'Yes, I know,' I said.

'Be honest, would you want this man teaching our child?'

'No, I wouldn't.'

'Was he enthusiastic, committed, good-humoured and hard-working?' she asked.

'Not when I saw him, he wasn't.'

'Then you had to say so. Your job is not going round schools telling poor teachers that they are fine, that everything in the garden is rosy. If there were a member of my staff who was not up to scratch, they would be told and I would help them to improve. If they didn't improve then they would have to go. It's as simple as that. Isn't your job to tell the truth as you see it, which sometimes means being critical? Of course, you have to celebrate what is good in a school, tell teachers who are doing a good job that they are doing a good job and tell those who aren't, that they need to improve.'

'Yes, I know you're right,' I said. 'It's just that it was pretty unpleasant and for some reason I feel very down about the whole situation. Anyway, once I've got the report back and made it less trenchant, I'm sure I'll feel better.'

'You're changing the report?' she asked.

'Yes.'

'Do you think that's a good idea?'

'What?'

'Changing the report just because Sidney and David said you were too hard on this teacher. I think you have to stick to what you believe, grasp the nettle and face the consequences.'

'Christine!' I snapped irritably. 'I wish I had never brought the wretched matter up. I'm feeling even worse about it now.'

'OK! OK! You do what you think best,' she said, beginning to clear the plates away.

I lapsed into a moody silence. When Christine began washing the dishes, I crept up behind her and put my arms around her waist. 'I'm sorry I was sharp with you,' I said. 'It's just that I was really looking forward to a break from work. This thing is like a black cloud. But you're probably right. I do need to grasp this particular nettle. Anyway, I'm not going to think about it any more. Let's just enjoy the weekend.'

Christine turned and kissed me on the cheek. 'It will be a taboo subject,' she said. 'Oh, and speaking of nettles, tomorrow you promised to sort out the garden. Half the village seems to be out in their gardens, and there are bonfires everywhere.'

*   *   *

98

On the following Monday morning I made my way along the neat gravel footpath bordering the well-tended lawns in front of County Hall to retrieve the report on King Henry's College. Despite my promise, I had thought about it a great deal over the weekend and had decided to take David's advice and make the commentary on Mr Frobisher's lesson less forthright and critical. I did not tell Christine.

Each time I took this route across the formal gardens to the front of County Hall, I recalled the first occasion, over three years earlier, when I had arrived for interview for the post of Inspector for English and Drama. The huge, grey-stone edifice had overawed me then, as it did now. The interior of the building was also daunting: endless cold, echoey corridors, high ornate ceilings, polished wooden floors, huge marble statues, endless rows of oil paintings of stern-looking dignitaries and sepia photographs of former mayors and aldermen. It was like a mausoleum.

Mrs Savage's office was in the Annexe, a bright, modern block which clung to the older darker building like some pale brown parasite. On her door, emblazoned in large black letters, it stated 'MRS BRENDA SAVAGE, Personal Assistant to the Chief Education Officer'. Since my last visit, at the end of the previous term, there had been an addition. A small box had been fastened to the frame of the door encasing what appeared to be a set of miniature traffic lights—three circles in red, amber and green. Above were the instructions to press the buzzer beneath and then wait. Julie had warned me about this contraption which I had, in fact, already seen in operation at one of the schools

I had visited the previous year. The idea behind the ingenious device was for the visitor to press the buzzer to gain the attention of the person inside the office. The headmaster, or whoever was within the office, then had three options from which to choose. He would press a button and one of the options would light up. It was only when the circles were illuminated that the instructions could be seen: 'Engaged', 'Please Wait' or 'Please Enter'.

All very clever, but I had to smile. In the school where I had seen this before, it had worked well for the first few weeks, but then the headteacher became concerned that so few people sought to see him. The reason soon became clear when the caretaker, wishing to see the headteacher one day, duly pressed the buzzer and a few seconds later one of the circles had lit up. The caretaker, being a forthright fellow, thought he should draw the headmaster's attention to the message. It turned out that one rather inventive pupil, who had been sent to the headmaster for misbehaviour just after the installation of the device, had waited outside the room. Having nothing better to occupy his time, the miscreant had, with a penknife, carefully erased the black lettering which stated 'Please Wait' and substituted a phrase of his own by writing on the plastic with a black felt-tip pen, his alternative only being seen when the panel lit up. Visitors arriving at the headteacher's door, duly pressed the buzzer and the little circle lit up with the instruction to 'Piss Off!' What had amazed the headmaster was that not one pupil, parent or member of staff had seen fit to inform him prior to the caretaker's fortuitous arrival.

I pressed the buzzer on Mrs Savage's door and,

100

much to my amusement, every light lit up. I knocked and entered. Mrs Savage stood beside her desk, a clutch of papers in her hand. She was, as usual, immaculately dressed. That morning she wore a calf-length pleated blue suit with diamanté buttons, cashmere jumper and smart, impressively pointed black shoes. Her long nails were painted a pale pink and her face was heavily made up. There was the fragrance of expensive perfume in the air. One had to admit it, the woman looked stylish.

She glanced at me imperiously as I entered. 'I did ask you to wait, Mr Phinn,' she said irritably. 'I've not quite finished reading though this "Health and Safety" document for Dr Gore yet. He is in urgent need of it this morning before his meeting.'

'All your lights lit up, Mrs Savage,' I told her.

'I beg your pardon?' she asked witheringly.

'On your door. All your little lights, they lit up at the same time.'

'Well, that is most strange,' she said. She looked down at her desk and scrutinised a small box-like affair with buttons on the top.

'Not to say very confusing,' I added.

'Pardon?'

'All your little lights, illuminating together.'

'I hope you were not heavy-handed with my buzzer,' she said. When I just smiled, she sat down and continued. 'I shall ask the janitor to take a look at it. Now then, Mr Phinn, as I said, you will have to wait a moment while I finish reading this report. You may sit there,' she said, indicating the chair which was placed strategically in front of her desk.

I did as I was bid, and gazed around me. Her office was plush, warm, fully carpeted and equipped with comfortable state-of-the-art

101

furniture. Through the windows was a fine view of Fettlesham and beyond to the moors and distant purple peaks.

Mrs Savage put aside the report, and said briskly, 'Now, Mr Phinn, is there something you want?'

What a stupid question to ask, I thought. Would I be there in front of her if I didn't want anything? 'Yes, there is something I want,' I replied. The chair on which I was sitting was lower than her huge swivel chair, so I found myself staring up into her eyes. 'I would like to have back a report which I sent over on Friday, please.'

'Like it back!' she exclaimed, as if I had made some sort of improper suggestion. 'That is out of the question.'

'I don't see why,' I said. 'It hasn't been sent out to the school yet, has it?'

'As a matter of fact, it hasn't,' she replied curtly. 'County mail, as I am sure you are well aware, is despatched to schools on Tuesday afternoons.'

'So there should be no problem in my having back the report then,' I said.

'Ah, but there is, Mr Phinn,' she said, carefully folding her hands before her on the desk and presenting me with the all-too-familiar unpleasant smile. 'Once I have received the reports they cannot be returned.'

'Why?'

'Because they can't!' she snapped, a defensive defiance blazing in her eyes.

'But I can't see why there should be a problem in my asking for my report back. I need to amend it and make certain important additions.'

'Mr Phinn,' she said in an exaggeratedly patient

tone of voice, 'once a report is received in this office, it is duplicated. One copy goes in Dr Gore's in-tray and then placed on file and the top copy is despatched to the relevant school. There is no procedure for the return of reports. If inspectors started demanding their reports back as soon as they had completed them, we would descend into chaos and confusion in no time. So, it is quite out of the question for me to return your report.'

'In the three years I have been working as an inspector, Mrs Savage,' I told her, trying to keep calm, 'I have never requested the return of a single report and I very much doubt whether there will be another occasion for a very long time. However, it is extremely important that I get this particular one back.'

She gave me a look of flat finality. 'I am sorry, Mr Phinn, but there is not the slightest possibility of my surrendering that report.'

I drew a deep and exasperated breath. 'Is Dr Gore in?' I asked.

'I don't see how pertinent that is,' she said.

'I would like to ask him if he would authorise the return of the report.'

'Dr Gore is not available. He is extremely busy, particularly on Mondays, and without an appointment—'

'Tomorrow morning?'

'I'm sorry?'

'Could I make an appointment to see him first thing tomorrow morning?'

Mrs Savage gave a slight smile and her eyes narrowed in triumph. 'He is in London at a conference tomorrow morning.'

'Mrs Savage,' I said, gripping the edge of her

desk, 'are you going to let me have that report back?'

'No, Mr Phinn,' she said calmly. 'I am not. Procedures must be followed and—'

Without waiting to hear her out, I jumped to my feet and strode for the door. I slammed it behind me, setting off all three little lights in the process. 'Dreadful woman!' I muttered to myself between gritted teeth, as I marched down the corridor. 'Dreadful woman!'

Back in the inspectors' office I immediately telephoned King Henry's College. I had decided to have a word with Mr Frobisher prior to his reading the damning report and was planning to suggest that I call in at the school to discuss it with him later that week.

'Good morning, King Henry's College,' came a formal voice down the line. 'Mrs Winterton, school secretary speaking.'

'Oh, good morning,' I replied, with a sinking feeling in my stomach. 'This is Gervase Phinn from the School Inspectors' Division at County Hall.'

'Mr Phinn?' There was a sharp intake of breath.

'Yes,' I replied. 'May I speak with Mr Frobisher, please?'

'I am afraid not. Mr Frobisher is away today.'

'Have you any idea when he will be back?'

'No, I haven't.'

'What's wrong?' I asked. 'Is he ill?'

'He would hardly be off school if he were not ill,' came back the reply. 'It's the first occasion in my time at King Henry's that he has had time off. I believe he felt unwell after your visit last Friday.'

'Oh, I see.' My heart sank down into my shoes. 'Perhaps when he does return, you would ask him to contact me at the Education Office on extension 8989.'

'Yes, I can do that, Mr Phinn. I shall pass on your message to Mr Frobisher when he returns to school.'

'Thank you,' I said, placing the telephone down on the receiver with a dull empty ache in the pit of my stomach. Now what was I going to do?

CHAPTER SEVEN

The week ahead was so busy I did not have time to dwell on the fate of Mr Frobisher. Tuesday found me bright and early for a short inspection of Butterthwaite, a small rural school set in the most magnificent countryside. The two-room schoolhouse, sheltered by sycamores and ancient oaks, stood square and solid at the head of the dale. From the classroom window pale green pastures, dotted with grazing sheep and criss-crossed by grey stone walls, rolled upwards to the great whaleback hills and gloomy grey clouds in the distance. The scene had a cold and eerie beauty about it.

The school had no major problems and I was able to give the headteacher a positive evaluation. It was at the end of the day when I joined a sturdy-looking little boy with a healthy complexion who was standing at the classroom window, hands deep in his pockets, surveying the vast panorama which stretched out before him. He was about six or seven years old.

'Just waiting for mi mam to come,' he told me.

'She's offen a bit late. She 'as a lot to do on t'farm.'

'Well, I'm sure she'll not be long,' I said.

'Aye, well, I'm not goin' anyweer.'

'Beautiful view,' I said.

'It's not bad, in't?' He dug his hands deeper into his pockets. 'Autumn's comin' on,' observed the child like a little old man. 'Not be long afoor t'leaves start to fall and t'bracken turns gowld. Looks like it's gunna be a bad winter an' all. We 'ad a lot o'snow last year. Mi dad can't be doin' wi' snow.'

'I'm not over keen,' I said. 'And what's your name?'

'Andrew.'

'Well, it's certainly a beautiful view, Andrew,' I said. 'You're a lucky boy to live up here.'

'Aye, as I said, it's all reight. Better in t'summer than winter though, when tha can get out and about. Starts about this time o' year, does winter, when it gets cowld and wet and windy.'

'And what do you like best at school?' I asked.

'I likes to read and I likes number work. I'm good at sums.'

'Are you?' I thought I'd test him on his arithmetic. 'How many sheep can you see in that field?' I asked him.

'Eh?'

'Can you tell me how many sheep you can see in the field?'

'Aye, I can.'

'Well, how many can you see?'

'I can see all on 'em,' he replied.

I chuckled. 'No, I meant how many altogether. Could you count them for me.'

'Aye, I suppose I could. I'm good at countin'.'

'Perhaps you'd like to show me,' I persisted.

'Well, there's five Swaledales and six Texels, three hybrids and four hoggits.' He paused for a moment. 'That makes eighteen in total, dunt it? And don't ask me to count t'rabbits because they waint stay still long enough for me to tot 'em up.' A large and rusty old Land-Rover pulled up outside the school gate. 'Hey up, mi mam's 'ere.' With a wave he scurried off. 'Tarra!'

I saw him clamber up beside his mother, a large and cheerful-looking woman with ruddy cheeks. She gave him a great hug, strapped him in his seat and drove off.

*   *   *

On the Wednesday I visited a very different kind of school. It has always amazed me how I can be in a small idyllic place like Butterthwaite, nestling in clean grassy fells, and an hour later be in the middle of urban Yorkshire, staring up at the forest of factory chimneys and breathing in the acrid smell of industry. Crompton Primary School was an enormous proliferating structure on three levels. The school had originally been built in the late nineteenth century as a Board school to meet the educational needs of children of all ages: infants on the ground floor, juniors on the second and seniors on the top. It now catered for a large population of primary-aged children who lived in the dark and brooding northern industrial town of Crompton. With its shiny brick walls, greasy grey slate roof, small square windows, towers and turrets and enveloping high black iron fence, it resembled more of a prison or a workhouse than a school. It was a depressing sight: this huge, ugly structure surrounded by row upon row of mean back-to-back terraced housing, featureless warehouses, rubbish-strewn wasteland and walls defaced with graffiti.

The teaching staff had endeavoured to make the interior of the monstrosity as colourful and friendly as possible and had decorated the walls in the gloomy entrance hall with pictures of dramatic seascapes and idyllic rural landscapes, vivid posters, well-mounted children's poems and stories and vases of bright flowers but the place still felt unpleasantly cold and daunting. Perhaps it was the high, flaking ceilings, the hard shiny green tiles on the walls or the unpleasant smell of school dinners and cheap disinfectant. Whatever it was, the place felt unwelcoming.

Mrs Gardiner, the headteacher, was a stout woman in her late fifties with a large bust and remarkably narrow waist. She wore a long blue skirt and a plain white blouse buttoned up at the throat, and around her neck hung a pair of gold half-moon spectacles on a thin gold chain. She would not have appeared out of place in the school when it had been built for she looked for all the world like a Victorian schoolma'am.

After a tour of the building, I joined Mrs Gardiner in her room to discuss the day's itinerary. I was there to watch a range of lessons, assess the children on their reading, examine their writing and study the test scores. For the first hour, I sat in the staff room scrutinising the schemes of work, the teachers' lesson plans and a sample of children's work and after morning break re-joined the headteacher in her room. Our conversation about the deprivation and neglect endemic in Crompton was interrupted by the noise of excited chatter. That signalled the passing in the corridor of an infant class on its way to the hall for PE.

Mrs Gardiner rose from her chair in queenly fashion, popped her spectacles on the end of her nose, clasped her hands in front and stationed herself at the door. I joined her to watch the children's progress.

'Quietly and quickly, please, children,' commanded the headteacher, peering severely over the top of her spectacles. 'Less noise and more haste.'

One little straggler in grubby white shorts and vest limped into view. His head was held down so far his chin rested on his chest. I noticed the child's skin looked unhealthily pale and his untidy, greasy hair was clearly unwashed.

'In my room, please, Matty,' ordered Mrs Gardiner.

'What, miss?' asked the child, looking up and producing an exaggeratedly innocent expression.

'You know what.'

The boy puffed out his cheeks and exhaled noisily. 'I don't, miss.'

'Yes, you do, and less of the sound effects,' said the headteacher, standing back so he could enter her room. When he was standing there and staring up at her with large sad eyes, she held out the flat of her hand. 'Now come along, Matty, give it to me.'

'What, miss?'

'You know very well what. In your plimsoll.'

'There's nothing in my plimsoll,' the boy told her and looked down sheepishly.

'Matthew Dickinson,' sighed the headteacher,

'remove your plimsoll now. Come along. I haven't got all day.' The child thought for a moment and then reluctantly took off his shoe to reveal a pound coin sandwiched between his big toe and the next. His feet could have done with a good scrub. 'Give it to me, please,' the headteacher said. The boy plucked the coin from his toes and passed it up gingerly to Mrs Gardiner who scowled and tut-tutted. 'So you had it after all? Do you know, Mr Phinn,' she said, turning in my direction, 'we have been searching everywhere this morning for this pound coin.'

'I didn't mean to take it, miss,' moaned the child, his eyes brimming with tears and his bottom lip beginning to tremble.

'Of course you meant to take it!' exclaimed Mrs Gardiner. 'It didn't fly into your plimsoll by magic, did it?'

'I didn't mean to take it,' persisted the child. 'I didn't mean to take it.'

'Matty, how many times have I heard that phrase: "I didn't mean to"? I didn't mean to hit him, I didn't mean to break it, I didn't mean to call her those names, I didn't mean to use those naughty words. You never mean to, but you always seem to do it, don't you?'

'I won't do it again, miss.'

'And how many times have I heard that phrase as well?' asked the headteacher. The boy, his head down again, began to sob pathetically, his little shoulders heaving. He looked a pitiable sight. 'What do we call somebody who takes something that does not belong to him?'

'A mugger, miss,' moaned the child.

'And?'

'A burglar, miss.'

'And?'

'A robber, miss.'

Mrs Gardiner shot me a knowing glance which said: 'He knows all the words.' The headteacher fixed him with a stony look. 'I was thinking of the word "thief". That's what somebody is called who takes something that does not belong to him. A thief!'

'I'm not a thief, miss,' wailed the child. 'Don't call me a thief, please—'

'I'm afraid that is what you are, Matty, a thief. You cannot keep your hands off other people's property. You are always taking things which aren't yours. All morning we've been looking for that coin and all the time it was tucked away in your shoe.' The child sniffed dramatically. 'And you see this gentleman here?' continued Mrs Gardiner, turning again in my direction. The boy looked up, wiped away his tears with a grubby fist, sniffed again noisily and stared like a frightened animal in the headlight's glare. 'This is Mr Phinn and he is a very, very important person. Mr Phinn is an inspector.'

The boy howled pathetically. 'I won't do it again, miss, I won't. I promise I won't do it again.'

'Fortunately for you,' said Mrs Gardiner, 'Mr Phinn is not a police inspector. He's a school inspector. And when Mr Phinn came into our school this morning, he said what a lovely school it was—cushions in the Reading Corner and pictures, double mounted, on the walls. I wonder what Mr Phinn is thinking now.'

'I don't know,' wailed the child.

'No, neither do I,' said the headteacher.

Mr Phinn was in actual fact thinking: I do hope this interrogation will stop otherwise Mr Phinn will be in floods of tears along with little Matty.

'And what have you got to say to Mr Phinn?' said the headteacher, looking down severely on the little figure before her. 'What have you to say to him?'

The child looked me straight in the eyes before replying: 'Tough shit!'

*   *   *

'Matty, Matty, Matty,' sighed Mrs Gardiner later. 'Whatever am I going to do with him? He spends more time with Miss Percival, the social worker, and Ms Kinvara, the educational psychologist, than he does with his mother. He's such a sad little boy. Can you imagine a child of his age having to get himself up in the morning, come to school without any breakfast, unwashed, in the same coat he has had for two years and which is now far too small for him. A child so smelly that none of the other children will sit near him or play with him, a child who watches all the other mummies collect their children from school but who has to walk his lonely way home alone to a cold, empty house. Poor child hasn't a chance, has he? Is it any wonder he steals and spits and gets into fights. He's never been shown any different. You know, Mr Phinn, some children come from homes where there is acceptable behaviour, positive attitudes to others, where there's laughter and love and lots of books. And then there are some children, like Matty, who get nothing. Of course, it's the same old story: teenage unmarried mum, poverty, inadequate parenting, absentee father, string of stepfathers. There are drugs, of course, and, I suspect, violence.'

As she spoke, I thought of the words of Mrs Todd and her four boys, about how some children have every advantage in life and others none at all, and I thought of Andrew's mum, rosy-cheeked and smiling, greeting him after school with a hug. 'Whatever does one do about the Mattys of this world?' asked the headteacher, sighing.

'If I had a magic wand, I'd wave it, Mrs Gardiner,' I told her, 'but I haven't. I suppose you just have to keep on trying.'

The headteacher smiled and shook her head. 'Do you know, on his first day here, when he was not much more than five years old, I found Matty outside my door with his pants around his ankles. He was just standing there as bold as brass. "Who wipes the arses around here?" he asked me.'

'Oh, dear,' I said, attempting to suppress a smile.

'In assembly one day, a child dropped a coin which rolled down to the front of the hall and spun round and round. Matty shot out like a chased rabbit and stamped on it. "Foot off!" I shouted. "I saw it first!" he shouted back, snatching it up and popping it in his pocket. I dare not think what he imagined I said to him.' I was unable to prevent myself from chuckling out loud. 'Then there was the time a squirrel appeared in the tree outside his classroom window. Mrs Prentice, his teacher, was near enough to hear the conversation he had with another child. "Oh look," said the other child to Matty, "there's a squirrel up that tree. Let's tell Mrs Prentice." "Shut yer gob," Matty had replied, "she'll make us write about the bugger!" You know,

Mr Phinn,' continued Mrs Gardiner, 'if you didn't laugh, you'd weep. One day he climbed on top of the bus shelter and would not come down. When the school crossing patrol warden attempted to get him down he urinated on him. I mean, he's a full-time job. I've had to suspend him from school three times now. I hated having to do it, but I had no choice. The last time was when Mrs Prentice brought a snail in from her garden. She was getting the children to think of words beginning with the letters "squ" so they could write a little poem together. The children suggested "squishy" and "squelchy", "squiggly" and "squirmy". Matty comes out to the front of the classroom and brings the flat of his hand down on the poor creature. "Squashy," he announces. Whatever will become of him?'

Well, I thought to myself, there's little chance of his becoming a doctor, an architect, a linguist or a fine artist like Mrs Todd's talented sons. Poor Matty will probably end up in prison. 'I expect you've tried to get through to his mother?' I said.

'Oh yes, of course. She's a sad case, too. She's a simple soul and can't cope. I suppose she tries her limited best but she seems to attract the worst sort of man, that's why Matty reacts to men as he does, in that aggressive, suspicious way. He's had some very rough treatment at the hands of his mother's boyfriends, I can tell you. And, of course, all the bad language he's heard comes from them. I remember when I helped his mother fill in the details on the form when Matty started school. She's illiterate, you see. When we got to the section which asked about the child's parents, she told me, "Father not yet known".'

'Social services?'

'Miss Percival, the social worker, tries her best, of course, but she's over-stretched and, believe it or not, there are children worse off than Matty. Anyway, we persevere, Mr Phinn, we try our best and we can't do more than that, can we?'

'No,' I replied feebly, 'you can't.'

*   *   *

I did not meet Matty again until after lunch when I joined the infant class. Sometimes when I visited schools I would read the children a story. This was a good opportunity for me to assess the children's confidence and proficiency as speakers and how attentive they were as listeners. I could also test them on their knowledge of words and spellings.

I gathered the small children in a half circle around me in the Reading Corner, the grandiose name for a square of carpet, a couple of large coloured cushions and an easy chair. The infants' teacher, Mrs Prentice, sat at the back. My story was about Lazy Tom, a fat ginger cat with green eyes who slept for most of the day but got up to all sorts of adventures by night. I had just started the lively account when a large child with a plump face, frizzy hair in huge bunches and great wide eyes interrupted loudly.

'We 'ad a cat!' she shouted out.

'Did you?' I replied.

' 'E were really, really 'orrible. 'Ee killed birds.'

'I'm afraid all cats do that,' I told her. I then endeavoured to continue with the story. ' "Now, one bright sunny summer's day, Lazy Tom—" '

'And 'e killed mice, an' all!' the child shouted out. ' 'E used to bring 'em in t'house and play wi' em on t'carpet and then ett 'em up. 'E used to bite their 'eads off an' all and—'

'What's your name?' I asked the child.

'Tequila,' she replied. 'I'm named after a drink.'

'Tequila Sunrise,' I murmured.

'No,' pouted the child. 'Tequila Braithwaite.'

'Well, Tequila,' I said, 'I want you to listen to the story very, very quietly. You are spoiling it for everyone else. You can tell me all about—'

'But I were tellin' you about mi cat,' interrupted the girl.

'Well tell me later,' I said rather more sharply.

'Can't I tell you now?'

'No,' I replied, fixing her with the look only teachers use.

I managed to continue for a couple of pages, aware of Mrs Prentice, with the folded arms, sitting smugly at the back of the classroom and clearly enjoying my discomfiture. Anyone who thinks that a class of thirty lively infants is easy to handle, I thought to myself at that moment, should try reading them a story. There is always a Tequila. It wasn't long before the child was shouting out again.

'Our cat were called Max and 'e were really, really smelly and 'e scratched and hissed an' all.'

'Well, Lazy Tom was not like that,' I told her. 'He was a nice cat. "Now, one cold, dark night Lazy Tom crept down the garden path—"'

' 'E were run ovver by a bus,' announced Tequila.

'Who was?' I asked.

'Max.'

'Well, I am very sorry to hear it. "Now, Lazy Tom—"'

'My granny wasn't sorry,' said the child. 'She said it were good riddance. My granny dribbles in 'er

116

knickers.'

The teacher came to my aid. 'Tequila!' she snapped. 'Listen to the story!'

I managed to finish the account of Lazy Tom. The children listened, even Tequila, with mouths open and eyes (as we say in Yorkshire) like chapel hat pegs. Matty was the exception. He sat a little away from the other children, a small pathetic figure with his head down.

'And here's a picture of Lazy Tom,' I said, turning the picture book around so the children could see the fat cat with the bright ginger fur and large green eyes. Matty glanced up.

'My gran's gorra fur coat just like that,' remarked Tequila. 'But it 'ant gorra an 'ead on it.'

'Now children,' I said, deciding to ignore Tequila's latest snippet, 'I would like to ask you a few questions about the story.'

'Ask me! Ask me!' cried Tequila waving her hand in the air like a daffodil in the wind. 'I like questions.'

'No, I'm going to give someone else a chance,' I told her firmly. 'You've had quite a lot to say this afternoon, Tequila, and now it's somebody else's turn to speak to me. Now, just listen.' I smiled in the direction of a small girl with long plaits and a serious face who had listened to the story without a sound or a movement. 'What about you?' I said.

'She's shy,' Tequila told me. 'She dunt say owt.'

'She might, given the chance,' I said, breathing out heavily in exasperation.

'She won't, she's dead shy.'

'Well, shall we ask her?' I asked.

'I'm tellin' you, she never says owt. She never does,' persisted the child.

117

'Tequila!' exhorted Mrs Prentice.

The little girl at the centre of the discussion looked down coyly. 'What's your name?' I asked her gently.

''Er name's Eleanor,' Tequila told me, 'and she's dead shy. She never says owt. I'll tell you about 'er.'

'No, you won't!' I cried.

'But she won't say owt,' retorted the girl.

Then a loud and angry voice came from the side of the room. It was Matty. 'For God's sake, woman, shut yer gob!'

Tequila looked startled and never said another word that lesson.

When the bell rang for afternoon break, the children changed into their outdoor shoes, put on their coats and gloves. Tequila, I noticed, had recovered and was regaling the teacher with a story about her mother hoovering up a mouse the day before and then flushing it down the toilet. She wrapped herself up in a bright red coat with matching accessories. It looked as if butter wouldn't melt in her mouth. When she saw me she made a beeline in my direction.

'My teacher tells better stories than you,' she told me bluntly. 'I din't like that story of yours about that cat.'

'I think it's playtime, Tequila,' I told her. 'Why don't you go outside and get some fresh air.'

'I like my teacher,' she said. 'I heard 'er tellin' Mrs Gardiner I was "a right little madam".' With that she skipped off in the direction of the playground.

Matty took off his soiled plimsolls wearily and pulled on a pair of scuffed shoes and an old anorak with a ripped sleeve. Poor sad little scrap, I thought.

As I was heading for the staff room with the teacher, I noticed little Eleanor hovering outside the classroom door.

'Hello, Eleanor,' I said cheerfully.

'Can I tell you something?' she whispered.

'Of course. What do you want to tell me?' I asked, bending down and looking into the small dark eyes.

'My Auntie Rachel's got sixty-five roses.'

'Sixty-five roses?' I said. 'She's very lucky your Auntie Rachel, isn't she?'

The child shook her head. 'No, she's not. It's not nice having sixty-five roses.'

'I thought your auntie would really like so many beautiful coloured flowers with their lovely smell.'

'It's not nice having sixty-five roses,' she persisted quietly.

And then it dawned upon me. Her auntie had just died. These were the flowers at her funeral.

'Has your auntie died?' I asked gently.

'No,' said the child in a voice deep with indignation. 'She's got sixty-five roses!'

Mrs Prentice, hearing the exchange, and seeing my puzzlement and the child's, explained with a wry smile, 'She means cystic fibrosis, Mr Phinn.'

*   *   *

Driving back to the office that afternoon, I began to think of the children I had met during the last couple of weeks: John and Russell, Hugo and Alexander, Kirit and Roisin. All of them, I guessed, came from homes where there was justice and

119

honesty, joy and grace, compassion and love. And then there was Matty, that sad little boy with the grubby face and the tight little mouth. I thought about our own unborn child, and promised myself that I would make him or her as happy a child as possible. Christine and I had discussed names for our baby. If it were a boy, we thought we might call him Matthew. The name means Gift of God.

CHAPTER EIGHT

I arrived at the office one lunchtime a week later in rather a sombre mood. I still had little Matty on my mind and Mrs Gardiner's words 'Whatever will become of him?' kept interrupting my thoughts. Just what future lay in store for that sad little boy? Mr Frobisher had also reared his head again and the whole sorry business at King Henry's was still preying on my mind. The very last thing I wanted to hear was Julie's resounding laughter coming down the stairs.

'Someone's in a good mood,' I said gloomily, as I entered the room.

'And someone's obviously not,' came back Julie's quick riposte. She was perched on the end of a desk in a ridiculously short denim skirt and tight-fitting pink jumper, sharing something presumably very amusing with Geraldine. 'Why aren't you at West Challerton?' she asked bluntly. 'You're supposed to be running a course there this afternoon, aren't you?'

'Not until four o'clock,' I told her, heading for my desk. 'It's an after-school session. In any case,

I'm not running the course until next month. This is a planning meeting and it's the last thing I want today, I can tell you. Mr Pennington-Smith is not my favourite headteacher.'

'I sympathise,' said Geraldine.

It was a rare occurrence for the super-efficient Dr Mullarkey to be in the office. She would write up her reports at home, having put her young son, Jamie, to bed, and she tended to hide herself away in the Staff Development Centre at lunchtimes in order to catch up with the office paperwork without interruptions. She was a bit of a mystery was this pretty, slender young woman with raven-black hair and great blue eyes. We knew very little about her past and I had to admit that I, along with my colleagues, was intrigued to know who was the father of her child. Sidney—of course it had to be Sidney—had once brought up the matter of her little boy's parentage and received short shrift.

'My private life is my private life, Sidney,' Geraldine had told him sharply. 'I do not wish to discuss it.' And that was the end of the matter, but we still longed to know. 'So, what is your course about?' Gerry now asked me.

'Language and learning,' I told her, pulling a face, 'and I am not looking forward to it at all.'

'I never feel comfortable in Mr Pennington-Smith's company,' she said. 'He's forever blowing his own trumpet and criticising the former headteacher. You should be flattered he's asked you to run a course for him, Gervase. He doesn't strike me as the sort of man to listen to advice.'

'Tell Sidney about it,' I said, recalling his difference with the headmaster about the place of art and design in the curriculum.

121

'What happened with Sidney?' asked Geraldine.

'Don't ask,' said Julie. 'Get Mr Clamp on to that particular subject and you'll be here till the cows come home.'

'Julie's right, it's a long, long story,' I told her. 'Anyway, it's not Mr Pennington-Smith who has asked me. It's a newly-appointed English teacher who has been given the responsibility of arranging some training for the staff.'

'From what I have seen of the science department,' said Gerry, 'they need it. To describe them as moribund would be an understatement. Mind you, Mr Pennington-Smith is giving more time on the timetable for the sciences this year. That's one good thing.'

I could have described Sidney's reaction to this initiative but I had a lot to do so resisted the temptation.

'Well, I'd better get on with this little lot.' I picked up the heap of papers in my in-tray. 'Oh, by the way, Julie, I was hoping to have a word with Harold, if he's in.' I needed to talk to him about the Frobisher situation.

'He's been in since seven this morning,' Julie informed me. 'But he's not to be disturbed this afternoon for at least another hour. He's had Dr Gore, Councillor Peterson, Lord Marrick, various governors, everyone bar the Queen, on his phone all day. Something's going on at County Hall by the sound of it. All very hush-hush.'

'Sounds intriguing,' I said.

'There's been comings and goings all week,' said Julie conspiratorially. 'I've never seen County Hall so busy. It's been a beehive of activity. People buzzing about all over the place. The last time it was so hectic was when that headteacher ran off to Scarborough with the school secretary and the school fund. I was over in the Post Room early yesterday morning picking up your mail and that Derek—you know, the gangly lad with the spectacles and big ears—said he'd heard a real barny going on in Committee Room Two, Monday afternoon. Raised voices, slamming doors and banging on tables. And then Marlene on the switchboard said her hands were red raw putting calls through to Dr Gore. Of course, she wouldn't tell us what about, but something's afoot, you mark my words. Then I saw the Savage woman—the Queen Bee herself—buzzing about like somebody not right in the head, swirling about in her fancy outfit, jangling her jewellery and pretending to be somebody important.'

'I guess we'll hear soon enough,' I sighed, starting to sort through the papers.

'Are you all right, Gervase?' asked Geraldine.

'Yes, I'm fine,' I replied. 'Just a bit preoccupied at the moment. What's this?'

I had come upon a bright yellow sheet of paper with 'URGENT' printed in large black block capitals at the top.

'That's what we were laughing at,' said Geraldine. 'It's Mrs Savage's latest memorandum. You know she's been named as the "Health and Safety" contact in the Education Department?'

'Huh!' grunted Julie.

'Well, she seems to be taking her new role very seriously,' said Geraldine.

'She'll be in combat outfit next,' added Julie, 'going on courses for bomb disposal.'

'Listen to this.' Geraldine cleared her throat and

read from her copy of the yellow piece of paper: '"Urgent! Health and Safety Circular Number 1: Suspicious Packages. Should you discover a package, parcel, box, bundle, envelope, container or any other suspect receptacle"—Mrs Savage never uses one word when five will suffice—"with protruding wires and/or stains and/or powdery substances and/or residues which might be emitting unusual noises and/or has a strange odour, do not attempt to touch, loosen, open, move, shake or interfere with it, and under no circumstances must it be immersed in water. This constitutes a suspicious package."'

'You don't say,' said Julie sarcastically. 'I would never have guessed.'

Geraldine read on. '"Should you find such an item, contact the County Council Civil Protection Unit (the CCCPU) immediately on extension 2222 and inform the designated Heath and Safety Education Liaison Officer, Mrs B. Savage, on extension 6666."'

'She must think our brains are made of porridge,' said Julie. She turned to Gerry. 'I mean, who in their right mind is going to pick up a ticking box that smells and start shaking it? Just read him the next lot.'

'Well,' said Gerry, 'she then has a series of other important pieces of information. Listen to this. "The County now has its own nuclear fall-out shelter at Collington. The facility, for use by senior county council members"—that presumably doesn't include us—"in the case of nuclear holocaust or a national emergency, is situated to the rear of Roper's Salesroom, Furnival's Funeral Parlour and Kwik Cutz Hairdressing Salon. The official opening by Councillor George Peterson, Chair of the Planning and Development Control Committee, scheduled for December, has been postponed for the time being due to vandals damaging the shelter." It could survive a nuclear attack,' chuckled Gerry, 'but not the activities of the Collington vandals.'

'I remember once,' said Julie, laughing, 'when Mrs Savage sent a staffing bulletin round County Hall with an advert in it for a children's crossing patrol warden and added that application forms were also available in Braille.' She looked pointedly in my direction. 'And speaking of staffing bulletins, I notice that Dr Yeats's job is in the Staff Vacancy Bulletin this week.'

'So I believe,' I said casually.

The previous academic year Harold had informed the team of his intention to retire early. He had had enough, he told us. The pressures of the job, the late nights, the increasing workload were getting him down so he had tendered his resignation. Spurred by my colleagues in the office, but not by Christine who thought I had quite enough on my plate with a new wife and a new house, I had applied. I had not even been short-listed, never mind interviewed. I had, of course, been disappointed but had been reassured by both Harold and Dr Gore that they would look favourably on an application some time in the future when I had had more experience.

A new Senior Inspector, one Simon Carter, had been appointed. Even before he had taken up the post he had managed to alienate everyone at County Hall with whom he came in contact. The initial meetings ('to get to know each other') convinced us that he was a systems freak, a know-all and a singularly unpleasant piece of work. Mrs Savage, who initially had taken quite a shine to him, very soon changed her mind when she came under his spotlight and he began questioning her role, criticising her correspondence to schools and indicating that he would be reviewing all her work. He also informed her that she would, if he had his way, be moving out of her plush office. The confrontation between the two adversaries had reached a wonderfully dramatic climax in the top corridor of County Hall. Everyone was greatly relieved when Mr Simon Carter gave back-word and decided to take his considerable expertise and extensive experience elsewhere. Harold had been prevailed upon to remain in post until his replacement, still to be appointed, took up his position which would be at the beginning of the Summer term. The advertisement for the position was now in County Hall's Staff Vacancy Bulletin and would be placed in the educational journals and newspapers the following week. I therefore had a decision to make and it was not an easy one, not an easy one at all.

'You are going to apply, aren't you?' asked Julie, breaking into my thoughts.

'I've not decided yet,' I replied.

'You ought to,' said Gerry. 'I reckon you'd have a really good chance this time round.'

'Well, we'll see,' I told her, starting to open my letters.

'My, you are in a glum mood this afternoon, aren't you,' observed Julie. 'As my grandma would say, you've got a face like a pan of fat.'

'Julie,' I said sharply, 'I really do have to get on. I

came in the office to reply to my mail, deal with the telephone messages and finish a report, not to discuss my career.'

'Ooo, pardon me!' she said, sliding off the desk.

'Look, I'm sorry if I snapped but I really do have a great deal to do this afternoon and I have to see Harold before I set off for West Challerton.'

'Well, don't take him any problems,' Julie told me. 'He's got enough of those on his plate to keep him occupied all term. Thursday is his day for dealing with complaints. As I said, he's been in since seven and hard at it for most of the morning with hardly time for a cup of coffee. He was supposed to be slowing down but since he was asked to stay on it's as if he has another lease of life. Well, I'm going to the canteen for my lunch and will try and find out what's going on from Doris. She's sure to have heard something. She hears everything from behind that serving hatch.' Julie straightened her meagre skirt, stretched and headed for the door.

'Have there been any calls for me?' I asked her before she disappeared. 'I was hoping that a Mr Frobisher from King Henry's might have got back to me.'

'No, he hasn't called. There are about six or seven but only one urgent one,' she told me.

'Nothing from King Henry's, then?'

'No, but will you please, please ring that man with the loud voice. He keeps on calling and he's nearly sent me demented bellowing down the line. I never got a word in, so I don't know what his name is or what it was about. His telephone number is on your pad.' With that she departed for the canteen.

'Is there something wrong?' asked Geraldine when Julie had clattered down the stairs on the absurdly high-heeled stiletto shoes she was fond of wearing. 'You're not your usual cheerful self today.'

I told her about little Matty. 'There are some children,' I said, 'who will have every opportunity and advantage in life. They will be cherished, encouraged, supported and loved as they grow up and there are others, like that little boy at Crompton Primary School, who has and will have precious little. I just find it so very sad and depressing, that's all. I've met quite a few neglected children in my time. I just don't know why it's getting to me now.'

'Perhaps it's because you're to be a father,' said Geraldine. 'Becoming a parent changes your whole outlook. It really does. The things in life you thought were important—money, position, job, status—just pale into insignificance when you have a child. He or she becomes the centre of your world.'

'For some parents, maybe,' I said. 'I guess not for Matty's. As his headteacher pointed out, it's the same old story: unmarried mum, inadequate parenting, absentee father—' I stopped mid-sentence and wished that the floor would open and swallow me up. 'I'm sorry, Geraldine, I didn't mean—'

She laughed. 'Don't worry,' she said. 'I'm used to it. In an ideal world a child should have a mother and a father, but sometimes things don't work out. They didn't for me.'

'Does Jamie see his father at all?' I asked.

'No. Let's change the subject, shall we?' she replied quickly. 'So, what about Harold's job then?

128

Are you going in for it?'

'Part of me says, "Yes, it will be a tremendous challenge" and another part says, "Don't touch it with a barge pole."'

'Well, it's a decision only you can make,' she said.

'Yes, I know.'

We both got on quietly with our work for the next hour or so, which was thankfully clear of interruptions. At three o'clock I decided to see if Harold was free. I wanted to get his advice about King Henry's College and have a chat about the job at the same time.

*   *   *

Harold's office was large but always appeared cluttered and cramped. A row of ugly olive-green metal filing cabinets stretched along one wall, a set of heavy bookcases, crammed with box files, bulging folders, heavy tomes and thick reports from the Ministry of Education, filled the other. There was a square of carpet on the polished wooden floor and two hard-backed chairs. Harold's ancient oak desk, buried beneath a mountain of paper, faced a sash window through which one had an uninspiring view of the rear of County Hall. It was a world away from the plush office of Mrs Savage.

'Come in! Come in!' exclaimed Harold when I knocked and poked my head around his door.

'Could I have a quick word, Harold?' I asked.

'Of course, come in,' he replied, 'I wanted to speak to you anyway. Pull up a chair.'

'You look busy,' I said, nodding in the direction of his desk.

'Always am, dear boy. Every Thursday I set the afternoon aside to try and deal with all the problems, contentious issues and complaints which dear Dr Gore, in his wisdom, sends my way. He has an uncanny habit of passing the most awkward things on to me to deal with.' Harold gestured to a bright red folder before him. 'Still, I shouldn't complain. I shan't have this for much longer.'

'So there are a lot of complaints and problems?' I asked.

'Oh yes, but that's part of the territory of the Senior Inspector. For example, there's a letter here from an irate parent claiming compensation. Apparently his child's teacher simulated a volcanic eruption in class.'

'I'm sorry?'

'She used health salts, yellow powder paint and vinegar, and evidently created quite an impressive display. Unfortunately, she rather overdid the health salts and powder paint and one child arrived home like the Gingerbread Man, a bright golden colour from head to foot. The father wants to know who is paying for the cleaning of the child's clothes and what compensation will be forthcoming for the distress caused.'

'Silly man,' I said.

'Maybe, but I have to deal with it. It starts as a small complaint, then the local newspapers get hold of it and it's blown out of all proportion. Then I've received several letters about bullying which, of course, have to be taken very seriously, a couple concerning excluded pupils, and a letter from Sister Clare of the Sacred Heart Convent, complaining, in no uncertain terms, about the opening of a sex shop opposite the gates of the school.'

130

'I never realised you had all this to do.'

'And there's more. There's the headteacher who is convinced the head of the infant department is a witch and has put a curse on him and the French *assistante* who allegedly assaulted a sixth form student with a banana.'

'*A banana?*' I repeated.

'She was using some plastic fruit as visual aids to get her class to practise their French when a boy made some clever comment. The *assistante,* who can't have been much older than the boy himself, evidently threw this banana at him which unfortunately hit the boy smack between the eyes, knocking off his glasses, before rebounding to the teacher like a boomerang. From what the Chair of Governors says in his letter, Mademoiselle Régine caught the missile and received a standing ovation from the class.' I shook my head and smiled. 'I'm afraid the boy's parents did not see the funny side and have contacted a solicitor. I've just been speaking to the headteacher.'

'I can't see it standing up in court,' I said. ' "And what was the offensive weapon?" asks the judge. "It was a banana, my lord." '

'It may sound bizarre,' said Harold, 'but it has to be dealt with nevertheless. The hours I spend dealing with such issues.' He gave a great toothy smile. 'But not for much longer. I shall pass on all such matters, with a light heart, to my successor.'

'I see,' I said thoughtfully.

Harold assumed a grave expression. 'Now, I'm pleased you popped in, Gervase, because my biggest and most urgent problem this week concerns Hawksrill Primary School.'

'Hawksrill's a splendid school,' I said. 'What's

131

the problem?'

'Yes, I am told it's a very good school,' replied Harold, 'and the reports I have read bear that out. Well, the fact of the matter is, it's closing.'

'Closing!' I exclaimed.

'I'm afraid so. There was an Education Sub-Committee meeting earlier this week—went on until after eight in the evening. I had to sit outside in that draughty top corridor of County Hall for nearly an hour waiting to be called. It was a terribly contentious meeting, interminable arguments, acrimonious exchanges. Anyway, the long and short of it is that the Sub-Committee has decided, reluctantly I have to say, to close the school next year.'

'Why, for heaven's sake?'

'Well, I am sure you are aware that there have to be big cuts in the educational budget. Small schools like Hawksrill are not really viable. It's much more cost effective to have larger schools and close the ones in some of the very small villages. Hawksrill's building needs quite a deal of work on it. The roof's leaking, the toilets require some refurbishing and the perimeter fence needs repairing. The headteacher, Mrs Beighton, and her assistant, Mrs Brown, have both indicated that they are looking to retire in the near future so there would be no redundancies or redeployments. All in all, it's quite fortuitous.'

'It's not fortuitous for the children at the school,' I protested.

'Perhaps not,' said Harold, rubbing his chin, 'but they can be bussed the few miles to the neighbouring school. You see, Hawksrill only has about thirty children and the village has an ageing

132

and declining population.'

'Hang on, I live in Hawksrill,' I reminded him.

'Yes, yes, I know, and that is why I wanted to have a quiet word with you prior to the news getting out.'

'I don't like the idea of this at all, Harold,' I said. 'I'm not at all keen on any child of mine being bussed in and out of the village every day, particularly in winter along those twisting, narrow roads. One of the reasons Christine and I decided to live in Hawksrill was its lovely school.'

'Yes, I quite understand that, but there is really no alternative. Councillor Peterson and the Education Sub-Committee—'

'I might have guessed Councillor Peterson would have a hand in it,' I interrupted.

'He and the Sub-Committee,' continued Harold, 'considered all the options and reluctantly decided that five small schools, including Hawksrill, will be closed in the next academic year. I do see his point. It's just not economic to keep such small village schools open with dwindling pupil populations and the rising costs of repair and maintenance. I'm sorry, but there it is. The headteacher and the Chair of Governors will be informing the parents by letter next Friday. Then, no doubt, there will be a meeting with the governors, parents and other interested parties, which is likely to be a very lively affair if previous meetings of this nature are anything to go by. This will be followed by the appeals procedures, various further meetings and possibly a tribunal.' Harold smiled. 'Your child might very well be at secondary school by the time Hawksrill actually closes.' I didn't smile. I was feeling shell-shocked. 'Anyway, Gervase, I just wanted you to know before it hits the papers. Now, was there something you wanted to have a word with me about?'

'No, nothing,' I said, getting up. 'Nothing at all.'

*   *   *

I returned to the office even more depressed than before. Geraldine had gone but Julie was there, placing my typed letters on my desk along with a mug of coffee. I had to hand it to her. She was an excellent secretary, and—despite always being overworked—she was highly efficient and very organised. She had had, for a few weeks the previous year, a clerical assistant called Frank, a hard-working and good-natured young man, but when he had been promoted to work in Financial Services, he had not been replaced and she was back holding the fort single-handed.

'Have you rung that man with the loud voice yet?' Julie asked now.

'Pardon?' I asked.

'The man with the loud voice, who wants to speak to you urgently. Have you phoned him?'

'No.'

'Please would you do it? I'm sick of his bellowing down the phone at me.'

I sighed heavily. 'All right. I'll do it now,' I said. I stared at the notepad on my desk. It's amazing, I thought to myself, how life can suddenly change. One minute everything is right with the world and the next it has all turned sour. First Mr Frobisher, now Hawksrill school closing.

'So are you going to phone him?' asked Julie.

'Yes, yes,' I snapped. 'In a minute.'

'Right,' she said and left the office.

I dialled the number on the pad. 'Hello, my name is Gervase Phinn,' I said wearily when I heard the phone being picked up at the other end. 'I believe someone on this number wishes to speak to me.'

''Ello! 'Ello! Is that Mester Phinn?' came a thunderous voice down the line.

'It is,' I said, before holding the receiver at arm's length.

'Jacob Bannister, 'ere. Tha might 'ave 'eard of us. "JBB's Quality Animal Feeds".'

'No, I'm afraid not, Mr Bannister,' I replied, before stretching the receiver away from my ear again.

'We're very big in these parts!' he shouted. 'You might 'ave come across our vans with the slogan "Rearing is as easy as ABC, when you buy your feeds from JBB".'

'Well, I don't have much call for animal feeds in my line of work,' I told him.

'Eh?' he bellowed.

'I said, I don't have—What can I do for you, Mr Bannister?'

'Tha're like t'Scarlet bloody Pimpernel. I've been trying to speak to you for a couple of weeks. "They seek 'im 'ere, they seek 'im theer." Tha're never in.'

'No, I spend most of my time in schools, Mr Bannister,' I replied, rather piqued. 'That's what I do for a living.'

'Eh?'

'I'm a school inspector. I try to get into schools as much as possible. Now, what can I do for you?'

'I 'ear you do talks.'

135

I should have guessed. He wanted me to speak at some dinner or other.

Shortly after becoming a school inspector I had been dragooned into speaking at a charity event. The very persuasive nun, Sister Brendan, headteacher of St Bartholomew's School, had invited me to give a light-hearted talk at the school one evening to raise money for disadvantaged children. I had been delighted, and not a little surprised, to discover that my talk had been warmly received. Some weeks later I had received an invitation from the wonderfully named and very formidable Mrs Cleaver-Canning—or, rather, the Honourable Mrs Cleaver-Canning—to speak at her golf club Ladies' Night dinner. I had been recommended by a friend of hers who had heard me speak at some charity evening. Things had then snowballed and I was soon receiving invitations from Rotary Clubs and Women's Institutes, Soroptomist groups and Townswomen's Guilds, and all manner of luncheon clubs. These organisations generously supplemented the funds of several children's charities and my reception had been, without exception, very positive.

'Yes, I do speak at different functions,' I told Mr Bannister. 'But at the moment—'

'After dinner talks like t'one my brother's wife's 'eard you at, at t'Countrywomen's Association Dinner in Ribsdyke a couple o'months back? She said tha were a funny man.'

I was not feeling particularly 'funny' that afternoon. 'I've been called many things, Mr Bannister, but—'

'Eh?'

'I am rather busy at the moment,' I told him.

136

'Eh?'

'I said I am busy at the moment.'

'I don't want tha to speak this very minute, Mester Phinn,' he said.

I sighed. 'So would you like me to speak at a function?' I asked.

'Eh?'

'I said, would you like me to speak at a dinner?' I was raising my voice an octave higher.

'Aye that's t'idea. At Fettlesham Farmers' Club Dinner, December the first. We're raisin' money for T'Children's Society. For them kiddies what don't have much goin' for 'em.'

'Yes, I know The Children's Society,' I said. 'It's a very worthy charity.'

'Well,' shouted the speaker down the line, 'I know it's a fair bit off but I wants to get things soarted. To tell you t'truth we was let down by t'speaker we booked, cricketer for Yorkshire in t'dim and distant past. Never 'eard of 'im mi'sen. I'm a rugby union man. Anyroad, how're tha fixed?'

'I should explain, Mr Bannister—'

'Jacob!'

'I should explain, Jacob, that I am not a comedian. I don't tell blue jokes or anything like that.'

'Coourse tha dunt. We don't want owt like that. We want sommat funny wi'out being mucky. And my brother's sister said tha'd fit t'bill a treat.'

'It's December the first, you say.' I flicked through my diary. I was free but felt like saying no, such was the mood I was in. Then I thought of Matty. He was the kind of child The Children's Society helped.

137

'Are tha still theer?' roared the voice down the line.

'Yes, I'm still here,' I told him.

'So, tha'll do it?'

'Yes,' I replied, 'I'll do it.'

'Champion!' he roared, nearly bursting my eardrum. 'We meet at T'Marrick Arms in Chapelwatersthwaite at seven prompt. It's a bit difficult to find. Does tha know it?'

'Oh, yes, I know Chapelwatersthwaite,' I told him. 'I know it well.'

The very first school I had visited when I had become a school inspector had been at Backwatersthwaite in the neighbouring village. It had been the devil's own job to find and I had motored at a snail's speed up hill and down dale, along twisting narrow roads and through countless villages which all looked the same, until I had finally arrived at The Marrick Arms in Chapelwatersthwaite. I had got to know the pub pretty well in the next half hour—I must have passed it a good few times before I had finally found the right road to Backwatersthwaite. So, yes, I knew well the venue for the farmers' dinner.

'Now, it's nowt fancy,' shouted the speaker down the line. 'Tha dunt need no "penguin suit" or owt o' that sooart.'

'Right,' I said.

'Ee, I'm reight glad tha can do it, Mester Phinn. My brother's wife, 'er what's in t' Ribsdyke Countrywomen's Association, said tha were a real barrel of laughs.'

'Really,' I sighed.

CHAPTER NINE

'I am not happy, Mr Clamp,' complained Connie. 'I'm *not* happy at all, having harems of naked women cavorting about the place.'

'Connie,' replied Sidney, his beard bristling and his eyes flashing wildly, 'there will be no harems of naked women. There will be one woman, a single person, an individual, and she will be doing no cavorting, I can assure you of that.'

'I don't care how many of them there are,' retorted the caretaker of the Staff Development Centre, 'I just do not like that sort of thing going on on my premises.'

Connie, with her round, florid face, bright copper-coloured perm, brilliant pink nylon overall and the large multicoloured feather duster, which she invariably wielded like a field marshal's baton, resembled a huge, savage and exotic bird of prey. She was a blunt, hard-working and down-to-earth Yorkshire woman and she kept the premises spotless but she ruled the place with a rod of iron. Like many Yorkshire folk, she had strong and unwavering views which she was not afraid of expressing. She was, as they say in Yorkshire 'not backwards in coming forwards'. She had no conception of rank or status and treated everyone who entered her empire exactly the same, be he the exalted Minister of Education or a man to clear the blocked drains. She could be obstinate, difficult and outspoken but Connie possessed a great impulse for generosity and an intense pride in the work she undertook.

It was a warm Friday afternoon towards the end of September and I was at the Staff Development Centre, where all the teachers' courses were held, to direct a conference on the teaching of Shakespeare. I had arrived just after lunch to find Connie and Sidney in heated discussion in the entrance hall.

'Look here, Connie,' said Sidney, changing tack and forcing a smile, 'there will be nothing going on here. The person, in the singular, is not a striptease *artiste*, she is a model, a professional model, one who poses tastefully for artists to sketch, draw and paint.'

'But she'll have nothing on,' persisted Connie.

'Of course she'll have nothing on,' said Sidney, trying to contain his anger. 'She is a nude. Nude models do not generally get wrapped up as if they're going on an Antarctic expedition. They pose nude so artists can draw them. The whole point is for the artist to see them *au naturel*.'

'See them what?' asked Connie.

'In the natural form, unencumbered.'

'With nothing on,' persisted Connie.

'Yes, with nothing on.'

'Well, I don't like it.'

'And as for cavorting about the place,' Sidney explained, 'she will be static, stationary, immobile, motionless, inert, sitting on a chair.'

'She could be sitting on top of the Eiffel Tower for all I care, Mr Clamp,' said Connie, flourishing the feather duster like a wand. 'She still won't have a stitch of clothing on. She'll be displaying everything she's got to the world and his wife. Well, I think it's quite disgusting, grown men ogling a young woman and calling it artificated. I'm as broad-minded as the next person and I like nice pictures but they have to leave something to the imagination. Nobody can accuse me of being a Pharisee.'

'Philistine,' murmured Sidney.

'A what?'

'It's Philistine, not Pharisee.'

'What is?'

'Oh, never mind,' sighed Sidney.

'As I was saying,' said Connie, 'I'm not one of these Pharisees, but I draw the line at naked women.'

'You make it sound like Sodom and Gomorrah,' mumbled Sidney.

'There's no call for that sort of language, Mr Clamp, thank you very much!'

Sidney appealed to me. 'Gervase, please try and enlighten Connie. I have an art course coming up next week and I have a female model for the teachers to sketch as part of the figure-drawing workshop. Can you impress upon Connie here that I am not opening a Soho strip joint, a bordello or a night club for lap dancers?'

'Connie,' I said, coming to Sidney's defence, 'all the great artists painted and drew the naked female form—Picasso, Matisse, Goya, Leonardo da Vinci, Michelangelo—'

'All foreigners,' Connie interrupted. 'Well, of course, that doesn't surprise me one jot. But what I am surprised at, Mr Phinn, is you taking Mr Clamp's side. You, a newly married man with a baby on the way and liking that sort of thing.'

'What I'm trying to say,' I persevered, 'is that there's really nothing disgusting about it.'

'Well, you would say that,' replied Connie, in no

141

way mollified. 'You're a man. You're all the same when it comes to naked women. I've seen them on the buses gawping at all those newspaper pictures of half-dressed women and looking at the top shelf in the newsagents. I've seen my Ted at it. You can call it tasteful if you like, Mr Clamp, and try to talk me round until the cows come home. I think a young woman taking off all her clothes for men to have a good gander at is disgusting. Now, I'm broad-minded to the point of obscenity, but I draw the line at naked girls.'

'She is not a girl,' groaned Sidney. 'Miriam is getting on for sixty, for goodness sake.'

'Getting on for sixty!' gasped Connie. 'Well, she ought to be ashamed of herself, stripping off for people at her age. She ought to be going ballroom dancing or flower arranging at her time of life, not taking her clothes off for men.'

I left the two combatants and headed for the room where my conference was to take place. I wanted to check that everything was ready. I had thirty secondary school English teachers signed up for the afternoon and had asked the widely-published Shakespearean scholar, Lawrence Parry-Wilson, to give a keynote talk to be followed by questions. It had taken some persuading on my part for Professor Parry-Wilson to speak because, as he had explained to me, he was massively busy. I had felt pretty pleased with myself when he had finally agreed.

That feeling of elation soon disappeared when he opened his mouth. To say the lecture was dry and uninspiring would be an understatement. Professor Parry-Wilson's books were challenging, informative and readable but his skills as a public speaker were clearly very limited. He mumbled his way through a prepared text in wearisome detail, shuffling and scratching, grunting and grimacing. Sometimes he would stop, stare vacantly out of the window and then nod as if some unseen presence were speaking to him. I could see the teachers getting increasingly restless. When it came to the questions, I was the only one who raised a hand and, before answering, the professor scratched his beard, grunted and nodded thoughtfully, before finally launching into an almost incomprehensible sermon. I had allowed an hour for questions, hoping that a lively debate would ensue, but by three-thirty it was clear things were not going to improve, so I thanked the professor and closed the course.

I dreaded what the teachers' evaluation sheets would reveal. It would have been much better, I thought to myself as I headed for the kitchen for a cup of tea, to have had Mr Purdey of King Henry's College speaking to the teachers about how *he* taught Shakespeare. It would have been more interesting and a whole lot more useful.

'You've finished early,' said Connie, poking her head through the serving hatch in the kitchen. 'I thought your conference was due to finish at four.'

'It was, but we finished early.'

'I had to tell that man with the fuzzy hair and the goatee beard, him what did the talk for you, not to block my entrance at the front. He parked right in front of the red and yellow cones. It's a health and safety hazard parking there, as I'm always telling people. I might as well talk to myself all the notice they take. You would think that these clever people could read a simple notice, wouldn't you?'

'I'm afraid that was my fault, Connie,' I told her, coming into the kitchen. 'The car park was full and I said it would be all right for him to leave his car there.'

'Well, please don't in future, Mr Phinn. If there was a fire in the centre, a car parked there would be an impediment.'

I changed the subject. 'Has Mr Clamp gone?'

'He has, and I can't say that I'm sorry either. Naked women indeed!' Connie shook her head and took two mugs out of the cupboard. 'I'm going to have a word with Dr Yeats about this. It's not part of my job description, catering for that sort of thing. I mean I've got all sorts of people in the Centre. There's a Women's Institute meeting here next week on that day. It's enough to give the poor ladies heart attacks, confronted with a naked woman.' She spooned coffee into the mugs and clicked on the kettle.

'In my experience the WI are pretty broad-minded, Connie,' I said.

'How would you know?'

'My mother was in the WI. It's not all jam and Jerusalem you know.'

'Well, the WI are not that broad-minded, I can tell you. You wouldn't get them taking their clothes off and posing for anyone, not at their age anyway. And then there's that nun who's always in here on courses, that Sister Brenda. Suppose she's here when this model is stripping off and swanning around the place in her altogether.'

'I don't think an artists' model is likely to be swanning about the place in her birthday suit, Connie,' I said. 'I guess she'll stay put in the room.'

'Yes, well I don't like it and I've warned

Mrs Osbaldiston already about Mr Clamp's shenanigans.'

'Who's Mrs Osbaldiston?' I asked.

'Didn't I say? She's my neighbour is Mrs Osbaldiston and I've asked her to hold the fort while I'm off next week. She cleans at the High School. I've asked her to come in. I shall be away next Tuesday for three days.' She poured hot water into the two mugs and reached for the milk jug. 'You don't have sugar, do you?'

'No, thank you. You're away next week, did you say?'

'Yes, I'll not be in for a few days.'

'So you'll not be here for Mr Clamp's course?' I asked, picking up a mug.

'No, I won't and I'm glad I won't as well.'

I changed the subject. 'Are you going on holiday?'

'Not at this time of year, I'm not,' she told me. 'I'm taking my father's ashes to Dunkirk. It's something I promised him I would do, scatter his ashes where some of his pals had been killed, but I've just not got around to doing it.' Connie's father had died the previous year. 'He lived in a cellar for a week at Dunkirk, you know, with nothing but a pound of sugar and rain water until he managed to get out on one of those little boats. Do you want a Garibaldi biscuit?'

'No, thank you.'

'That's what brought his stutter on, you know. He always said he wanted to rest with those pals of his who never made the journey home. He was a Dunkirk Veteran. I'm going with my Ted to scatter his ashes.' Connie sniffed and took a sip of coffee. 'Oh, look at me now, I'm getting all weepy.'

145

'He was a brave man, Connie,' I said.

'He was the best father you could hope for, was Dad. Never raised a hand to me, never used a bad word. He was always there for me, he was. When you're growing up you spend most of your time trying to get away from your parents, don't you? You always think you know better. You always think they're forever nagging you and not letting you do this, that and the other. When I was a girl, I had to tell Dad where I was going and who I was meeting. I had to be in by a certain time and woe betide if I came in late. I couldn't wear this skirt or that make-up.' She took a sip of coffee and sighed. 'You never really appreciate your parents when you're young. It's only when they're dead do you realise you never can get away from them. They're always going to be with you in your thoughts and in your memories. And when they're dead, you stop being a child, don't you?' Sometimes Connie uttered the most profound thoughts. 'Oh, I nearly forgot, you have a message.'

'From whom?'

'That Mrs Savage at County Hall. The one who sounds as if she's got a potato stuck in her mouth. She said to phone her immediately.'

'Now what does she want?' I sighed.

'I don't know, but she said it was urgent. She's got a tongue as sharp as a butcher's knife, that one, and a look as cold as a cemetery. I've had confrontations with that woman before now, parking that fancy red sports car so it blocks my entrance, flouting health and safety regulations.'

'She's been put in charge of that at County Hall,' I told Connie.

'Of what?'

'Health and safety.'

'Well, she's the last one to tell people about health and safety. Mind you, it doesn't surprise me at all. People without much substance always rise to the top like froth on the top of coffee.' She stared for a moment at the mug she was holding. 'I think this milk's off. Anyway, I wouldn't bother phoning now. Let her wait until Monday.'

What an end to the week! It had been full of trials and tribulations and it would, no doubt, end on an acrimonious note. Ignoring Connie's advice, I headed for the office with a sinking heart to telephone Mrs Savage.

'You wanted to speak to me, Mrs Savage?' I said rather formally when I finally got through.

'Yes, I did,' she replied icily. 'Dr Gore wishes to see you.'

'When?'

'At once.'

'I see.' I resisted the urge to ask what about but I had a shrewd idea it concerned the wretched report on King Henry's. 'Well, I'll be there presently.'

'May I impress on you, Mr Phinn,' continued Mrs Savage, 'that it is a matter of utmost urgency. I take it the course you have presumably been directing has now finished?'

'Yes, it has.'

'Well, in that case, could you return to County Hall ASAP?' Without waiting for a reply she continued. 'I will inform Dr Gore that you are on your way.' With that she thumped down the phone.

I sat back on the chair, sighed and shook my head. 'She gets worse,' I murmured to myself.

Connie appeared at the door with my mug of coffee. 'It's getting cold, this,' she said.

'Sorry Connie,' I told her. 'I've got to go. I've got an appointment.'

*   *   *

Dr Gore, Chief Education Officer for the County of Yorkshire, peered over the top of his small, gold-framed spectacles and then, resting his hands on the large mahogany desk in front of him, smiled like a contented cat.

'And how are you, Gervase?' he purred, steepling his long fingers in front of him like a judge about to pass sentence.

'I'm very well, Dr Gore, thank you,' I replied, attempting to hide my nervousness.

'Good, good,' the CEO murmured. He stared for a moment and nodded thoughtfully. 'And how is that lovely wife of yours? Is she keeping well?'

'Very well, thank you, Dr Gore,' I replied.

'And when is the baby due?'

'The end of March.'

'"Whan that Aprill with his shoures soote, The droghte of March hath perced to the roote."'

'Er, yes.'

'Chaucer.'

'Yes,' I replied, wishing he would get on with it and put me out of my misery.

'Well,' he said after a weighty pause, 'I'm sure you are wondering why I sent for you.'

'Yes, I *was* wondering,' I replied, getting more and more tense.

'I was speaking to Mr Nelson last week,' he said casually. Here we go, I thought. 'He's in the same Rotary Club as I am, you know. He's next year's District Governor, as a matter of fact. You're not a

148

Rotarian are you, Gervase?'

'No, no, I'm not.'

'Wonderful organisation is Rotary. "Service before Self"—that's our motto. Do you know, we raised a thousand pounds last year for a sensory garden at St Catherine's Special School?'

'Really?'

'Anyway, Mr Nelson mentioned you had paid a visit to King Henry's College recently.'

'Yes, I did,' I said.

'Took a bit of a look at the English department, I believe.'

'I did, yes.'

'I gather you were not impressed with one particular teacher?'

'About the report, Dr Gore—' I started to say.

'Ah yes, the report,' said the CEO, resting his elbows on the desk and peering at me over the top of his small, gold-framed spectacles. 'Mr Nelson said that he had never read a report quite like it.'

'Oh dear,' I mumbled.

'I must say that when I read it, it was, how shall we put it, rather direct and to the point. You certainly didn't pull any punches.'

'I would like to say, Dr Gore—' I began again.

He leaned back in his chair. 'But, of course, that's as it should be.'

I stared at him. 'I beg your pardon?'

'I said, that's how it should be.'

'It is?'

'Why, yes. I want my school inspectors to give clear, honest and objective assessments of what they see. To tell me how it is. You wouldn't be doing your job if all you did was say that everything was fine. I have to say that sometimes the reports

149

which land on my desk are very bland. I recall Mr Carter, who was to have taken over from Dr Yeats, was very critical of the lack of focus and clear issues for action in some of the inspectors' reports. Yes, I too thought your report on King Henry's was excellent. Well done.'

'Mr Nelson thought it was an excellent report?' I asked, dumbfounded.

'Yes, indeed. We didn't, of course, discuss the report at our Rotary meeting. That would have been entirely inappropriate. Mr Nelson merely mentioned it was extremely well written and to the point. Just wanted to put in a good word on your behalf.'

'I see.'

'I did read through the report with the others this morning and I must say you certainly have got to the nub of the problem in the English department. I rang up Mr Nelson to have a word and from what I gather the head of department at King Henry's, Mr Frobisher I believe his name is, has become rather tired and a little cynical over the past few years, not incompetent or anything like that but, to use common parlance, past his sell-by-date. He can, I believe, be quite difficult at times. When Mr Frobisher returned to school last week—evidently he had been away ill for the first time in living memory—the headmaster asked to see him and it was not a very good-humoured meeting, by all accounts. Mr Nelson was quite taken aback with Mr Frobisher's reaction but rather pleased with the outcome. The teacher concerned has decided to take early retirement which certainly suits Mr Nelson. He can now appoint someone more dynamic and enthusiastic.'

'I see,' I mumbled, hardly able to take in what I was hearing.

'So, your report was extremely effective.' Dr Gore paused and stared again over his glasses. 'You know, Gervase, when you applied for the Senior Inspector's post last year, one reservation I did have about you was that you might not have the mettle to be quite as critical as sometimes it is necessary to be. You're an enthusiastic enough young man, you get on with people, have a pleasant manner, you are hard-working *et cetera* but I had that nagging doubt whether or not you could be forceful enough to grasp the nettle. Sometimes one has to have a critical word, say the unpalatable. I think you have proved that you can.'

'Thank you, Dr Gore,' I said. I suppose I should have felt happy and relieved but for some reason I felt even more depressed. My report had been the means to end a teacher's career.

'Anyhow,' continued the CEO amiably and smiling widely, 'it wasn't about King Henry's that I wanted to see you.'

'No?'

'No,' he repeated. 'I have a little job for you.'

'Oh,' was all I could muster up to say.

I was well acquainted with Dr Gore's 'little jobs', having been given quite a number of them in my time with the Education Department, and they were never 'little'.

'You are, no doubt, aware that I sit on several major national committees and working parties. One is the "European Intermediary Education Initiative"—the EIEI.'

'Oh,' I said.

'EIEI enables teachers and inspectors to visit

other European countries to study and compare the education systems there.'

This didn't sound too bad, I thought to myself and I quite cheered up. A week in Sweden or Spain or a few days touring the schools in Germany or France sounded a 'little job' I could very much enjoy.

'Next term,' continued Dr Gore, 'there will be a small group of inspectors from various European countries visiting the county to look at the education we provide. It is all funded by the EIEI.'

'Oh,' I said again. It was beginning to sound like the chorus to 'Old Macdonald had a Farm'.

'I would like you to arrange for our foreign colleagues to visit a number of different schools so they may observe some lessons and talk with teachers.' My hopes of a continental expedition were dashed. 'In addition, you could perhaps set up a couple of meetings at the Staff Development Centre with invited headteachers and governors to talk about the education system over here and maybe organise an informal evening reception. That sort of thing. You can enlist the help of your colleagues and, of course, Mrs Savage will liaise with you and be on hand to deal with all the administration. The European inspectors will only be with us for a few days and shouldn't number more than three or four, so it's not a massive undertaking. Does that sound reasonable?'

'Fine,' I replied, thinking of all the extra work it would involve just when I knew my mind would be on the forthcoming happy event. Christine would need all the support and help I could give her in the months running up to the birth of the baby.

'Good, good,' murmured Dr Gore. 'Well, thank

you for coming to see me.'

Mrs Savage was waiting for me in the outer office. She had a smug expression on her face. 'It's just as well you didn't get the report back after all, isn't it?' she drawled, with ill-concealed satisfaction.

*   *   *

I arrived back at the inspectors' office to find Sidney regaling Gerry about Connie, the Staff Development Centre and the nude model. His colleague sat trapped behind her desk trying to look interested, her head cupped in her hands. No wonder Gerry avoided the office. Sidney stood before her waving his arms about him, spluttering and shaking his head, as if performing on a stage.

'I intend to speak to Harold about this,' he was saying. 'The woman is a cleaner, for goodness sake, not a director of studies. She's there to polish pipes, scrub floors, dust shelves, clean toilets, not dictate what goes on in the Centre or who visits. She's a megalomaniac. She's like Hitler in pink.' He paused in his diatribe to greet me. 'Oh hello, Gervase. You will, of course, vouch for what I say. I was telling Gerry here about the fracas at the Staff Development Centre earlier this afternoon. I merely asked Connie to ensure the heating was on next week. As you know, she usually doesn't start the boiler until mid-November and the first frost. It was so cold there last year I could hear my bones clicking. I certainly don't want Miriam—she's my model by the way—turning blue. And what do I get? "Of course, Mr Clamp. I'll make sure it's nice and warm for you. No problem at all." Do I heck! I get accused of opening a brothel.'

'Oh come on, Sidney,' I said, 'you know perfectly well what Connie's like.'

'Yes, I do indeed know what Connie is like and I don't like it. It's about time somebody told the woman what's what.'

'What?' asked Gerry.

'What's what, that's what!' exclaimed Sidney.

'She needs humouring, that's all,' I said. 'You just seem to wind her up.'

'I wind *her* up,' he cried. 'The woman does not need humouring, as you put it. She needs sacking, that's what she needs,' retorted Sidney.

'Sidney,' said Gerry gently, 'don't get in such a state about it. Try and keep calm and don't get all worked up—'

'Keep calm!' he exploded. 'I am incapable of keeping calm in the face of such naked aggression, if you will excuse the unintended pun. I shall see Harold about this. He needs to have a strong word with her and remind her of her role. He needs to put the cards on the table. She either toes the line or she goes. She's getting far above her station. *Au dessus de sa gare*, as one might say.'

'I think poor Harold has quite enough on his plate at the moment,' I observed thoughtfully, 'without another problem winging its way. The new term had barely started and you began bombarding him with a problem. First West Challerton High School—'

'What's been the problem there?' asked Gerry. 'I wish someone would tell me.'

'Don't ask!' snapped Sidney.

'The science and technology departments certainly need sorting out,' she said, 'but one thing I *am* pleased about is that the headmaster has, at

154

last, agreed to allocate more time for physics and chemistry.'

'Don't get me started on that,' warned Sidney. 'Please don't get me started on that.'

'Having sorted out the problem at West Challerton,' I continued, 'you now want Harold to sort out Connie. No wonder he's ready to retire.'

'Gervase,' said Sidney petulantly, 'that is Harold's job. He is, after all, the Senior Inspector. He is paid more than we—pittance that it is—to deal with these problems. It is his role to sort things out. As David's old Welsh grandmother would no doubt be moved to say: "He who collects the honey and the roses must bear the stings and the thorns." Should you take over from him, then you will be in the hot seat, fire-fighting for us.'

'That's if I apply,' I said.

'Of course you're going to apply. Just because you were unsuccessful before and didn't even get on the shortlist doesn't mean they'll reject you again.' Sidney was nothing, if not blunt. 'They're probably thinking "better the devil you know" after the last fiasco.'

'Thanks, Sidney,' I said. 'You have such a way of making people feel better.'

'I agree with Sidney,' said Gerry. 'I think you have a fair chance of getting the job this time.'

'That's if I want it, this time,' I replied.

CHAPTER TEN

I spent a fairly uncomfortable weekend with the knowledge that Hawksrill School might be closing

155

but decided I was not in a position to pass on the news which Harold had given me in confidence. Christine and the village would know soon enough.

On the following Tuesday, I arrived at the Staff Development Centre early. I had received a memorandum from Mrs Savage the day before asking me to meet her to discuss the EIEI initiative. 'It is imperative,' she had written, 'that we put our heads together ASAP so that wheels can be put in motion.' She had noted, having looked though my engagement sheet for the week, that I was to visit St Helen's Church of England Primary that morning, a school just a few miles from the SDC and therefore, 'it would not greatly inconvenience you to meet me at 0815'. Such was the tone of sharp command in the memo that I was minded to ignore it or reply that I was far too busy, but then I thought that it would be better to get the meeting over and done with. In any case, I wanted to make a start on this 'little job'. There was a lot to do. I replied, therefore, that I would be at the SDC at the designated time.

It was a particularly cold morning with what they call in Yorkshire 'a cheeky wind' as I drove along the twisting road from Hawksrill in the direction of Fettlesham. I stared in wonderment at the endless green and grey landscape wrinkled with rocks which stretched ahead of me. The views in the Dales are stunning and never cease to fill me with awe. I love travelling in this vast sprawling county with its soft green valleys and soaring fells, stately cathedrals and dramatic ruins, dark pine forests and vast, empty moors, flooded with bright purple heather in autumn. Every journey is different and every scene has a unique beauty. I slowed down to watch a formation of geese flying overhead, honking noisily as they went. Off to their wintering grounds, no doubt. What a place to work, I thought.

The Staff Development Centre was eerily quiet that morning. I was used to Connie standing sentinel in the entrance hall. She would arrive well before anyone else and watch from her vantage point in the kitchen, eagle-eyed and stony-faced. Then, at the sight of visitors, she would scurry down the corridor to greet them. Perhaps 'greet' was not the most appropriate word to use, for Connie would stand there, statuesque, feather duster poised, a shimmering pink apparition with a facial expression which could curdle milk.

I discovered Mrs Osbaldiston in the kitchen scrutinising a wodge of papers and shaking her head thoughtfully. She was a lean, elderly woman with tightly curled, silver-white hair, a small thin-lipped mouth and an amazingly wrinkled in-drawn face. A multi-coloured apron, depicting some large and gaudy flowers, enveloped her small frame. She was wearing slippers. As I approached I detected a curiously pervasive smell of mothballs.

'Good morning,' I said cheerfully. 'You must be Mrs Osbaldiston.'

She looked up from the papers and maintained a carefully blank expression. 'Are you Mr Camp?'

'No, I'm Gervase Phinn, the English inspector,' I replied.

'Oh, I was expecting Mr Camp, the art man.'

'It's Clamp.'

'What is?'

'The name of the art man. It's Clamp, not Camp. He'll be along later.'

'I thought he was Camp.'

'No, no, Clamp, as in clasp, vice, fastener.'

'And who did you say you were?' she asked, screwing up her eyes.

'Mr Phinn,' I replied, extending a hand. She raised a small cold hand and placed it in mine as a queen might to a courtier.

'Good morning,' she said, with an anxious look. 'There's been telephone calls for you this morning. I arrived well before eight o'clock and that phone started ringing as soon as I'd got through the door and it's never stopped. I thought I was here to clean, not answer calls.'

I explained to Mrs Osbaldiston that Julie, the inspectors' secretary, would phone through the numbers if there was anything urgent or ask callers to get in touch with me directly at the Centre.

'I've made a note of them on a pad in the office. I've not touched a thing yet, and it's already five minutes past.'

'Well, I'll go and make the calls and leave you to it. Have you everything you need?' I should not have asked.

The old lady huffed, tutted and then shook her head. 'Ee, what I need, young man, is a cup of strong sweet tea and a long sit down, that's what I need.' The poor woman looked as if the troubles of the world had been heaped on her small round shoulders. Then she turned her attention to the papers. 'There's nothing on this list what Connie left me about answering telephone calls or about any English courses here today. She never said you was to be in this morning, just that Mr Camp. I don't think I could cope with anything else, I really don't.'

158

'No, there isn't an English course on today,' I reassured her. 'I'm here to meet someone.'

'Connie's left this list of instructions as long as my arm,' Mrs Osbaldiston told me, with the expression of one suffering from chronic constipation. 'I just don't know where to begin, I really don't. There's so much to do. I mean, I only said I'd do a bit of dusting and wiping and keep things tidy and ship-shape to help out, but my goodness just look what she's left me.' She prodded the papers. 'I clean at the High School but I'm not expected to do all this. It'd take an army of cleaners to do this little lot that Connie's left me.' She flourished the list. 'I can't stretch, what with my bad back. There's no question of my bending what with the legs, and I can't over-exert myself what with my angina. Connie knows I'm allergic to bleach, and floor polish brings me out in a rash.'

Perhaps she is in the wrong line of work, I thought to myself. 'I really wouldn't worry, Mrs Osbaldiston,' I told her, 'Connie's a perfectionist.'

'Tell me about it,' she said. 'I lives next door to her. Inside her house is like Buckingham Palace and her garden, you should see her garden! The lawn's like a billiard table. There's not a flower out of place and she uses scissors on the Virginia creeper.' Mrs Osbaldiston clearly looked distressed. 'Then there's this Mr Camp. Connie's warned me about him and his goings-on. She said he wants watching.'

'Oh, he's not that bad.'

'Connie says he leaves a trail of debris and destruction wherever he goes and now he's got these naked women coming in. I really wish I hadn't agreed to do this but Connie's so . . . what's

159

the word?'

'Persuasive,' I suggested.

'Exactly.'

'Well, there are no naked ladies, just one artists' model and when Mr Clamp arrives, which shouldn't be too long now, he will deal with that.' I smiled and patted her arm. 'So don't worry, Mrs Osbaldiston. You make yourself that nice strong cup of tea.'

This proposal resulted in a remarkable transformation, as I guessed it would. The old lady visibly mellowed and a small smile came to her thin lips. It is a known fact that in Yorkshire, whatever the problem, the prospect of a cup of tea seems to have a remarkably calming effect. One might be dragged out from under the wheels of a ten-ton juggernaut, emerge half-drowned from a flash flood, stagger smouldering from a burning building, and a cup of tea is the first thing suggested.

'That would be very acceptable,' said Mrs Osbaldiston, sounding a whole lot happier. 'I think I might just do that.'

'By the way, have you put the water urn on yet?' I asked.

'No, I haven't.' She glanced at the papers in her hand. 'Oh dear, here it is, look, at the top of Connie's "To Do List". I should have put the water on at eight. She says here that people will be wanting a cup of tea or coffee when they arrive. First thing she asks me to do and I gets it wrong.'

'Well, you put out the cups and saucers in the lounge area and I'll see to the water before I make the calls and don't worry, Mrs Osbaldiston, everything will be fine.' She left the kitchen, mumbling to herself, to arrange the crockery in the lounge.

I filled the huge metal urn with water, switched it on and headed for the office. On the desk was a list of scrawled numbers: no name, no message, just the numbers. Connie's practice was to write neatly and legibly in the 'Messages' book the date, the time of the call, the number, the speaker's name, the subject of the call and any other relevant details. She was meticulous. All I had before me now was a list of five or six scribbled numbers, some of which were indecipherable. I sighed. Come back Connie, I said to myself as I rang the first number.

'Hello,' came a voice down the line.

'Oh hello, my name is Gervase Phinn. I believe someone on your number has telephoned to speak to me this morning.'

'Do you know who?'

'I don't, I'm afraid.'

'Was it Miss Precious, the headteacher?'

'Ah, is that Barton Moor Parochial School?' I asked.

'It is.'

'Yes, it must have been Miss Precious.'

A moment later the headteacher's voice came on the line. 'Hello, Mr Phinn. This is a pleasant surprise.'

'Did you not call me this morning, Miss Precious?'

'No, I've only just arrived.'

'I think someone called me from your number,' I told her.

'There's a mystery,' she said. 'I wonder if it was Mrs Durdon.' I doubted very much if it would be

Miss Precious's assistant, a small mousy, nervous little woman into whom I seemed, for some reason, to put the fear of God. It would be hardly likely that she would be contacting me early in the morning. 'I'll ask her if you like,' said Miss Precious. 'She's only down the corridor.'

'No, no, don't bother her, Miss Precious. I'm sure the person will ring back.'

'No trouble at all, Mr Phinn,' said the headteacher, and I heard the line go dead. A moment later Mrs Durdon was on the phone.

'Hello, Mr Phinn,' she said in a hushed voice. 'I did ask the receptionist who answered the phone at your end to tell you to ask for me personally. I didn't want Miss Precious to know.'

'Oh, I'm sorry,' I tried to explain, 'but—'

'It's just that Miss Precious retires at the end of the term and I wanted to invite you to a surprise party. I hope she doesn't suspect. You might have let the cat out of the bag. I shall have to think of some good excuse for you ringing me.'

'Well, I'd love to come, Mrs Durdon, if I am not busy.'

'Best thing for me to do is put it in a letter. It was most unfortunate Miss Precious answering the phone. I don't think your receptionist sounded very "with it" this morning.'

The tell-tale click-clack of high heels on the hard corridor floor outside the office heralded the arrival of my unwelcome visitor.

'I must go, Mrs Durdon,' I said. 'I look forward to hearing from you.'

'Good morning,' I heard Mrs Savage say beyond the office door.

Then I heard the morose tones of Mrs

162

Osbaldiston reply, 'Mornin'.' Then she added, 'You're early, aren't you?'

I was tempted to show myself at this point but resisted the temptation, deciding instead to eavesdrop. This was going to prove interesting.

'I beg your pardon,' replied Mrs Savage curtly.

'I said you're early,' said Mrs O.

'No, I am not,' came another curt reply. 'In fact, I am prompt. I am always prompt. I said I would be here at eight-fifteen and if I am not mistaken that is the exact time on the clock in the corridor.'

Mrs Osbaldiston did not sound in the least daunted by the cold and superior voice. 'Well, I was told you'd be here at nine. I've got it on my list.'

'And who are you, may I ask?'

The sharp, authoritative tone was clearly lost on Connie's locum. 'Mrs Osbaldiston.'

'And?'

'And what?'

'What is your function here?'

'My function?'

'What exactly do you do?'

'What do I do?'

'Am I in an echo chamber?' asked Mrs Savage.

'You're in the Staff Development Centre,' Mrs Osbaldiston informed her. 'And for your information, I'm filling in for Connie, the caretaker. She's in France scattering her father's ashes at Dunkirk.'

'Really,' said Mrs Savage wearily.

'I'm holding the fort, so to speak, doing a bit of cleaning and that.'

'I see.'

'And, as I said, I have it on my list that you'd be arriving at nine. Anyway, now you're here, do you

163

want to see where you'll be? You're in the end room where it's warmer and more private. I've pulled the curtains as well. I'm sure you don't want people gawping at you through the window. I'll put a cushion on your chair before you start posing. I suppose being sat on a hard wooden chair for any length of time must be uncomfortable on the nether regions, specially if you have no clothes on.'

'No clothes on!' snapped Mrs Savage. 'Whatever are you talking about?'

I nearly betrayed my presence with a burst of laughter but smacked my hand over my mouth. Mrs Osbaldiston had mistaken Mrs Savage for the nude model. I could visualise the scarlet lips pursing in disapproval and the dark eyes flashing.

'Well, I was told you'd be taking your clothes off for Mr Camp,' continued Mrs Osbaldiston blithely.

'Taking my clothes off for Mr Camp!' repeated Mrs Savage. 'What *are* you talking about? Have I entered Bedlam?'

'No, I've just told you, this is the Staff Development Centre,' replied Mrs Osbaldiston calmly.

'Do you know who I am?' asked Mrs Savage.

'The nude model, aren't you?'

'The *what?*' spluttered Mrs Savage. 'I am Mrs Savage, Personal Assistant to Dr Gore.'

'Who's he?'

'Dr Gore is the Chief Education Officer.'

'Can't say I've heard of him,' replied the old lady. 'Any road up, I thought you was the nude model.'

'Do I look like a nude model?' asked an exasperated Mrs Savage.

'I don't really know,' said Mrs Osbaldiston

stubbornly, 'I've never seen one.'

At this point I decided to enter the fray and emerged from the office, attempting to keep a straight face. 'Good morning, Mrs Savage,' I said seriously.

Mrs Savage was attired in a scarlet jacket with silver buttons, tight-fitting black skirt, long dangling silver earrings and high-heeled patent leather shoes. It was very like the ensemble Julie had worn some weeks earlier when she had attended the Health and Safety meeting. I told myself not to smirk.

'Mr Phinn,' said Mrs Savage, drawing her lips together into a thin line. 'This . . . this person here, was under the misapprehension that I was some sort of . . . of model.'

'Really?' I said innocently.

'I thought I had entered Bedlam.' The eyes in the stony visage glowed with anger, the mouth remained small and tight.

'I told her it was the Staff Development Centre,' said Mrs Osbaldiston blithely, more to herself than to me. 'I don't know where she wants to be. Anyway, you'll have to deal with her, Mr Flynn. I've got lots to do.' With that she waddled off, mumbling to herself, 'And I never did get that cup of tea.'

The meeting with Mrs Savage was short but not very sweet. I agreed to nominate certain schools for the foreign inspectors to visit, prepare some briefing papers and devise a programme, and Mrs Savage announced that she would organise the travel and accommodation, and deal with the administration.

'And do keep me up to speed, Mr Phinn,' she

said in a hectoring tone, as she rose to leave. 'I will arrange a further mutually-convenient meeting to tie up any loose ends just prior to their visit.'

'Very well,' I replied, wishing she would high-tail it off back to County Hall.

'And I shall be having a word with Dr Gore about nude models at the Staff Development Centre,' she told me. 'I assume it is Mr Clamp who has organised this. The man gets worse.' I did not reply. 'I am afraid that particular colleague of yours sails very close to the wind at times. By the way, I sincerely hope that the caretaker—that Connie woman—has cleared things before having time off to visit France. She can't just take leave when she wants to and it is up to the office to arrange replacements, not her. Personnel will be informed of this as soon as I get back to County Hall. I shall also be having words with Dr Gore about that other cleaning woman whom I encountered this morning.' She stroked out the creases in her skirt. 'Now, I must return to the office,' she continued, as if I were deliberately detaining her. 'Dr Gore is finalising arrangements for the appointment of Dr Yeats's successor this morning, specifically organising the interview panel . . .' She paused, as if awaiting some sort of response, but I remained tight-lipped. 'The advertisement for the post of Senior Inspector has gone into the Staff Vacancy Bulletin and will appear in the educational journals and national newspapers later this week.'

'Yes, I believe so,' I said.

When Mrs Savage had departed, I bade my farewell to a harassed-looking Mrs O. and headed for the door. In the car park I discovered a lean woman climbing from an extremely old and rusty car. She could have been Mrs Osbaldiston's twin sister: tightly curled greying hair, small down-turned mouth and an amazingly wrinkled in-drawn face.

'Excuse me,' she said, 'is this the Staff Development Centre?'

'It is,' I replied.

'I'm here to see Mr Clamp,' she told me. 'I'm the artists' model.'

*   *   *

St Helen's Church of England Primary School was a square, grey-stone building with small mullioned windows, a very impressive heavy oak door and a high shiny slate roof. It had been built in the latter part of the eighteenth century following the bequest of a wealthy landowner for the education of his estate workers. It was still continuing to serve the two villages of Kirby Crighton and Kirby Ruston and a few children from the nearby United States Air Force Base at Ribbon Bank. It was situated in a very advantaged area, and houses in the vicinity were amongst the most expensive in this part of the county. I had visited the school during my first year on such a nippy day as this when the trees were beginning to turn golden.

Mrs Smith, the headteacher, greeted me at the door and ushered me into a small entrance area. On the wall was a large photograph of all the teachers, governors and ancillary staff and another of all the children, sitting up smartly and smiling. There were also pictures and prints, potted plants and a large dried-flower arrangement. It looked a cheerful and welcoming place. 'It's very nice to see you again, Mr Phinn,' said Mrs Smith. 'You'll find we've grown quite a bit since your last visit to us.'

I had given the school a very good report on the last occasion and this visit was to see if standards in English had remained high.

'A victim of your own success, eh, Mrs Smith?' I suggested.

'One would like to think so,' said the headteacher, clearly pleased with the flattering observation, 'but it is rather the result of more American children attending from the base. And there are some real characters, as you'll see.'

On the way to the infant classroom, the headteacher told me about Esther. 'She's a remarkable little reader and has the vocabulary of an eleven-year-old. I've never come across a child like this in all my teaching career. She's just six and can read virtually anything. Her mother's a lecturer at York, her father a colonel in the United States Air Force which, of course, explains a lot. Esther is an amazingly fluent reader. She simply devours books. I should say she is gifted.'

'What do her parents say?' I asked.

'Oh, they seem to take it in their stride. They certainly don't want her pressurised or anything like that, no special provision or extra work and, I must say, I have to agree with them. Young children should enjoy their childhood. I do, however, need some advice on suitable reading material for such a gifted infant.'

I have, on my visits to schools, very often been told by a teacher that a particular child is 'gifted' or 'talented' or 'exceptionally able'. It generally turns out that the child is bright or intelligent but it is rare to find a child of really outstanding ability.

168

Einsteins are extremely rare. I smiled at Mrs Smith and said I would speak to the child and hear her read.

I discovered little Esther at a table splashing paint on a large sheet of pale yellow paper. There were three egg-shaped, bright-pink figures complete with long spindly arms, fingers like twigs and great beaming smiles. They all had tummy buttons.

'Hello,' I said.

'Oh, hi!' the child replied, looking up and smiling. 'How are you?'

'I'm fine,' I said, leaning over and scrutinising her picture. 'Now, who are these interesting people in your painting?' I asked.

'There's Daddy,' Esther told me, gesturing with the brush. 'He's the large one. There's Mommy in a bikini and the little one is me. We're on the beach in France. Have you been to France?'

'Yes, I have.'

'It's cool, isn't it?'

'It is. Now, Mrs Smith tells me you are a very good reader,' I said.

'Yeah, that's me!' she replied.

'Would you like to read to me?'

'I don't mind,' she said. 'I like reading. I've got lots and lots of books at home. I have my own library in my bedroom.'

'I'm sure you have,' I said, 'and I bet you have a bedtime story every night, as well.'

'I sure do. Daddy and Mommy take it in turns. I have a cuddle and a bedtime story every night. Daddy says stories are very good for children.'

'Your daddy's right,' I told her.

'Daddies always are,' she told me pertly. 'Shall I

get my reading book?'

'No,' I said, 'perhaps you would read one of mine.'

I carry around with me in my briefcase various documents and books: standardised reading tests, non-verbal assessment sheets, word recognition lists and also a few books of varying difficulty to test children's reading ability. The reading scheme books, with which the children learn to read, have familiar characters and settings, repeated words and phrases to give children confidence and security but the good reader is able to be confronted with an unknown text and read and understand it. I presented little Esther with a book suitable for a seven-year-old.

'Gee, this looks too easy,' she told me, examining the cover and flicking through the pages.

'Easy?' I repeated. 'I'll be very surprised if you manage to read it.'

The child gave me the kind of melancholy smile a Mother Superior might bestow upon an erring novice. 'May I have a harder book, please?'

'OK,' I said, reaching into my briefcase, 'let's try another one.' I selected a book suitable for a nine-year-old. 'Now, if you find this a bit hard, don't worry. It's a book for older children.'

She stared at the cover for a moment. 'Shall I start from the beginning?' she asked.

'Yes please.'

'From the very beginning?'

'From the very beginning,' I repeated.

The child tilted her head, stared at the large black stamped box at the very top of the cover page and then she read: 'Property of Yorkshire County Council, Education Department, Schools

Inspectorate.'

I shook my head and smiled.

Later that morning in the nursery, I met Imogen. She looked like a china doll: golden curls, huge blue eyes and a flawless complexion. The child was casually turning the pages of an early reader. Each page displayed an object: house, bus, church, man, woman, dog, car and so on, beneath which was the word in large black letters. 'Will you read it to me, please?' she asked.

'Of course,' I replied, amused by such a confident little thing.

'I know some words,' she told me, 'but I can't read all of them.'

When I had finished reading the book, I wrote the word 'car' on a piece of paper. 'Now,' I said, 'can you read this word for me?'

'No, I can't,' she replied.

'It begins with a curly "c". Would you like to have a guess?'

'No, I can't read it.'

'Let me give you a clue,' I said. 'Your daddy or mummy might drive you to school in it in the morning.'

'Oh yes!' she cried. 'You mean Wolls Woyce.'

*   *   *

The older children were in the middle of a discussion when I joined them after morning break. Their teacher, a round, jolly woman in an orange skirt, white blouse and green cardigan, greeted me warmly and ushered me to a chair at the front of the classroom. She looked like a walking flag of Ireland.

'Now, this is Mr Phinn,' she told the children. 'Some of you might remember him. He visited us before, didn't you Mr Phinn?'

'Yes. I did,' I said.

'And Mr Phinn is very interested in children's reading and writing, aren't you, Mr Phinn?'

'Yes, I am,' I said.

'And today we are writing a cautionary tale. We've been reading a story about children who did not do as they were told and as a result they all came to a sticky end.'

'Oh dear,' I said.

'There's the disobedient boy who did not listen to his father and played with fire, despite being warned of the danger, and ended up burnt to a crisp. It's not as gruesome as it sounds,' she said in an undertone. 'Nothing gratuitous. And the girl who ignored her mother's cautions and played near the river bank. She came to a watery end. Then there was the boy who went near the railway line, ignoring all the signs that warned him of danger. That had a very unfortunate outcome. Now, before they write their own cautionary tales, Mr Phinn, the children are describing an accident they have had because they have not taken sufficient care. Let me see. Katy, would you like to tell our important visitor what you are going to be writing about?'

'Miss,' said the girl enthusiastically, 'when I was little we went to a pizza parlour and I sniffed some pepper up my nose.'

There was a ripple of laughter. 'It's not funny, children,' said the teacher seriously. 'The pepper might have gone right down into Katy's lungs. It could have been very serious, couldn't it, Mr Phinn?'

'It could,' I agreed.

'And I couldn't stop sneezing and coughing,' continued the child. 'My mum went bananas—'

'I think a better phrase to use would be "became very angry", Katy,' interrupted the teacher.

'She became very angry and said what a stupid thing to do. We had to go home and my dad said I would not do that in a hurry again.'

'I think your father was right, Katy,' said the teacher. 'Don't you, Mr Phinn?'

'Yes, I do,' I agreed.

'David, what about your accident?' asked the teacher, looking at a small boy near the front.

'Miss, I swallowed a marble,' said the boy.

There was another ripple of laughter. 'Good gracious!' exclaimed the teacher. 'That was a very silly thing to do and could have been very dangerous. You could have choked to death, couldn't he, Mr Phinn?'

'Yes, indeed,' I said.

'Miss, I was pretending it was a sweet,' continued the boy, 'and I popped it in my mouth and swallowed it by mistake. I started to cough and my mum had to smash me on the back really really hard and—'

'I think a better phrase to use would be "strike firmly" or "slap heavily", David,' interrupted the teacher.

'So, my mum had to strike me firmly on the back but it wouldn't come up, so I had to go to hospital. The doctor gave my mum this paper to get some medicine—'

'Prescription,' interposed the teacher.

'Gave mum this prescription to get some medicine and it was thick and pink and had a horrible taste and—'

'Tasted unpleasant,' prompted the teacher.

'And it came in a big brown bottle and I had to take it for a couple of days and then one morning I was sitting on the toilet and there was a "clunk" and I shouted down the stairs, "I've got my marble back!" and my dad said, "Leave it alone!" and—'

'My goodness, David,' said the teacher hurriedly, 'what a to-do. I think we've heard quite enough about your unfortunate accident, haven't we, Mr Phinn?'

'Yes,' I said, wishing that the teacher would not constantly keep referring to me for an opinion.

'Just one more, before we get on with our writing,' said the teacher, turning to a large, friendly-looking boy with cropped hair and large ears. 'Scott's from America, Mr Phinn. All the way from Tennessee. Come along then, Scott, what was your accident?'

'Well, I guess the worst accident I had was when I was riding my bike on the sidewalk—'

'We call it "pavement" over here, Scott,' interrupted the teacher.

'Oh yeah, pavement, and I came to this slope. I was pedalling so fast I just could not stop. I put on my brakes but I carried on skidding and sliding until I hit one of those great white things in the middle of the road—'

'Bollards,' said the teacher.

'Straight up, miss,' said the boy. 'I really did.'

CHAPTER ELEVEN

One of the great joys of being a school inspector is the opportunity of meeting so many interesting, unusual and sometimes truly bizarre people. And Mr Maurice Hinderwell was certainly out of the ordinary.

I arrived at Scarthorpe Primary School one bright October morning to undertake a half-day's follow-up inspection. The small school was a squat, dark, stone building, tucked away behind the ancient Norman church of St Mary the Virgin and partially hidden by a towering oak tree with branches reaching skywards like huge arms. It had been in the spring of the previous year when I had visited Scarthorpe, to take a look at the standards in reading and writing, and I had found it to be well managed and held in high regard by the parents. There had been a few recommendations for improvement and I was here that morning to see that they had been implemented.

As I approached the building now, I recalled the first occasion, eighteen months before, when I had driven up that twisting ribbon of road. Behind me, in the valley bottom, rolling green pastureland dotted with ewes and their lambs contentedly cropping the lush grass had stretched into the distance. Before me an ocean of bright green young bracken had swept upwards to a belt of dark pines and beyond to the rocky tops. Above, the sky had been a vast canopy of pale blue. It had taken my breath away. What a glorious place to live, I had thought. It was a very different scene now, but equally magnificent in its autumnal beauty. Through the windscreen appeared a sea of fading crimson heather, the bracken on the slopes was beginning to turn and the distant felltops were now a pale purple in the early morning light.

I had been driving behind a tractor for some time along the narrowest of winding roads so arrived a little later than expected. The bell had just gone for the start of the school day so, not wishing to interrupt the headteacher's assembly, I headed for the staff room. There I discovered, sitting in the corner of the room, a small man in an incredibly creased grey suit, loud spotted bow tie and small shiny boots. He was balancing a cup of steaming coffee on the arm of the chair with one hand and holding a chocolate biscuit in the other.

'Nice morning,' he said jovially as I entered.

'Yes, indeed,' I replied. 'It's beautiful.'

To my amazement, the little man posted the whole of the chocolate biscuit into his mouth and crunched noisily. Clearly he was not a member of staff or he would have been at assembly. I decided he was a governor or a book representative or, more likely, here to see about the plumbing or electrics.

'I'm here to inspect the school,' I told him. 'I'm a school inspector.'

'Oh, yes?' he said, spitting bits of biscuit in my direction. I sat in the chair the furthest away. He made no effort to introduce himself. 'I wouldn't like that job myself, school inspector,' he told me, poking a bit of irritating biscuit from his teeth. 'Too much like hard work. All those reports to write. And I don't suppose you're very popular either. Having you in must be like a visit from the KGB.'

176

He took a great gulp of coffee and smacked his lips noisily. 'No, it can't be the most rewarding line of work, school inspecting.' Before I could enlighten him, he continued. 'Most important thing for me is job satisfaction, not money or status or long holidays or fancy perks. It's job satisfaction, knowing that you're doing something worthwhile and challenging, a service to the community. That's something *I've* got—job satisfaction. I love my work. I get up every morning raring to go. Yes, it's a very satisfying job, is mine.'

I just had to ask: 'And what exactly do you do?'

'Have a guess.'

'I haven't a clue.'

'I'm the County Pest Control Officer.'

'Indeed—I see.'

'I deal with pests: cockroaches, bed bugs, rabbits, moles, bats, wasps, ants, beetles, fleas, every pest imaginable. You name it, I kill it. You'll be pleased to hear we don't include human pests like VAT officers, traffic wardens, tax investigators and'—he paused for effect—'school inspectors are not on the list either.' He chuckled at his own witticism.

'So the school has a problem with pests, has it?' I asked.

'Rats.'

'I beg your pardon?'

'The school. They've got rats. Quite a colony by all accounts.' I shuddered and pulled a face. 'Got a call last week from Mrs Fox, the headteacher. Now there's a name to conjure with. I do foxes as well, you know. Anyway, she was in a right old state. Got her knickers in a real twist. Teachers were in a panic, dinner ladies hysterical, governors complaining, caretaker a nervous wreck and parents up in arms. Rats have this effect on people, you know. Kiddies weren't worried, to be honest. Quite took to the rats they did, watching their antics. They were running up and down the climbing frame in the playground, scuttling across the wall, burrowing behind the bicycle sheds, paddling in the waste near the dustbins. The rats, I mean, not the kiddies.'

'It sounds frightful,' I said. I must have looked horrified.

'No, no, as I said to Mrs Fox, I'll soon have the little buggers—pardon my French. Mind you, some of them aren't so little. They can grow to the size of small rabbits, you know. I do rabbits as well. Your average rat grows to about a foot long and weighs about a pound, but you can get them much bigger. But I'll get them, oh yes, I'll get them.' He took another gulp of coffee before adding philosophically, 'I always do.'

'Well, good luck,' I said.

'It's not a matter of luck,' my sharp-faced companion informed me. 'It's more a matter of skill, intuition and know-how. You have to appreciate how rats think, you see.' He sipped the remains of his coffee and then licked his lips. With his dark inquisitive eyes, small pointed nose, protuberant white teeth and glossy black hair bristling on his scalp, he did not look so dissimilar to the creatures he had come to exterminate. 'I think of all the pests I have to deal with, the rat is my favourite. He's a much greater challenge than your average cockroach or your bed bug.'

'Really?'

'Aye, it's a fact. Intelligent creatures are rats, but I have to exterminate them. It's a fact of life.

They're walking death traps,' he told me, his small eyes flashing. 'One in ten rats carries *Leptospira* which can lead to a whole host of very unpleasant diseases, you know.'

'You don't say.'

'Oh, but I do,' he chuckled to himself. 'Penicillin and other antibiotics have little effect against causal organisms like leptospirosis. One of the varieties of leptospirosis is called Weil's disease, you know. Very unpleasant that. Very unpleasant indeed. It's contracted through rats' urine, often found in contaminated water, and is fatal more often than not. They urinate eighty times a day, do rats. Did you know that?'

'No, I didn't,' I replied weakly.

'And one in ten rats carries *Listeria* and *Cryptosporidium*, both of which can cause very nasty gastroenteritis. You could be ill for weeks with a dose of that, on and off the lavatory, diarrhoea, vomiting, spitting blood. Of course, humans are very susceptible to all these horrible diseases that this particular rodent can carry. Rat urine and faeces get everywhere. They like to live near kitchens where there's lots of cooked food and waste. I don't eat out much myself. I say, is there another chocolate digestive going?'

'Oh dear,' I sighed. The morning had started off so well. I was beginning to feel quite ill.

'One in twenty-five rats has the Hantavirus antibody,' he continued blithely, 'which can lead to haemorrhagic fever. That's a killer. Once you've got that, mate, you're dancing with death.'

I quickly passed over the packet of biscuits. I was by now fascinated by the gruesome account. 'It's fortunate then,' I said, 'that there aren't so many

179

rats about.'

'Not so many about!' he squeaked derisively. 'Not so many about! There's seventy million in this country alone, that's how many. There are more rats than humans on this planet, over six billion of the buggers—pardon my French. Rats have sex twenty times a day and can give birth every four weeks. One in twenty domestic premises are infested with rats and that's a conservative estimate, so I'm kept pretty busy, I can tell you. You think there aren't so many because you don't see them. They're elusive creatures. But they're there all right. Watching, waiting, breeding and spreading disease wherever they go. You see, your rat is very clever, he's devious, quick-witted and adaptable. You're never more than fifteen feet away from a rat. Rats' teeth are harder than aluminium or copper. They can gnaw through cables, climb brickwork, get into cavity walls and swim up toilet U-bends. You could be sitting there, reading your paper, minding your own business—if you'll excuse the pun—and up he pops.' I shifted uncomfortably in my chair. 'They can squeeze through a hole no larger than my thumb and will eat almost anything.' He took a sizeable bite out of the biscuit he had plucked from the packet and crunched noisily. 'Very nice digestives, these. Will you have one?' I shook my head. He polished off the biscuit. 'Then there's what we call in the business your "intermediate vectors", like fleas.' He became suddenly quite animated. 'Now your flea is a fascinating creature. The distances they can spring is quite mind-boggling. The danger is that they feed off the rat, sucking its blood, and then pass on the rat's disease to you. That's how the Black Death started.'

I suddenly began to feel rather itchy. 'How will you dispose of the rats?' I asked, scratching my scalp.

'Traps and poison, simple but effective. You know, I have a certain respect for *Rattus*. He's quite amazing. Body like a coiled spring, calibrated senses, razor sharp incisors, jaws of steel, superb night vision, fast mover, brilliant swimmer and agile climber. I almost admire him in a funny sort of way.'

'Well, you certainly seem to enjoy your work,' I said.

'I love it. Every day is different, every day has its share of exciting challenges.'

Thankfully, the bell for the end of assembly sounded. My companion rose to his feet, brushing the crumbs from his trousers. He placed the empty mug on the side and stretched his arms widely. 'Well, I shall have to make a start, I suppose. I need to reconnoitre, find the right place to lay my poison and set my traps. Mrs Fox has been explaining things to the children in assembly. She felt it would be best coming from her. She thought my explaining things might frighten the kiddies.' Having heard him, I could well see her point. 'Now, I know you inspectors like to look into everything in a school but a word of advice. Don't go poking about in the undergrowth, pushing your fingers into holes or lifting anything suspicious-looking. There'll probably be a trap or poison in there.'

'I won't,' I assured him.

'Anyway, nice meeting you, and if ever you do need anything disposing of—and I don't include your mother-in-law in that list—then phone

Maurice Hinderwell at the County Pest Control Unit in Crompton. Service with a smile, that's me.'

I little thought that morning at Scarthorpe School that I would one day quite soon be requiring the services of Mr Hinderwell.

The Mrs Fox I remembered from my last visit was a large, cheerful woman with a foghorn voice. On this morning, however, she was very different. She appeared so careworn and subdued that I suggested to her that I cancel my visit and return at a later date when the problem with the rats had been resolved. She sighed with relief and readily agreed to my suggestion.

'Oh yes, that would suit very well, Mr Phinn,' she said. 'Was it not Hamlet who said that "troubles come not in single spies, but in battalions"?' I knew exactly how she felt. 'First we had the blocked drains, then the leaking roof, then an outbreak of scabies and an infestation of head lice. And then'— she took a deep breath—'the rats arrived. Parents are beginning to think this school is cursed. A school inspection would just about finish us off.'

'I'm very happy to fix another date, Mrs Fox,' I told her, 'and return when the rats have gone. I have plenty of paperwork to catch up with back at the office and I'm running a course this afternoon so that will give me the chance to go through my notes.'

'It's ironic, really,' she sighed. 'We were about to start rehearsals for the Christmas play next week. Well, that will have to be cancelled. There's no way I'm staging that particular piece of drama.'

'What was it to have been?' I asked.

'*The Pied Piper*,' she replied, giving me a weak smile.

182

So I departed, my mind full of the frightening facts about disease-ridden rodents, giant blood-sucking bed bugs and acrobatic fleas.

*   *   *

I was not in the most positive frame of mind as I walked into the entrance of West Challerton High School later that day to direct the staff-training course. The previous year, one of Dr Gore's 'little jobs' had been for me to take part in a Ministry of Education initiative called 'Language and Literacy for Learning'. English inspectors from selected education authorities had been given the task of observing a range of lessons in a sample of secondary schools, to assess how effective teachers in different subject areas were in using questions, developing reading competence, organising group work, encouraging discussion and teaching writing skills such as summary and note-taking. The inspectors were also instructed to examine how teachers evaluated pupils' work. From this 'pilot' survey, it was found that the questions asked and the written work set in the classroom could very well act as barriers to communication between teachers and their students. A fully-blown national project had emerged and each secondary school in the country was now asked to devise a 'Language and Literacy for Learning' policy. All teachers were required to explore the issues in the Ministry of Education's detailed report through courses, subject-based workshops and working parties in order that an understanding of the theory could be translated into practice.

The second-in-charge in the English department

was a dynamic young teacher called Miss Mullane. She had been asked by the headmaster to lead on this project, produce guidelines and organise training sessions and it was she who had asked me to address the staff. I had observed Miss Mullane a couple of years before, when she had taught at the ill-named Sunny Grove Secondary Modern School, a dark, grim building set in a wretchedly depressed inner-city environment, scarred with graffiti and ankle-deep in litter. The atmosphere in her classroom had been such a contrast. It had been bright and warm and the pupils had responded well to her outstanding teaching. I had kept in touch with her and had been pleased when she had been put in charge of the 'Language and Literacy' initiative and been only too happy to accept her invitation to speak to the staff.

When I saw Mr Pennington-Smith sweeping down the corridor towards me in his black academic gown, I had a presentiment that my course would not go all that well. I could quite understand the headmaster wearing his gown for a speech day or when the pupils were in school but wondered why he still had his symbol of authority draped around him. It was not really conducive to a training course for teachers.

'Aaaahhh, Mr Phinn,' he intoned, 'you've arrived. The staff are waiting for you in the school hall.' He gave a weak smile. 'It's never easy delivering these training courses, is it?' he said as we walked together down the corridor. 'Most of the staff feel they could be better occupied than sitting in a draughty school hall at the end of the day, listening to a lecture on language and learning. Most of them do not see the relevance for their subject areas. I have to say, I have a deal of sympathy with that view. The Ministry of Education, in its wisdom, seems to invent these initiatives, churning out discussion papers, frameworks, guidelines and unwieldy reports that rarely get read. These people in their ivory towers in London have not the first idea of the amount of work that goes on in schools.'

'I have to admit, Mr Pennington-Smith,' I said, 'that when I was asked to take part in the pilot project, I too felt very sceptical but I have changed my mind. I think this initiative is worthwhile and well overdue. I am convinced that school failure begins with the inability of young people to master spoken and written English. Teachers of all subjects need to be aware of the process by which their students acquire information and know something about the reading demands of their own subjects.'

'There is none so zealous as a convert,' remarked the headmaster. We stopped at the entrance to the hall and he rested his hand on my arm. 'If I may proffer a little advice,' he whispered in my ear. 'We don't want thought-showers, brainstorming, bullet point presentations, group work and plenary sessions and could you make your talk amusing and entertaining?'

'Make it amusing and entertaining?' I repeated.

'We don't want anything heavy or rigorous.'

This was going to be such an ordeal, I thought to myself.

At this moment, Mr Pennington-Smith was waylaid by a teacher, no doubt attempting to give his excuses for not staying for my talk, so I had a minute or two to recall Sidney's reminiscences which he had imparted that afternoon in the office prior to my departure for West Challerton.

'You will find, Gervase,' he had said, 'that there are some teachers who derive a perverse satisfaction from trying to wind up anyone who attempts to train them. There's the very noisy one who arrives just after you've started your lecture, who bustles into the room, apologising profusely for being late, drops his papers, makes a real fuss finding a seat and finally decides on a chair at the very front right under your nose. He will then shuffle and yawn and grunt and sigh deeply during your presentation and make frequent comments behind his hand to the person sitting next to him. Occasionally, he will distract others who are attempting to listen by passing little notes along the row, chuckling and watching for their reaction. Then there's the one who, when asked if there are any questions, enquires when we are breaking for lunch or who asks if anyone has a spare pencil, and the one with verbal diarrhoea whom you can't shut up and rambles endlessly off the subject to everyone's annoyance.'

At this point in Sidney's outpourings, I had pushed away the notes I had been attempting to read through, and gave myself up to listening to him until he ran out of steam. 'There's the one who looks as if he's in a coma, who stares at you unnervingly, without the trace of a smile, and who, when you explain the exercise you wish them to tackle, informs everybody in a loud weary voice that he has done it before and it doesn't work. Of course, there's the one who falls asleep and the one who ignores the "No Smoking" sign and the one who has a digital watch which goes off at regular intervals. Then there's the downright rude person. Once I was half way through making a point when some individual from the back shouted out "Bullshit!" I had the presence of mind to reply, "Yes, I got the name, but what was the question?" Oh yes,' Sidney had told me, 'I've seen them all.'

Not all, as I was soon to find out.

Mr Pennington-Smith, having finished his conversation with the teacher, motioned me forward to the door of the school hall. Inside, I was greeted by Miss Mullane.

'It is really good of you to come,' she said brightly. 'We're all so much looking forward to your talk.'

From a quick look at the assembled teachers, nothing could have been further from the truth. They appeared about as interested as waxwork exhibits and sat in rows facing the stage, arms folded and faces like death masks. I predicted that my talk would not be rapturously well received.

The headmaster called for attention and introduced me. In the front row was a woman sipping noisily from a large mug and wearing a T-shirt on the front of which was emblazoned in large red letters the slogan: 'Give a man an inch and he thinks he's a ruler!' Her neighbour was knitting furiously and looking at me as she might her former husband who had deserted her for another woman, leaving her to bring up the ten children. My introduction was followed immediately by a few whispers, assorted sighs and a sea of icy stares from the assembled staff.

Then, in a feeble attempt to start the proceedings off on a light-hearted note, the headmaster started with a joke. 'What's the difference between an

187

inspector and a sperm?' he asked no one in particular. None, least of all myself, bothered to respond, so he provided the answer. 'A sperm has a two million to one chance of being human.' There was not a titter. At this point, a man in a tracksuit covered in bright badges opened a newspaper with a flourish and someone sitting at the end of a row slithered out.

It was time for me to start which I did as cheerfully as I could, outlining what I intended doing during the hour-long session. The clacking of the knitting needles, the sipping of the tea and the rustling of someone's newspaper were soon accompanied by further sighs and tuttings.

'Education these days,' I began enthusiastically, 'is rather akin to the opening lines of a favourite novel of mine: "It was the best of times, it was the worst of times." These are the opening words of the novel, *A Tale of Two Cities* by Charles Dickens.' I stared pointedly at Madame Defarge in the front row but she clacked on regardless.

The afternoon, needless to say, was not a great success. I had felt like a Christian in an arena full of lions. I declined the headmaster's invitation to join the few remaining staff for a cup of tea and prepared to depart.

'Our speaker next week is a Miss de la Mare,' Mr Pennington-Smith informed me as he escorted me down the corridor to the exit. 'She's one of her Majesty's Inspectors, you know. Very high up at the Ministry of Education, I'm reliably informed.'

'Yes, I do know her,' I said. 'She's an excellent speaker and has a formidable intellect. I am sure she will go down a bomb.'

'She's addressing the staff on the topic "Creating

a Vibrant Curriculum".'

'That should be fun,' I replied, pitying the poor woman.

'I hope so,' replied the headmaster, smiling widely and showing me to the door. 'I do hope so.'

*   *   *

I arrived home later that evening, after a particularly tiresome governors' meeting, tired, hungry and not in the best of moods. I found Christine sitting at the kitchen table, seemingly awaiting my arrival.

Before I could even say hello she flourished a newspaper and asked, 'Have you seen this?'

I could see it was a copy of the *Fettlesham Gazette* so guessed at the contents.

'No,' I replied, taking off my coat and throwing my briefcase on the table. 'I need a whisky.'

'They're closing the village school.'

I took a deep breath, poured myself a generous measure of whisky, took a gulp and replied. 'Yes, I know.'

'*You know!*' she gasped.

'Yes.'

'How long have you known?'

'About a week,' I told her, taking a sip from the glass.

'Why didn't you say anything?'

'Christine, you know I can't discuss office matters at home.'

'Even when it affects us so personally?'

'Look, Chris,' I sighed, 'I didn't say anything because, well it was said to me in confidence and, anyway, I knew how you would react. I felt exactly

189

the same when Harold dropped the bombshell but, as he explained, there's got to be real savings in the education budget next year and Hawksrill is one of the county's smallest and most uneconomic schools and—'

'I don't believe I'm hearing such claptrap.' I had never seen her quite so angry.

'I felt exactly the same as you, and I told Harold that, but there is really nothing we can do. Both Mrs Beighton and Mrs Brown are retiring soon, so closing Hawksrill means they will not have to pay redundancies or re-deploy anyone.' I could hear myself echoing Harold's words.

'Hell's teeth! All you government people can think of are your costs. Saving redundancy here, killing off jobs there. What about the children? What about *our* child? How can you just sit back and let them close the school? The school your child would go to?'

'There's nothing I can do,' I said, draining the glass. 'If I could wave a magic wand and keep the school open, I would, but the decision has been made and that's that.'

'That's a defeatist attitude if ever I heard one,' Christine said angrily. 'Well, I do not intend to let a bunch of miserable councillors, pathetic education officers and petty officials at County Hall close the school without a fight.' She thumped the kitchen table so hard my glass fell over. 'There are such things as appeals, protests, demonstrations, sit-ins and pressure groups.'

'I can't be part of any pressure group,' I told her, picking up my glass and pouring myself another whisky.

'Why?'

'Because I'm on the other side of the fence, that's why.'

'It seems to me that you're sitting *on* the fence, not the other side of it.'

'Look, I'm one of those pathetic education officers and petty officials at County Hall to whom you've just referred. I'm an officer of the County. There's no way I can be part of a pressure group, can I?'

'Even if your child's future is at stake?'

'That's not very fair, Christine. If there were anything I could do—'

'Well, there's no point in discussing it any further. I think you've made your feelings perfectly clear. There's the remains of a cottage pie in the oven. I'm going to bed.'

'Christine,' I sighed, 'can't we talk about this?'

'There's nothing to talk about. By the way, Harry Cotton called earlier.' Harry was our nearest neighbour and could be a real pain in the neck.

'What did he want?'

'Rats.'

'Rats?' I repeated.

'We've got rats at the back of the house. He's seen them running along the fence. Good night.'

*   *   *

Christine had been asleep when I went to bed, and we had got up in silence. Now, at breakfast, we stared at each other sheepishly across the table.

'I'm sorry,' Christine said, 'I was just so shocked. I did rather overreact.'

'I should have told you,' I replied. 'You were right.'

'No, *you* were right. If something is told to you in confidence you shouldn't be discussing it. I don't talk about the children at my school with you so why should I expect you to talk about confidential matters with me. And it was unfair of me to say you were sitting on the fence. I've had time to sleep on it and you are quite right. You can't be seen to be favouring one school just because your child is to attend it. That would be unfair on the others. No, you have to keep well and truly out of it.'

'I'm glad you see that, Christine,' I said. 'You see, if Hawksrill were the only one to be reprieved, it would smack of my pulling a few strings, using my influence for personal advantage.'

'I know that,' she told me. 'I'm agreeing with you. You really don't need to justify yourself.'

'Well, I'm glad that's sorted out,' I said.

'Of course, that doesn't stop *me* from getting involved, does it?' said my dear wife, looking at me directly with her large blue eyes. 'I really meant what I said last night. I do not intend to let them close the school without a fight.'

There was nothing I could say, but I sensed dark storm clouds forming on the horizon.

CHAPTER TWELVE

The following Saturday morning found me at the Staff Development Centre. Christine hadn't mentioned the proposed closure of the school in Hawksrill since we had talked across the breakfast table but I knew, from what my colleagues in the office had said, that things were moving forward at a dramatic pace.

I could hear Connie clunking and clanking behind the hatch in the kitchen. The volume was such that I knew she was not in the best of tempers. I took a deep breath, popped my head charily around the door and said, 'Morning, Connie.'

'Oh, it's you,' she replied, looking up glumly before returning to her furious attack on the dishes in the sink. 'Why are *you* here today?' she asked. 'It's Saturday. I thought I had the place to myself for once.'

'I wanted to sort out the room for next week's course,' I told her, 'and put up a book display while the place is quiet. Anyway, you're a one to talk. What are you doing here? You should be in your caravan at Mablethorpe this weekend, not slaving away on a Saturday. I would have thought you see enough of this place.'

'You're right. You wouldn't get me in here on a weekend normally but you should have seen the state of this building when I came in yesterday. Three days away from the place and it's like a tip. Do you know, I'm having to wash all these cups and saucers again. Filthy they were. They couldn't have seen a drop of hot water. Just rinsed and put back in the cupboard, they were. Dried sugar in the bottom, tea and coffee stains round the rims. And the state of my floors and toilets! She was less than useless, Mrs Osbaldiston. I should never have asked her to fill in for me. When I walked through that door yesterday I thought a tornado had hit the place. I've had to work all day Friday to get the floors and toilets shipshape. Today is the kitchen's turn. I want everything right for Monday.'

I quickly changed the subject. 'How was

France?'

She drew her lips together into a tight thin line and glared at me. 'Don't ask,' she said.

'Oh dear,' I said. 'Not too good then?'

'Not too good?' she repeated. 'Not too good? It was a nightmare from beginning to end.' She withdrew her hands from the soapsuds and wiped them vigorously on a towel. 'We got on the ferry at Dover and the sea started to heave. Up and down, up and down, like a rollercoaster. Mountainous it was. I thought I was going to die. If I vomited once, I vomited ten times. It was worse than that trip to Ireland a couple of years back. It was awful. When we finally arrived in Calais, you would not believe what happened.'

'Wouldn't I?'

'No, you would not.'

'What did happen?' I asked, intrigued.

'I was intercepted, that's what.'

'Intercepted?'

'Intercepted by this little French customs official. Ignoranus he was. Out of all the people going through, he picks on me. I mean, I ask you, do I look like a terrorist or gun-runner? Rootles through my bag, he did, probing and prying, laying everything out without a by-your-leave. All my personal accoutrements exposed to the world. "And what's this?" he asks me, holding up the urn. "That is my father," I told him. Course he didn't understand, did he? Well, they don't these foreigners. "What is in the pot?" he asks. "It is not a pot, it's an urn, and it contains the remains of my dear departed father," I tells him. He takes the lid off, looks inside, pokes his big nose in and starts to sniff. "What is in this pot?" he asks again. "It is my

194

father," I tells him, "and kindly stop sniffing him, he's not that pope puree stuff." "I shall have to take a sample," he says. "Over my dead body," I tells him. At this point a nice old priest in a black hassock comes to my assistance. He was leading some sort of pilgrimage to a weeping virgin in Brittany with a group of old ladies in tow. Anyway, he starts jabbering on in the lingo to the horrible little man in the black uniform. "He thinks it might be an illegal substance," he tells me at last. "That's no illegal substance," I says, "it's my father in there and kindly ask him to stop interfering with him." "He thinks it might be drugs," says the priest. "Drugs!" I says. "Do I look like a drug-runner?" "He wants to take a specimen," says the priest, and I says, "Tell him that if he lays so much as a finger on my father, I'll be across that counter. And tell him I'm here to scatter my father's ashes at Dunkirk. And," I adds, "tell him if it wasn't for the likes of men like my father defending *his* country from the Nazis in the last war, extinguishing himself on the battlefields of Europe, Adolf's lot would be goose-stepping up and down Calais, instead of him."'

'Oh dear,' I sighed.

'I don't think the priest told him that though.'

'I guess not,' I murmured.

'The priest said not to make the horrid little man angry or be obstructive or he might insist on a strip-search. Well, that was the last straw. I asked the priest to tell him to hand back my father or there would be fireworks.'

'So what happened?' I asked.

'He just sort of smiled did the priest, the way that they do. Anyroad, he gets my father off of the

Frenchman. They're very persuasive are clerics, aren't they? He blesses my father, which was very nice of him, and me and Ted go on our way—and not before time.'

'So you managed to scatter your father's ashes after all,' I said.

'No, I didn't. I was so hot and flushed after that run-in with the customs man and loaded down as I was with bags and duty free and I don't know what else, I only dropped the urn, didn't I?'

'Oh no, Connie!' I gasped.

'Just slipped clean out of my hands on the sea-front, smashed to smithereens before my eyes and Dad was blown out to sea. He was there one minute, gone the next. So I never did get to leave him with his pals at Dunkirk after all. Wasted journey, it was.'

'Well, if it's any consolation,' I told her, 'there are many people who ask for their ashes to be scattered on the water, to be washed out by the sea, carried forever in the currents of time.'

It was clear from her expression that Connie was far from reassured. 'Well, it *isn't* any consolation. I didn't want Dad flushed out to sea on the currents of time. It wouldn't have suited my father at all. He hated water, couldn't swim and was sick on the boating lake at Scarborough.'

'Well, you're back now, Connie.'

'Oh, I'm back all right!' she exclaimed. 'And what do I come back to? Scuffs on my floor, chips out of my plates, dirty cups, dust on my shelves, marks on my walls and my toilets—well, I could have wept. She was about as much use as a chocolate teapot, Mrs Osbaldiston. Didn't do a hand's turn, as far as I could tell, all the time I was away.'

'Well, she is getting on a bit, Connie,' I told her, 'and she does have a lot of ailments.'

'The only ailment Mrs Osbaldiston has is a dose of idleitis. She never lifted a mop. Of course, it's like the old saying: "When the cat's away—"'

'How do you mean?'

'Mr Clamp's filled all the walls with rude pictures of his nudes and very ugly and off-putting they are as well. And then I had the shock of my life.' Connie sucked and blew and pursed her lips. 'Near the art room, staring at me from the wall, smiling like a Chester cat is Mrs Osbaldiston. He only used her as a model as well. Mrs Osbaldiston! No wonder she got no work done. Sitting there she is, like the Queen of Sheba.'

'Mrs Osbaldiston, a nude model?' I exclaimed.

'No, no, she's a Primitive Methodist. She wouldn't do anything like that. No, she was fully compost mentis in a floral overall and holding my feather duster, as large as life.' Connie plunged her hands back into the soapsuds. 'Anyway, I took her down and put her in the ladies' toilets. Best place for her.'

'Well, you can have a rest tomorrow,' I said.

Out of the soapsuds came the hands and Connie dried them on the towel. 'Chance'd be a fine thing. Last Sunday I was in the middle of putting the Yorkshire puddings in and there was a knock at the door. I've had a lot of these Jehovah's Witnesses round recently on a Sunday, ever since they opened a church near us. Nice enough people—very polite, smartly dressed, very friendly—but they always appear when I'm in the middle of doing something. Anyway, on the doorstep there were these two men in grey suits with black briefcases. Here we go again, I thought. "I'm sorry," I says, "I can't speak to you at the moment, I'm very busy." "Can we just have a moment of your time," said one of the men, "to tell you what we believe?" "No, you can't," I says, "I don't want to be unprepossessing, but I've got a pan of hot fat in the oven. I'm just about to put my Yorkshire puddings in." Course, they wouldn't take no for an answer. "It'll only take a minute," says one of them. They're very . . . what's the word?'

'Persistent.'

'Persistent, that's it. "Look," I says to him, "I've heard what you've got to say before and I've read the booklet you pushed through the door and the only thing you and me have in common is God. Nothing else." Well that took the wind out of his sails, I can tell you. "Oh," says he, looking all taken aback, "you'll not be voting Liberal Democrat then?" I felt such a fool.' Connie brushed down the front of her pink nylon overall. 'Well, I can't stop here talking all day. I've got the floor to do in here yet.'

After I had set up the book display and before leaving, I popped into the ladies' cloakroom. I could not resist having a quick look at the portrait of Mrs Osbaldiston. On the far wall, between the cubicles and the basins, was a large picture of a stooping little woman of raddled appearance, arrayed in a bright multicoloured overall and looking imperiously from the canvas. I had to smile. Knowing Connie as I did, that is where Mrs O. would stay, overseeing the ladies' ablutions.

I left the Staff Development Centre that morning in a much better frame of mind.

*   *   *

That afternoon I decided to tackle the garden at the back of the cottage. Harry Cotton, my nearest neighbour, had already been across to see me to offer his usual unsolicited advice, this time on the pruning that needed to be done to the shrubs and trees, how I might improve the mossy, weed-infested lawn, what I should do about the overgrown bushes and with numerous other horticultural suggestions necessary before winter set in. The rats, of course, had arisen in the course of our conversation.

'Must have been about four or five of 'em runnin' along that fence o' yourn as large as life. Big as babby badgers they were,' he had told me, almost gleefully. 'It's all very well you gettin' this 'ere 'inderwell chappie out to set traps and put down poison and t'like, but rats are very resilient creatures. They'll be back. Make no mistake about that. I know all abaat rats. I were brought up wi' 'em. There's nowt I don't know abaat rats. Tha wants a dog or a couple o' cats. They'll sort your rat problem out. Take my Buster, for example. Border terrier she is, and as tough as owld boots. I was only talkin' to George Hemmings a week back and 'e says 'is Patterdale bitch is ready to whelp. I could get you one o' those pups, if tha likes. Can't beat a terrier. My Buster's a rare little ratter. By, she can't 'alf shift if she sees a rat or a rabbit. She brings me a rat into t'kitchen every day. Just nips t'back of its neck as soon as it shows its scabby little face.'

Harry had banged his stick on the ground as though knocking a rat on the head. He was an old

199

man with a wide-boned, pitted face the colour and texture of an unscrubbed potato, a sharp nose with flared nostrils and a shock of white hair.

'Well, I don't think Christine would be all that keen about having a dead rat brought into the kitchen every day, Harry,' I had replied.

'Better a deead rat in your kitchen, than an army of live ones infestin' your garden,' he had said. 'That's what I always says.' I wasn't sure I agreed with that.

'I'll think about it,' I had told him. 'Mr Hinderwell, the Pest Control Officer, is coming out to have a look. I'll see what he says.'

'Suit yourself,' Harry had said. 'But I'll tell thee this. He can put all t'traps and poison down in t'world but they'll be back. Mark my words, they'll be back. Tha wants a dog or a couple of cats, that's what tha wants. Ted Poskitt's cat's just had kittens. I could get you a couple o' them, if tha prefers cats.'

'That's really good of you, Harry,' I had said, 'but I'll see what Mr Hinderwell suggests.'

'Mebbe it's just as well. Old Mrs Poskitt probably wouldn't let you have one anyroad. She's not kindly disposed to thee at t'moment.'

'Why?' I'd then asked. 'What have I done to upset Mrs Poskitt?'

'Her granddaughter, little Bethany, goes to t'school what you're closing.' Oh, don't let's get onto that subject, I'd thought to myself, but Harry, true to form, had refused to let it lie. He was as tenacious as his Border terrier.

'Aye, it's a rum do about t'shutting a school what's been 'ere in 'awksrill for countless centuries.'

'It's a Victorian school, Harry,' I had told him, 'so it's not much more than a hundred years old and I should point out that I am not personally responsible for closing it. It's the County Council and I'm as angry about it as anyone. Have a word with your local councillor and get him or her to complain.'

'Local councillor!' my companion had snorted. 'Local councillor! You mean Horace Witherspoon. I was at school with Horace. He were a two-faced little bugger then and he an't changed. I don't have owt to do wi' politicians, never 'ad and never will. They're all t'bloody same. My owld dad used to say politicians are like bananas. They start off green, then they turn yella and end up bent.'

'Yes, well I don't have any influence,' I had told him.

'That's as may be, but people in t'village are up in arms abaat it.'

'So I hear,' I had sighed. Although Christine had kept deliberately very quiet about the whole matter, I had heard from Harold that there had already been a great deal of activity from the residents of the village. It was also clear to me that Christine's stated intention to take the matter further was not an idle threat.

'Well, I'll get on,' Harry had said and he had ambled off to give someone else the benefit of his uncalled-for advice and words of wisdom.

Maurice Hinderwell had been very helpful but he had agreed with Harry that the rats would return, without a shadow of doubt.

'You have to destroy their habitat,' he had advised, nodding sagely. 'Take that derelict building you've got at the bottom of your garden.

That's where they'll likely be, out of sight, breeding and spreading disease. There'll be nests of them in there, where it's dry and dark. Plenty of food for them as well by the looks of it. Putting out a bird table full of nuts and bread is inviting rats. My advice to you is knock it down and lawn it over. Barn, I mean, not the bird table. Then your rats will move somewhere else. That old building takes up half your garden anyway and it's an eyesore.'

*   *   *

So, on this Saturday afternoon I made a start on demolishing the old building. It was not big enough to be called a barn, and it was bigger than a shed. It must have been some sort of outhouse, a store perhaps. One wall had completely collapsed and another was dangerously tilted. The exposed beams were rotten and little remained of the grey slate roof. It was a peculiar oblong building of dark stone with oddly narrow windows not like any of the outbuildings I had seen in the area, which were mostly built of limestone with red tiled roofs and had plain square windows.

I worked all afternoon and soon all that remained was a pile of rubble. I was surveying my handiwork when Christine appeared with a mug of tea.

'For the worker,' she said.

'Thanks.'

'My goodness, it's all gone,' she said, clearly impressed. 'The garden looks a lot bigger, doesn't it?'

'Yes, and much better without that old building.'

'What are you going to do with all the stone?'

202

she asked. 'The garden's too small for a rockery, isn't it?'

'I have an idea,' I told her. 'I thought we might have a wall across the back. Remember last year when those two sheep got through the fence and into the garden. You certainly weren't too pleased with what they did to your plants. Well, I thought a drystone wall with flowering shrubs and creepers, sweet peas perhaps, against it would be ideal there.'

'Good idea,' she said. 'Now, I'm off to the School Action Group meeting,' she said. 'I'll see you later.'

We had been assiduously avoiding the subject of the school closure thus far, but she had spent most of the morning on the telephone so I wasn't surprised about the meeting.

It was later that evening when my knee began to hurt. One of the rotten beams from the old building had suddenly fallen and, in an attempt to avoid it crashing down on top me, I had leapt smartly to the side and fallen heavily, cracking my knee in the process. Later that evening the knee had swollen to the size of a pomegranate.

'I really don't know why you had to do the demolition yourself,' chided Christine, examining the knee. 'We should have got a builder in to do it.'

'Think of the expense,' I said. 'I'm just about capable of knocking a couple of walls down.'

Christine gave a wry smile. 'Are you?' she asked. 'It looks dreadful. You had better see the doctor about that.'

'I had worse bangs than that when I played rugby. It's not nearly as bad as it looks.'

Would that that had been the case.

203

Tom Fields, the drystone-waller, arrived bright and early the following Saturday. Christine had met him at the meeting of the School Action Group the previous week. She had arrived home with two bits of news. First, that she had been made chairman of the village's action committee to fight the school closure and, following a brief but somewhat heated argument, we had agreed that there would be no further discussion of the subject between us. Secondly, she had met Tom Fields and once she had convinced him that I was not the demonic inspector intent on demolishing his child's school he had agreed to build our wall. He had been let down over a job when some stone hadn't arrived, and we were fortuitously able to take the slot.

I found him staring beyond the small garden taking in the spectacular view: the dark and distant fells, the bronze belt of the dead bracken, the rolling green fields sweeping down to the river, the limestone outcrops gleaming bone-white in the early sunlight, the scattering of grey farmhouses and hillside barns, and the endlessly criss-crossing drystone walls.

'Tha's a grand view 'ere and no mistake, Mester Phinn,' he told me.

I had rather expected an ancient, grizzled character in some sort of traditional outfit—flat cap, corduroy trousers tied at the knee with string, thick tweed jacket and spotted neckerchief—but Tom Fields was a young man dressed in a bright blue overall. He had a ready smile and long blond hair tied back in a ponytail. He didn't look old enough to be the father of a child of school age.

He turned his attention to the remains of the old outhouse. 'And tha's got a grand bit o' stone 'ere, an' all.' He placed his hands on his hips and surveyed the small mountain of rubble. 'Cost a pretty penny this would to buy and o' coourse then tha'd 'ave t'added expense of 'aving it brought in. Some on it will want a bit o' dressing but there's plenty 'ere for what I've got to do. A wall across t'back will look champion, it really will. Just as it used to do.'

'What do you mean by that?' I asked.

'Oh, there'd 'ave been a wall 'ere afore. All t'fields were walled at one time. But when they fell down, some of 'em newer farmers just replaced t'wall wi' fencing, sometimes using t'bits of t'old wall to patch someweer else. That's what's happened 'ere, tha sees.'

'Well, I'm glad to be putting it back, then.'

'Aye, and tha's got more than enough stone 'ere to mek a reight champion wall, not too 'igh as it'll spoil tha view, not so low as it'll let t'sheep in.'

'It's the remains of the derelict building which used to be in the corner of the garden,' I told him.

'Oh aye?'

'So how big will the wall be?' I asked.

He looked at me as if I were some sort of simpleton. 'What I've just said—'igh enough to keep t'sheep out and low enough not to spoil tha view. Like them what were built in owlden days. My walls are a touch higher but not a deal different—not much more than four foot high. They'll be t'same arrangement of throughs, fillings and top-stones as there 'as been for centuries— abaat a yard wide at t'bottom lessening to a touch

205

ovver a foot at t'top.'

'And how long will it take you to do?' I asked.

'Same time as it did for wallers two or three 'undred year ago, abaat seven yards a day. I'll 'ave yours finished within t'week.'

'That's excellent,' I said.

By the following Sunday, the small garden at the back of Peewit Cottage was transformed. Tom Fields had finished as he'd promised the previous day and the wall was magnificent. Straight and solid, it looked as if it had been there for centuries. I had pruned the trees and shrubs, cut down the dead flowers, dug up the weeds, turned over the soil, burnt the rubbish and prepared the ground where the building had been. I would sow grass seed there next year. I heard the garden gate click and a moment later Harry Cotton appeared around the side of the cottage. He was accompanied by his bristly little dog with large black eyes and a very hairy face.

'Hello, Harry. Hello, Buster,' I said. 'Have you had a nice time away?'

Harry had told me he was going to spend a few days at his sister's and had asked me to keep a neighbourly eye on his cottage.

'Aye. It were reight enough wi' our Bertha, but it's allus better in yer own 'ome, in't it? She dunt shurrup, that's 'er trouble and there's nowt she dunt know abaat.' Two peas in a pod, I thought, smiling. 'She 'as a view on everything, our Bertha and it's all nowt abaat owt. It's like 'aving a conversation wi' a bloody Gatling gun.' He poked into some shrubs with his gnarled walking stick. 'Got rid o' your rats then, 'ave you?' he asked, regarding me balefully.

'Yes, I think so,' I replied. 'Maurice Hinderwell caught about six in his traps and has put some poison down, so keep Buster well away. I should think that that will be the last of them. He reckoned that they were breeding underneath the old outbuilding.'

'Oh aye,' said Harry, approaching my new drystone wall which he patted as he might a pet animal. 'Nice bit of work this. Very nice.' His terrier nosed along the base of the wall. 'I reckon she can smell a rat. Got a nose for 'em.'

'I doubt it very much, Harry,' I said.

'Aye, well we'll see,' he said, as ever the prophet of doom.

'So, my wall meets with your approval, does it?' I said, not wishing to start up a discussion about rats.

'Who did it for thee?' he asked.

'Tom Fields.'

'Oh well, 'is family's been building drystone walls since time o' Vikings. I thought it were one of 'is.'

'He's made a splendid job of it.'

Harry remained staring at the wall for a good long time before saying, 'I'm surprised they let you pull that owld chapel down, tha knaas.'

'What old chapel?' I asked.

'That what were in t'corner o' your plot.'

'You mean the old outhouse?'

'Nay, it were no outhouse. It were t'owld Wesleyan chapel. Built seventeen 'undred and summat. One o' oldest chapels in t'county, so they say.'

'It was a chapel?' I said, my mouth dropping open and my heart sinking into my boots. 'I thought it was just some sort of outbuilding.'

'Nay, not that 'un,' Harry told me, rubbing the

207

whiskers on his chin.

'It was a chapel?' I repeated.

'Did nob'dy tell thee?'

'No, they didn't,' I said in a shocked whisper.

'I don't suppose there would o' been much point in Tom telling thee, if tha'd already knocked it down.'

'Did he know?' I asked.

'I reckon he did. But he's a drystone waller not a church builder. He couldn't 'ave put it back together ageean, if that's what tha's thinkin'.'

'What do you mean, put it back together?' I said. 'There was hardly anything standing. I had no idea it used to be a chapel. This is terrible.'

'Aye, it is,' agreed Harry. 'Probably got some sort of preservation order on it. Could 'ave been a listed building, tha knaas.'

'I don't believe it,' I said. 'I just don't believe it.'

This was like a re-enactment of an episode which had occurred when we had first moved into the village. I had taken over an overgrown allotment, spent many a Saturday clearing it of the thick briars and twisting brambles, overgrown bushes and rampant weeds, only to find that I had cleared the wrong plot, one that was rented by Albert Tattersall, a friend of Harry Cotton's.

'You see, owld Albert kept it on for t'gooseberries,' Harry had been quick to point out to me as he had surveyed my handiwork, 'and, of course, the blackcurrants?'

'Gooseberries? Blackcurrants?' I had cried. 'What gooseberries and blackcurrants.'

'Them what would 'ave been growin' on them bushes which you dug up and are now burnin' on tha bonfire,' Harry had observed.

208

I had eventually persuaded Albert, after a good few beers in the local pub, the Golden Ball, and the promise of some fresh vegetables, to let me take over the allotment.

Now, here I was again with Harry, the Job's comforter *par excellence*, describing how once again I had put my foot well and truly in it. 'Tha's probably just pulled down a building of gret 'istorical hinterest,' he remarked casually.

'It was derelict,' I said feebly.

'Sometimes we get American Methodists dropping in to t'village to have a look at it. I don't suppose they'll be calling in to view a wall even though it used to be an 'istorical shrine.' I was speechless. Then Harry rubbed more salt in the wound. 'On t'anniversary of Wesley's death, t'local minister, Reverend Jessop, held a service up here, as I recall. Old Mrs Olleranshaw, who 'ad cottage afoor thee, was very big in t'chapel and asked t'minister to come out and conduct a special service. They do say that Wesley himself preached 'ere and that—'

'Mary Queen of Scots slept here on the way down to her execution and Guy Fawkes hid in the cellar!' I cried in desperation.

'I don't know owt about that,' said Harry, looking puzzled. 'But I s'pose they might 'ave.'

'Please, Harry,' I pleaded, 'don't go on.'

'I reckon you'll be having a visit from George Hemmings. He's on t'Parish Council tha knaas and is very keen on preservation. Then I expect 'istorical people from York will be up to see thee. And it won't be long afore Horace Witherspoon starts tekkin up t'case, pokin' his fat nose in and causin' trouble. I shouldn't be at all surprised if tha

209

were prosecuted and fined.'

'Harry!' I snapped. 'Please do not go on about it. I'm feeling pretty bad about this as it is.'

'I won't say another word,' he said, 'but I reckon tha'll be even more unpopular in t'village when they 'ears abaat this.'

'Yes, I suppose I will,' I sighed.

'They'll be thinking that tha wants t'school closed so tha can knock it down to use t'bricks for an extension to t'cottage.'

CHAPTER THIRTEEN

'Well, I must say, you might have done your homework, old boy.' It was Monday morning in the office and I had just told Sidney and David about my disastrous weekend and the demolition of the Methodist chapel. Sidney was his usual unsympathetic self and I soon wished I had kept the whole sorry business to myself. 'This county is crammed full of old ruins,' he announced, leaning back on his chair and placing his hands behind his head. 'You can't turn a corner without finding an abbey or priory or castle or some medieval church or other. It's not Milton Keynes, you know. You should have guessed this charming and antiquated little construction would be of historic interest.'

'It was a ruin, Sidney,' I told him, 'not a charming and antiquated little construction, as you put it. It was a broken-down ramshackle building with two walls and no roof. I've looked through the deeds of the cottage and there is nothing about any Methodist chapel on my property.' I was trying to convince myself that I was blowing things out of all proportion. 'It's called an outbuilding and if it were a listed building it would say so—wouldn't it?'

'It's in the National Park, your cottage, isn't it?' remarked Sidney, leaning even further back in his chair.

'Yes, it is. Why?'

Sidney sucked in his breath dramatically. 'Well, they slap preservation orders on everything from a pigsty to a cesspit in the National Park. You can't change a tile on your roof without permission. You know, I did warn you, Gervase, before you bought that crumbling pile that you would be far better off in a smart riverside apartment or a modern town house in Fettlesham, within walking distance of the office. Now, I'm no expert on the matter—'

'Well, there's a first,' remarked David, looking up from his papers and over the top of his spectacles. 'You're an expert on every other blessed thing.'

'But, what I will say,' continued Sidney blithely, 'is that I well recall the hoo-hah when they knocked down those derelict outside toilets at the little school at Tarncliffe. You know the school, Gervase, next door to the rather attractive little grey-stone Primitive Methodist chapel where John Wesley was reputed to have preached. They were pre-Victorian, by all accounts, these privvies, and the only examples of their kind in Yorkshire, possibly in the country. Everyone thought they were an eyesore—the headteacher, Miss Drayton, her assistant, that rather fussy Mrs Standish, all the governors and parents. They were small, smelly, damp and disgusting and they harboured rats, just like your old building. Well, no sooner were they down than up jumps the local historical society and claims they were unique and had been used by many a famous person passing through, if you will excuse the unintended pun, on their way to York and were of unimaginable historical importance. They were hoping to put up one of those blue plaques saying, "Emily Brontë sat here".'

'Take no notice, Gervase,' David reassured me. 'Nothing will come of it, mark my words. He's just winding you up. You might give old Perkins in the County Architects' Department a ring, though, to be on the safe side. He's a very good-hearted sort is old Perkins. Been in the county for ever. He's big on old ruins, Fellow of the Royal Historical Society and he's a Methodist lay preacher. If anyone will know about this chapel, he will.'

'I would advise you to keep very quiet,' said Sidney. 'Mentioning it to someone like old Perkins is inviting trouble. If I were you, I would admit nothing or blame vandals. They've managed to incapacitate the nuclear fall-out shelter in Collington, from what I hear. A chapel would be a piece of cake for them after that. I would just plead ignorance.'

'I don't know what has got into you today, Sidney,' said David, smiling. 'You freely admit you are not an expert and then you start pleading ignorance. Are you on some sort of medication?'

Sidney didn't deign to answer.

'I seem to be having a real run of bad luck at the moment,' I told my colleagues. It was true: first it was King Henry's, then the Hawksrill school closure, then the rats, then the chapel and my knee was no better either. Whatever next? I hadn't long to wait.

The first visit of the week was to Manston Church
of England Parochial School, a quaint, two-storey
stone building which nestled in a small village on
the extensive estate of Lord Marrick. Valentine
Courtnay-Cunninghame, 9th Earl Marrick, Viscount
Manston, Baron Brafferton, MC, DL, was one of
the most colourful and unusual characters it had
been my pleasure to meet; a delightfully cheerful,
good-natured and somewhat eccentric peer who
loved the Dales as passionately as any farmer. This
portly, red-cheeked character with his bombastic
walrus moustache and thick hair shooting up from
a square head looked as if he had walked straight
out of the pages of an historical novel.

The last time I had visited the school I had
accompanied Lord Marrick, who was the Chairman
of the Governing Body. The children had been
fascinated when this outlandish-looking figure had
marched through the classroom door, moustache
bristling, and thundered, 'Morning, children!' We
had sat together beneath a small marble plaque
bearing the name of one of his distinguished
forebears—the Dowager Countess Marrick—who
had endowed the small school a century or so
earlier.

As I sat in the corner of the same classroom
now, beneath the same marble plaque, making a
few preliminary notes on the state of the building
and the display of work, I became conscious of a
small boy, aged about seven or eight, observing me
from a little way away. I could feel his eyes taking
in every detail of my appearance. Eventually he

213

approached me.

'May I ask you what you are doing?' he inquired.

'I'm writing about your school,' I replied, looking up and smiling.

'I see.'

'I'm a school inspector.'

'Yes, I know. Our teacher told us you would be visiting us today and that you would be looking at our books and listening to us read.'

'I'm Mr Phinn,' I told him.

'Oh, I'm Benedict,' he replied, holding out a small hand which I shook formally.

'Well, Benedict, shouldn't you be getting on with your work?'

'I've done it. When we've finished our writing, we're allowed to select a book from the Reading Corner. I was on my way there when I thought I'd stop and say hello.'

His manner and speech were amusingly old-fashioned for one so young.

'Well, that's very nice of you, Benedict,' I said.

'Mrs McGuire—she's our teacher, but you probably know that already—well, Mrs McGuire says there are much better words to use than "nice".'

'I'm sure she's right,' I said, chuckling. 'I'll try to remember in future.'

'And that there are much more interesting words to use in our stories than "said". Do you like stories, Mr Phinn?'

'I do,' I replied.

'Would you like to see some of mine?'

'Perhaps later, Benedict,' I told him. 'I'm a little busy at the moment.'

'Righto, I'll get along then and choose a book. I

like poetry, you know. I love the rhymes.' He thought for a moment and then said, 'Do you know, Mr Phinn, we've had a very interesting conversation, haven't we?'

'We have, Benedict,' I replied, 'indeed we have.'

He then patted me gently on the arm and said, before departing for the Book Corner, 'We must do lunch sometime.'

*　　　*　　　*

One reason for my visit that morning was to see the recent changes which had been made to the building to accommodate a disabled pupil who had recently started at the school. Ramps had been built, doors had been widened to allow the wheelchair to pass through, classrooms had been re-arranged and a disabled toilet and a stair lift had been installed. It all looked very impressive and the headteacher and her assistant were well pleased.

I met the child in question over lunch. She was a small girl of about seven or eight, a cheerful, chattery little thing with curly red hair and a wide smile. I soon discovered that she was as bright as a button.

'Mr Phinn, are you very important?' she asked between mouthfuls of lasagne.

'No, not very,' I replied.

'Mrs McGuire told us that you were a very important person.'

'I think she was exaggerating, just a little bit.'

'My grandpa's a very important person,' the child told me.

'Is he?'

'He wears a wig, you know, and a long red dress.'

'Does he?'

'And shiny shoes with high heels and big silver buckles on the front.'

'I see.' I had visions of a drag queen but I suspected I knew what her grandfather did.

'He's a judge, you know,' she informed me.

'Yes, I thought he might be.'

'And he locks naughty people up.' She took a gulp of water from the plastic beaker. 'My daddy's not a judge, but he's very important.'

'Is he?'

'He cuts people up,' the little girl said, nodding gravely.

'I see.' Now I had visions of Jack the Ripper but I guessed her father was probably a surgeon.

'He's a sort of doctor, you know,' she told me.

'Yes, I thought he might be. But what about you?'

'Oh, I'm not very important,' she said, in a matter-of-fact voice.

'Well, I think you are and I bet your teachers and your parents think you are too and that grandpa of yours. I reckon he thinks you are very special as well.'

'My first name is India and I'm named after a country,' she told me.

I leaned across the table and whispered confidentially, 'Well, my first name is Gervase and I'm named after a yoghurt.'

The child giggled. 'You're not really named after a yoghurt, are you? People aren't named after yoghurts.'

'When my mother was expecting me, India,' I told her, putting on a very serious expression, 'she had a passion for a particular French yoghurt called

"Gervais", and for broccoli. I think I did pretty well with the name she picked, don't you?'

'I know what you are, Mr Phinn,' said India, giggling and pointing a little finger at me.

'Do you?'

'You're like my grandpa, Mr Phinn. You're a tease. He takes me for long walks and tells me about all sorts of things, my grandpa, and sometimes he teases me, like when he said he was swallowed by a whale and it took him to the South Seas and he was stranded on a desert island and met these pirates. He's a lot of fun, my grandpa.'

I bet he's not a lot of fun in the courtroom, I thought to myself, in his wig, long red dress and buckled shoes. There would be no teasing then. 'And do you like to be teased, India?'

'Yes, I do rather, it's fun. That's if it's not cruel. Grandpa says you shouldn't tease people about the way they look.'

'No, it's not nice to tease somebody in that way,' I agreed.

'Mrs McGuire says there are much better words to use than "nice", Mr Phinn.'

'So I believe,' I replied. 'Benedict's already had a word with me about that.'

'And grandpa says that we're all different and that's why the world is such a wonderful place. "Big or small, short or tall, black or white, dark or light, God loves us all." That's what grandpa says.'

'He's a very wise man, your grandpa, India,' I told her.

'They've put special ramps in the school for me, you know,' said the little girl proudly.

'Yes, I know.'

'And a special toilet and a stair lift.'

217

'And are you managing to use them all right?' I asked.

'Oh yes, they're fine, but the toilet is a bit of a nuisance. You see, they've made the toilet seat about as high as the seat on my wheelchair. Well, my wheelchair has foot-rests which are quite high off the ground. That means when I'm sitting on the toilet my legs sort of dangle down. It's quite uncomfortable. Then the washbasin is on the wall opposite to the towel. I wash my hands and then have to wheel over the other side to dry my hands. I think it would have been a good idea for the builders to have had a word with me before they put the toilet in.' She thought for a moment. 'But, I'm very pleased really and everybody's very nice here—whoops! I mean very friendly. It's people outside school that get on my nerves a bit.'

'In what way?' I asked.

'I just wish they would believe me when I tell them things.'

'What do you mean, India?' I asked.

'If I'm in my wheelchair in a shop and someone comes along, a grown-up that is, and says, "Are you all right?" and I say, "Yes, I'm fine, thank you," then they always say, "Are you sure?" and I say, "Yes. I'm sure." Then I start to wheel myself along and they say, "Here, let me help you," and I say, "I'm all right, really. I can manage." And then they say, "It's no bother," and then they push me along.'

'Well, India,' I told her, 'you've given me quite a lot to think about.' And indeed she had.

I have met a number of disabled youngsters over the years and, without exception, they have been good-humoured and extremely positive. The problems faced by India, of course, are not

218

unusual. Access is often denied to those with disabilities and they face a whole raft of challenges and hurdles, in particular achieving the independence they so desire. The difficulties faced by the disabled are not of their own making; they are the result of the way they are treated by the able-bodied.

In my first year of teaching, I remember meeting John, a seventeen-year-old with cerebral palsy. John's condition made it hard for him to control his muscles and movements and sometimes he would shout out involuntarily. He was a highly intelligent boy with a wicked sense of humour and a permanent smile. He would career down the corridors of the school like a charioteer at the Roman games, totally fearless and at a frightening speed. He took part in as many sports as he could, acted in the school drama productions, sang in the choir and annihilated anyone foolish enough to take him on at chess. He despised the word "spastic" with all its negative connotations.

I recall one memorable occasion, in a General Studies lesson, when we were debating the depiction of people on the television and in films. John, as always, brought a fresh perspective to our discussions. 'How many disabled people,' he had asked, 'do you see on the screen? And if they do appear, how many are different from the stereotypical long-suffering, permanently cheerful invalid in the wheelchair who shows everyone else what courage and suffering are really like? And,' he had continued, 'how many of these roles are actually played by disabled actors?'

Before going on to university, John received the prize at the school's Speech Day, for the best examination results in his year. He sped across the school stage, executed a perfect turn in his wheelchair and came to a skidding halt in front of a startled Lord Mayor who was presenting the awards. John received the silver cup, his certificates and a book token for his outstanding academic achievement.

'While I have this opportunity, your worshipful,' he had said, 'may I ask you to use your influence to get a better ramp fitted in the public library.'

The headmaster later remarked that the Cambridge dons did not know what they were letting themselves in for.

During the afternoon break, I wandered around the playground with Mrs McGuire. The children, well wrapped up against the cold, were clearly enjoying the fifteen minutes of freedom from their studies.

'It's so good to see the children skipping and playing hopscotch and other traditional games,' I told her. 'So many have disappeared.'

'Indeed,' replied Mrs McGuire. We paused at the edge of the playground. 'Every time I look at that view,' she said, 'I tell myself how very lucky I am to be teaching here. It's so fresh and clean and peaceful.' We stared together at the pale green fields with grazing sheep, stretching away beneath a cloudless blue sky.

Later that afternoon I sat with the headteacher to talk about the day I had spent in the school and India, of course, cropped up.

'My goodness,' sighed Mrs McGuire, 'you would not believe the difficulties we had getting the powers that be to agree to the alterations to accommodate that one little girl. The school was only built a little more than a century ago and it's not listed or anything but you'd think it was York Minster or Skipton Castle, the trouble we had obtaining permission to make the minor changes to the structure, to install the stair lift, widen the doors, things like that. I mean, it wasn't as if we were taking a sledge-hammer to some religious shrine and knocking down something irreplaceable.' She must have seen the expression on my face. 'Are you all right, Mr Phinn?' she asked. 'You've gone quite pale.'

*   *   *

I decided to take David's advice and when I got back to the office that afternoon I went in search of old Perkins—or Jasper Perkins, to be correct—in the Architects' Department. Mr Perkins was a delightful and erudite gentleman whom I discovered poring over a large map in a small office tucked away at the very rear of County Hall. I explained about the chapel and waited in trepidation for his considered opinion.

'Do you like to be teased, Mr Phinn?' he asked, echoing my words to India earlier that day.

'I'm sorry, Mr Perkins?'

'Teased. Do you like your leg pulled?' He chuckled. 'I think you've got friends with very vivid imaginations or ones that enjoy a little ruse. Firstly, speaking as a lay preacher of some thirty years, I know of no Methodist chapel on your property. There are two chapels in Hawksrill, if my memory serves me aright. I've preached at both. There's the Primitive Methodist on Shire Lane and then the Wesleyan Methodist on Snig Hill. As for the

Reverend Jessop conducting some sort of service up where you live, I think it extremely unlikely. He's not in the best of health and he's got quite enough on, managing the two chapels in the village, without taking on a third. He did attempt to amalgamate the two chapels, you know, but traditions die hard and both congregations dug their heels in. But, that's another matter. Anyway, Mr Phinn, I am pretty certain that there was no third Methodist chapel in Hawksrill. Now, speaking as an architect, you would have been made fully aware when you purchased the property that this was a listed building or a site of particular historical interest. There have been a few occasions when some buildings have been demolished by accident and one or two that have slipped through the net, but they are very few and far between. I think you can rest assured that you won't be locked up for the desecration of a church.'

'Thank you so much, Mr Perkins,' I said, shaking his hand vigorously. 'You don't know what a weight you have lifted off my shoulders. I owe you a drink.'

Mr Perkins raised an eyebrow and gave a wry little smile. 'I'm a Methodist, Mr Phinn, remember.'

There would have been a veritable spring in my step as I made my way down the top corridor of County Hall that afternoon had it not been for the swollen knee which was still extraordinarily painful. I had ignored Christine's advice about going to the doctor but now determined to make an appointment just as soon as I got back to the office.

I stopped in my tracks, however, when I turned a corner. Outside Committee Room One, a group of councillors was huddled around a loud gesticulating individual in a baggy tweed suit. Although he had his back to me, I recognised instantly the bull neck which overlapped the collar, the mop of unnaturally jet black hair and the bombastic voice. It was Councillor George Peterson. I had come across Councillor Peterson a good few times before and he always managed to make my hackles rise with his clever comments and tasteless observations. There seemed no way that I could avoid him but I was going to make a determined effort anyway. So I quickly continued down the corridor, limping but walking on the balls of my feet so my heels would not betray my presence and looking down as if I were preoccupied in some knotty problem. I sailed past the cabal and thought that I had not been seen, but as I reached the top of the long curved staircase, a voice echoed down the corridor.

'Hey! Hey! Mr Phinn. Not tryin' to avoid me, are you?'

I turned round to face the group and gave a watery smile. 'Councillor Peterson.'

'You were goin' at a fair lick. I'll walk across to t'inspectors' office wi' you. I've got a meetin' with Dr Yeats.' He turned to his companions. 'We'll raise it at t'next meetin', Horace,' he said to one of his fellow councillors, before striding towards me. 'This is a right carry-on about these school closures, in't it?' he said as we descended the stairs together.

'Yes, it's very unfortunate,' I replied, negotiating the steps.

'What's up wi' yer leg?' he asked.

'Oh, I had an accident,' I told him. 'I banged it.

Nothing serious.'

'Aye, well, I was just sayin', it's a right carry-on about these school closures.'

The least I said the better, I thought. 'Yes, it is.'

'We've just 'ad an hextrahordinary meeting of the Sub-Committee about it. It's a right can of worms and no mistake.' He made no attempt to hide his anger. He puffed out his cheeks, shook his head and grimaced theatrically.

'Feelings are running very high,' I remarked, looking into the red meaty face.

'Too right, they are, and I'll tell you what school is t'fly in t'ointment. It's Hawksrill. Everybody bar the cat and its mother is gettin' in its two pennyworth about t'closure of that particular school and it's turning very nasty.'

'I'm sorry to hear that.'

'We've 'ad countless late meetings of t'Sub-Committee, letters of protest, pictures in t'paper of people wi' placards. That Chairman of Governors, Reverend Braybrook, has put it on t'agenda of t'full Education Committee and when *'e* gets started there's no stoppin' 'im. 'E thinks 'e's in 'is pulpit.' Those in glass houses, I thought. 'We've 'ad t'local member of parliament writin' me notes and Lord Marrick grumbling at me down t'phone and next week, blow me, if one of these HMIs isn't comin' up from London to see me about it—woman with a funny name and a very sharp manner.'

'Miss de la Mare?'

'Aye, that's 'er. Anybody'd think I was doin' this to be awkward. Anyroad, I don't suppose I should be tellin' you all this.'

'And why is that Councillor Peterson?' I

enquired.

We stopped at the bottom of the stairs. 'Because it might get back to t'opposition.'

'Meaning?'

'Meanin' that that wife of yours and 'er protest group are causin' all t'trouble, stirrin' things up.'

My hackles began to rise but I kept calm, breathed out slowly and looked him in the eye. 'I can assure you, Councillor Peterson, I have not discussed the situation with my wife or anyone else, for that matter. Like you, I guess, I keep County Council business to myself and do not talk to her about such things.'

'That's as may be, but that wife of yours gave me a real grillin' at t'public meetin' and you don't even 'ave kiddies at t'school.'

'No, but we will have or would have had, I should say. People in the village feel very strongly about the school closing. It's at the very heart of the community and it's used for all manner of activities and events. More importantly, Hawksrill is an excellent school as all the reports show. In fact, it's one of the best schools I have visited.'

'Yes, yes, I know all that, but it's small, very small and it's too uneconomical to keep it goin'. What your wife and these protestors don't seem to realise is that we 'ave to cut costs. I don't want to close a school any more than you do, but we 'ave to save money somehow and that's t'top and bottom of it. You should per'aps 'ave a quiet word with your wife and tell 'er to go easy.'

'Councillor, gone are the days when a husband tells his wife what to do.' I was certain that the councillor himself did not go around giving orders to Mrs Peterson. She was the headteacher of

Highcopse County Primary School and a fierce and formidable woman.

'I am sure you realise, Mr Phinn, that should she keep up this pressure, it could make it tricky for you.'

'In what way?'

'Well, if you were to get Dr Yeats's job, you'll be t'one that 'as to deal wi' t'closures. 'As that crossed your mind?'

'Yes, it has,' I replied.

'I mean, you can't be on t'side of t'angels and drink wi' t'devil and it's not goin' to do much for marital harmony, you at loggerheads with your wife about Hawksrill School, is it?'

'That situation will not arise,' I assured him.

'Oh, but it could. After the last fiasco when we appointed that Mr Carter who gave back-word—and I never really took to 'im—then you might find yourself t'new Senior Inspector and that means that you'll 'ave to deal with all this. It'll be you who's in charge of closin' t'school.'

'I repeat, that situation won't arise,' I told him. I looked him in the face. 'You see, I don't intend applying for Dr Yeats's job. Good afternoon, Councillor Peterson.'

With that I limped off towards the car park.

CHAPTER FOURTEEN

'Are you doing anything this Saturday?'

The question, from the Head of the English Faculty at The Lady Cavendish High School for Girls, took me rather by surprise. I had observed

Miss Bridges's lessons the previous year and judged them to be some of the best I had ever seen. I had rather expected this diminutive schoolma'am with the pale, indrawn face, dark eyes and thick iron-grey hair scraped back into a tight little bun, to be a rather dry and crusty individual and that her lessons would be dull in the extreme. Appearances can, of course, be deceptive, and the talented Miss Bridges turned out to be lively, amusing and immensely enthusiastic. She was quite clearly idolised by the students she taught and their examination results were outstanding. Now, here she was on the phone asking me out.

'Saturday?' I said.

'That's right. Are you free this Saturday? Let me explain. I am taking a party of senior girls to see the Royal Shakespeare Company's matinée performance of *King Lear* at Stratford-upon-Avon and I have a couple of spare tickets. Two students can't come at the last moment. It's such a pity to let the tickets go to waste and I thought, since you are something of a Shakespeare *aficionado,* you and your wife might care to join us. I did so enjoy meeting you when you visited LCHS last year. Also, it would be good to have some more adults with us. Our girls are extremely sensible, of course, but one never knows when emergencies might arise and it's always good to have another pair of hands.'

'Well, that's very kind of you, Miss Bridges,' I said, flicking though the pages in my desk diary. 'Actually, Christine and I don't have anything on this Saturday. I'm sure she would love to come. I certainly would. I haven't seen a Shakespeare play for some time. It will be a real treat.'

'Splendid!' cried Miss Bridges. 'Well, that's

settled then. If you could be at the school for eight of the clock prompt, that will give us ample time to travel down to Stratford in time for the matinée performance.'

Christine was distinctly lukewarm when I mentioned it to her that evening. 'It's not a barrel of laughs, *King Lear*, is it?' she said gloomily. 'We could both do with being cheered up this weekend, not thoroughly depressed. It's all doom, gloom, treachery and murder, isn't it?'

'Well, no, it's far from a comedy,' I agreed, 'but it's sure to be a superb performance and a day out, away from school closures and reports and listed chapels, will buck us both up. Anyway, it will take a lot to depress me at the moment. Deciding not to apply for Harold's job has made me almost light-headed. I feel like celebrating.'

I had thought long and hard about applying for the Senior Inspector's post. I was flattered, of course, that my three colleagues in the office were keen for me to try my hand again, and Dr Gore's comments, when we discussed the King Henry's College report, had led me to believe that I would be in with a serious chance this time. But then I had seen Harold's desk which overflowed with reports, letters of complaint and all manner of official documents. I remembered his talking about the numerous problems he had to solve— 'Sometimes,' he had said, 'I feel like a glorified agony aunt'—and, of course, the endless late night meetings. I had seen how wearied he had become by all the pressure and stress, and how much he was looking forward to his retirement. This time, I had not taken long to come to the conclusion that Christine was right and that I should not apply. I had quite enough on my plate with a new wife, new house, and a baby on the way. Maybe another opportunity would arise one day, when things were more settled.

'I really am pleased about you not going for the job,' said Christine now, giving me a peck on the cheek.

'So, are we on for Stratford?' I asked.

'Would you mind awfully if I didn't go?' Christine said. 'It's just that Baby Phinn is a bit tiring at times and my bladder is a bit unpredictable in my present condition. I need to be in close proximity to a loo. I really couldn't face a long coach journey at the moment.'

'Of course!' I cried, 'I never thought. I'm sorry, darling. I'll ring Miss Bridges and tell her we can't go.'

'I'm the one who's pregnant,' said Christine. 'You go. I've got lots to do. It will take you out of yourself. You deserve a bit of a break. Actually, I thought I might do a bit of early Christmas shopping in Fettlesham this weekend before all the crowds start.'

'Are you sure you don't mind me going?'

'Of course I don't mind.'

So, early on the Saturday morning, I duly arrived at the car park of the vast, mock-Gothic edifice with its ugly redbrick towers and turrets, which was The Lady Cavendish High School for Girls. I had contacted Miss Bridges, asking her to find someone to take Christine's place. The Head of the English Faculty, wrapped up like an Arctic explorer, greeted me warmly and introduced me to her colleagues, Miss Pike and Mrs Roache.

'Quite a fishy collection of teachers,' she said,

chuckling, 'and now we have Mr Phinn. Very apt. We're just waiting for Mrs Todd, who's gone to powder her nose, then we can be on our way. Mrs Todd used to teach at the big comprehensive and is covering for a teacher on maternity leave. I thought she might like to step into the breach and join our party. I believe you met her when you inspected King Henry's in September.'

'Yes, I did,' I replied.

'You caused quite a stir, I hear,' said Miss Bridges, a wry smile on the small lips.

'I don't know about that.'

'Well, whatever they said about you,' said Miss Bridges, 'I found you very agreeable.' Which made me wonder just exactly what they *had* said about me. I guess the staff thought I was something of a 'hatchet man'. 'Mrs Todd's husband's a surgeon at Fettlesham Royal Infirmary, you know,' continued the teacher, 'and she has four very clever sons.'

'So I believe,' I said.

'Ah, here she is now!' cried Miss Bridges. 'Shall we get on the coach? The girls are aboard already and are excited to get going.' She looked for a moment at the craggy-faced individual with an enormous protruding stomach and greasy black hair slicked back on his head, who was leaning by the door of the coach and puffing mightily on a large pipe. Clouds of evil-smelling smoke filled the air. 'I do hope the driver will be all right,' she added *sotto voce*. 'All our regular drivers were already booked—some important football game, I believe.'

'I'm sure he'll be fine,' I said.

'Are we all set then?' the driver shouted as Miss Bridges, her colleagues and I approached him.

'All present and correct, Mr Mitchell,' the teacher told him, waving her hand in front of her face to diffuse the smog.

'And 'ave all t'girls paid a visit before they got on? I don't want to 'ave toilet stops all t'way down. Last school party I took, they were on and off t'coach like a fiddler's elbow. They were jumping on t'seats, running up and down t'aisle, dropping litter, pulling faces out o' t'winder, mekkin an 'ell of a racket. I tell you, school parties are not my idea of fun. OAPs, now, they're t'best.'

'I have made certain that the girls have all done what is necessary, Mr Mitchell,' Miss Bridges assured him. 'And you can be certain there will be no jumping up and down or unnecessary noise.'

'And you've mentioned t'litter?'

'I've mentioned the litter.'

'And told 'em not to stand up and block mi view?'

'They are well aware of that, too.'

'And there's no smoking on t'coach,' he said, exhaling a cloud of pungent smoke.

'No smoking,' repeated the teacher. 'Very sensible. It's such an unpleasant habit.'

The pointed remark was lost on him and he blew out another cloud of smoke. 'And they know where t'sick bucket is?'

'All has been explained,' said Miss Bridges impatiently, 'so could we make a move, do you think?'

'Because cleaning vomit off seats is not something I take kindly to and t'last school party I 'ad on 'ere—'

'Shall we get going?'

I could see by Miss Bridges's twitchy manner and

231

increasingly exasperated countenance that she was getting irritated.

The driver looked to be in no great hurry. He blew out his cheeks, tapped his pipe on the side of the coach and looked at the sky with a martyred expression on his face. 'Looks like rain,' he said grimly.

I climbed up the steps of the coach and faced rows of young women all in identical clean white blouses and yellow ties, dark green pinafore dresses and matching berets which displayed, in gold, the Lady Cavendish school badge. A hush descended, and as I made my way down the aisle to sit in my designated seat on the back row next to Mrs Todd, I felt thirty pairs of eyes trained on me.

Miss Bridges was the last on the coach. She did a quick head count, smiled widely and said, 'Well, girls, I think we are all set. As you will have observed, we have a gentleman with us for the trip, in addition to our driver, of course. Some of you might recall seeing Mr Phinn when he visited the school last year to carry out an inspection. Do make him feel welcome, won't you? He's something of an expert on the bard so you may like to ask him about the play we are to see. I am sure he is a mine of information.' She turned to the driver. 'Lead on, Macduff.'

'Eh?'

'We can go now, Mr Mitchell, when you are quite ready.'

As the coach wound its way in an autumn drizzle down the long gravel drive and through the ornate wrought-iron school gates, I sat back, sighed contentedly and looked forward to a relaxing journey. We passed the enormously vulgar statue of the founder of the school, Sir Cosmo Cavendish, standing, legs apart on his plinth, glowering at the world. A pigeon sat on his fat head.

It wasn't long before Mrs Todd raised the spectre of Mr Frobisher. 'He was not the easiest man to get along with, you know,' she told me. 'I'm sure you must have found him difficult?'

'Well, I only met him the once and, to be frank, inspectors are rarely received with open arms.'

I thought it best to be very guarded in what I said to Mrs Todd. Discussing a teacher with another, despite the fact that he had left the school, seemed to me to be highly unprofessional. I therefore contented myself with nodding and grunting.

'I think the bottom line was that the man lacked a sense of humour, which to me is perhaps the most important characteristic in a good teacher. He found difficulty in relating to the members of his department and to the older students. Some of the older boys ribbed him unmercifully.' I began to feel quite sorry for the man. 'He took everything so very seriously. Of course, his home life isn't at all happy, I gather. His wife isn't a well woman and I think she is rather demanding and possessive. I only met her the once, at a music recital, and I had to endure a diatribe about how disappointed she was that her husband never made it to headship, how he could have been more ambitious and how undervalued he was. She told me that all he ever seemed to think about these days was his clocks.'

'Clocks?'

'He collects clocks,' Mrs Todd told me. 'He has quite a collection I believe.'

I felt even more sorry for Mr Frobisher as the

story unfolded. I thought of Christine and all her support and encouragement. How lucky I was.

'Your visit certainly threw the cat amongst the pigeons, I can tell you,' continued my companion, 'but it had the desired effect. Mr Frobisher upped and resigned. They've just advertised for the head of department position.'

'So I hear,' I said. I attempted to change the subject. 'Teenage boys can be difficult to handle,' I observed.

'And girls,' she added.

'Yes, and girls.'

'My philosophy with regard to adolescents going through that problematic stage in their lives,' Mrs Todd informed me, 'is to back off, lighten up and calm down. It's always worked with my four boys. Life is too short to get all worked up about an untidy bedroom, the occasional backchat and the odd drunken night out. It's a phase they go through, a young person's reach towards adulthood.' Appearances can indeed be deceptive, I thought. Mrs Todd, elegant, middle-aged, immaculately dressed, someone who would not have looked out of place at a Mothers' Union meeting, did not look at all like the easy-going and unflappable person I was now hearing.

'Well, you certainly handled your students well,' I told her. 'Your class was extremely well-behaved.'

'I have had a lot of experience,' she told me. 'I started my teaching career in a very tough inner-city boys' school. It was a baptism of fire. The stories I could tell! The boys were always at great pains to shock me, a young woman teacher straight out of college, and were rather disappointed and not a little surprised when I didn't rise to their little games. I recall once, a boy named appropriately Duane Pratt, arriving at my room with a condom over his head.'

'A condom!' I exclaimed.

The two girls in front turned round and gave me a very strange look.

'Yes,' said Mrs Todd, without the slightest trace of embarrassment. 'He was a small, silly little boy and I guess someone had put him up to it. He wasn't clever enough to think of it himself. Anyhow, he walked in with this bright-pink condom stretched tightly over his head like a cap. He looked like Noddy sitting there at the front desk grinning inanely at me.'

'Whatever did you do?'

'Nothing.'

'Nothing?'

'Nothing,' she repeated. 'The class all waited for my outraged reaction but I just ignored him, gave out the books and started the lesson.'

'You just ignored him?'

'I most certainly did. I could see it was not the most comfortable of headgear and it wasn't long before he began to find it somewhat constricting. His face took on a sort of red tinge, I remember. I should think a condom on one's head would be quite painful after a while. The silly boy sat it out, right through to the end of the lesson. He didn't want to lose face with his pals, you see. When the bell went and he headed for the door, I called him over. "Duane," I said, "do you know, you have given a whole new meaning to the term 'dickhead'."' I spluttered with laughter and the girls in the seats in front of us giggled. 'I am a teacher, Mr Phinn, who does like to have the last laugh.'

After a couple of hours we stopped at a service station on the M1 for us all to stretch our legs. The girls and staff dispersed in the direction of the Ladies, the coach driver disappeared, presumably for a smoke somewhere, and I headed for the telephones because I was anxious to know that Christine was all right. I felt a bit guilty about leaving her at home while I was out 'gallivanting', as my mother would have said. I was the last back on the coach because I had had to wait behind a long queue of people at the telephone kiosks, and it was only when the coach was speeding along the motorway that I realised that I wanted to go to the lavatory. As the coach steadily clocked up the miles, I became increasingly uncomfortable and kept crossing and uncrossing my legs to try and ease the pain in my complaining bladder.

'Are you not comfortable there, Mr Phinn?' asked Mrs Todd, after witnessing my contortions.

'Yes, yes, I'm fine,' I said, giving a pained smile. 'I've got a bit of a knee problem, sort of twinges. An old rugby accident. Cartilage trouble.'

'You should get it seen to. My husband's a surgeon at the hospital. He's always telling me that torn cartilages are one of his specialities.'

'Yes, I intend to,' I said.

The discomfort got worse and worse. I just had to go to the lavatory or I would burst.

'I suppose we'll be stopping for lunch soon,' I said casually to Mrs Todd.

'Oh no,' she replied. 'We shan't be stopping now until we get to Stratford. We'll eat our sandwiches there on the lawn in front of the theatre, just by the river. I love the waters of the Avon, don't you?'

'Yes, indeed,' I mouthed.

The pain in my bladder was becoming unbearable. I just had to go to the lavatory. Then I thought of the most horrendous scenario: me standing by the side of the road doing what I had to do with thirty girls and four women teachers staring out of the coach window in amazement. The embarrassment, the indignity, the shame! No, I would have to think of something.

I teetered down to the front of the coach until I was on the step next to the driver.

'Oi!' he cried. 'Nobody's supposed to come beyond that point back there. There's a notice. "Don't distract the driver when the vehicle is in motion." It's a safety hazard.'

'This is an emergency,' I whispered.

'Oh, bloody 'ell!' he exclaimed, beginning to brake. ' 'As someone been sick?'

'No, no. I have to go to the toilet.'

'Toilet!' he exclaimed loudly.

'I have to go,' I whispered in his ear. 'I'm desperate.'

'Didn't you 'ear what I said when we was setting off? I said make sure—'

'Yes, yes, I know, and I'm truly sorry but I'm fit to bursting.'

'Well, I can't just stop 'ere and there's no services on this stretch of motorway. You'll just 'ave to cross your legs and wait till I get to a caff.'

'I can't wait,' I said between gritted teeth.

'Well, I'm not stopping on t'hard shoulder. I'd get done for that.'

'Look, I really am desperate.' There was a pathetic pleading in my voice. 'Please.'

'Well, I'll tell you what I can do. I'll get off and

go via Coventry. There's a car park and toilets in t'
cathedral precincts.'

'Oh, thank you, thank you,' I said.

'But you'll 'ave to clear it with t'missus back
there.'

I tiptoed down the aisle until I arrived at Miss
Bridges. 'I was just talking to the driver, Miss
Bridges,' I said casually, 'since I thought it might be
a good idea to break our journey at Coventry and
see the wonderful cathedral.'

'Oh, I don't know. It's not on the programme,'
said the teacher.

'I know, but this is an opportunity not to be
missed. Have you been to Coventry Cathedral,
Miss Bridges?'

'Well, no, I haven't.'

'The cathedral is quite stunning and we have
plenty of time.'

'I don't think we have, Mr Phinn,' said the
teacher, looking at her watch.

'Miss Bridges, I really do think we should break
our journey at Coventry. It would only take half an
hour and it really is well worth a visit.'

She looked a little daunted. Perhaps the tone of
my voice was a trifle threatening. 'Well, if you really
think so.'

'Oh, I do, I do!' I exclaimed.

Ten minutes later, the longest ten minutes in my
life, we pulled into the car park by the cathedral. I
nearly cried when I saw the GENTS sign. As soon
as the coach came to a halt, I leapt down the steps
and shot off like a man pursued by a charging
rhinoceros. To my dismay, I heard Miss Bridges's
voice behind me.

'Follow Mr Phinn, girls. Follow Mr Phinn. He's

238

heading for the cathedral.' I turned and to my horror saw thirty girls in green uniforms running across the car park in my direction.

* * *

It was on the journey home that I made a fool of myself again. We had stopped at another service station for a short break and what Mr Mitchell described as a 'toilet stop'. I did not like the way the bus driver, emphasising the phrase 'toilet stop', looked pointedly at me.

I was heading back to the coach when I was approached by a very distressed-looking young woman.

'Excuse me,' she said, 'I'm most terribly sorry to trouble you, but I wonder could you assist me?'

'Yes, of course,' I said. 'How can I help?'

'Well,' explained the woman. 'I've been really, really silly. I'm in a terrible fix. I just can't get into my car. The key won't work in the lock. I've tried and tried but it just won't open the door. Are you any good with keys?'

'Oh, it's probably frozen up,' I told her, smiling reassuringly.

'But it's not that cold, is it?'

'Locks can be temperamental,' I told her. 'Don't worry, I'm sure with a bit of manipulating I'll get the door open for you.'

'Thank you so much,' she said.

Her car, a small red Toyota, was parked near the coach. I took the key from her, twisted and turned, pushed and pulled, but to no avail. 'It just doesn't seem to work,' I said.

'This is awful,' moaned the woman. 'I'm off to

239

see my mother in Nottingham and she worries so. She's not on the phone, you see. And all my work papers and handbag and everything are in the car.' Her eyes began to fill up. 'I don't know what to do.'

'Don't worry,' I said. 'We'll get it open.'

I tried another door, again twisting and turning, pushing and pulling. Then there was a snap.

'Dash it!' I exclaimed. 'I've broken the key off in the lock.'

'Oh no,' groaned the woman. 'Now what do I do?'

'Look,' I said, 'there's an RAC man in the service station. I'll get him.'

On the way back to the main building, I stopped at the coach and explained the situation to Miss Bridges and the bus driver. Neither seemed all that pleased.

'So 'ow long are we going to be waiting 'ere?' asked Mr Mitchell, puffing out his cheeks and looking heavenwards with a martyred expression. 'I've got a schedule to keep.'

'And the girls' parents will get worried if we are not back on time,' added Miss Bridges.

'Yes, yes, I know,' I told them. 'This will only take a moment. I'll get the RAC man and leave him to sort it out.'

If only it had been that simple.

The RAC man and his young colleague scrutinised the lock. 'You've broken the key off,' the older one concluded.

'Yes, yes, I know,' I said. I felt like saying, thank you for telling me the blindingly bloody obvious.

'Oh yes, snapped clean off. It's no good being heavy-handed with keys, you know,' he told me, like a headteacher chastising a naughty schoolboy.

240

'These mechanisms are very delicate.'

'And Toyota cars are the devil's own job to get into,' added his young companion.

'Can you get into the car?' I asked.

'Oh, I can get into the vehicle all right,' said the older man, smiling.

'Thank goodness for that,' I sighed.

'You should have come to me in the first place.' He stared at the lock for what felt like an inordinate amount of time. 'There is, of course, the small problem of needing the key to drive and you broke it off.'

'Oh dear, yes,' I said.

'You should have come to us first thing,' said his companion, 'then this wouldn't have happened. Are you a member of the RAC, by the way?'

'Yes, I am,' I replied.

'And are you fully covered for roadside recovery and for home assistance?'

'Yes, I am.'

'Could I see your membership card, please sir? I do need to make a note of the number.'

'But this is not my car,' I explained.

'It's mine,' piped up the woman, who up to this point had been watching the proceedings in silence with a doom-laden expression on her face. 'I just asked this gentleman to help. I wish I hadn't now.'

'Some help, breaking the key off,' mumbled the older man.

'Are you in the RAC, madam?' asked the younger man.

'No, I'm not,' she replied, 'I've always meant to join but—'

'The times we've heard that, eh, Jack?' said his colleague, shaking his head. 'It's only in emergencies like this that people wished they were in the RAC. Save them a whole lot of time, grief, trouble and money if they had joined in the first place.'

'Look,' I said, 'could you sort this out? I am with a party of thirty schoolgirls and really have to—'

At this point, two traffic policemen arrived. 'What's the problem?' asked the taller of the two.

'We're trying to get in this car,' explained the older RAC man. 'Bloke here broke off the key in the lock.'

'Who broke the key off in the lock?' asked the taller policeman.

'I did but—' I started.

'I told him,' said the RAC man, 'that it's no good being heavy-handed. He should have come to me in the first place, then this wouldn't have happened.'

'It's easy to say that after the event,' piped up the woman.

'Are you sure it's the right key?' the other policeman asked me.

'It's not my car,' I said.

'Not your car?' he repeated. 'Well, what were you doing trying to get into it?' He reached for his pocket book.

'It's this lady's car,' I said.

'Yes, it's my car,' explained the woman.

'And this man was trying to get into your car, was he, madam?'

'Yes, that's right,' she replied.

'I see.' The policeman flipped open the covers of his little black book.

'No, no, you don't see,' I spluttered. 'This lady stopped me as I was coming out of the service

242

station and asked me to help her. She couldn't get into her car. The key wouldn't work.'

The situation was rapidly descending into farce. Then the greasy bus driver arrived.

'Look,' he said to me, 'can we get moving? I've got a schedule to keep.'

'And who might you be?' asked the smaller of the two policemen.

'I'm 'is driver. There's thirty girls waiting for 'im.'

The crowd which surrounded the small red car was now joined by an elderly couple. They looked worried and confused.

'What's wrong?' asked the old man.

'This man's broken the key off in this lady's car,' said the older of the RAC men.

'Her car?' exclaimed the old man. 'It's *my* car!'

Out came the policeman's notebook again and as he flicked it open there was a sort of shriek from behind us.

'Oh, my goodness!' cried the young woman. 'It's the wrong car. We've been trying to get into the wrong car.' She pointed to an identical small red Toyota parked further down the line of cars. 'That's mine. I recognise the radio aerial.' Then with a weak smile she said to the semi-circle, 'I'm awfully sorry. I feel such a fool.'

'If you'd all like to accompany me into the service station,' said a solemn-faced policeman. 'I'll need to take some statements.'

*   *   *

'So did you have a nice time?' asked Christine when I staggered through the door later that

243

evening.

'It was memorable,' I told her. 'Memorable.'

CHAPTER FIFTEEN

'Well I think it's very strange, very strange indeed,' said Sidney, twisting a large paper clip out of shape. 'I cannot recall any other occasion, in all my time in the school inspectorate, when this has happened. It is without precedent.'

It was Friday afternoon and Harold had called a meeting for all the team at the Staff Development Centre to consider a new initiative from the Ministry of Education. Discussion, however, centred on the appointment of the new Senior Inspector.

'I must admit,' agreed David, who rarely endorsed anything Sidney had to say, 'I think it is highly unusual for an appointment to be made and not tell us who it is.'

'The appointment has *not* been made,' said Harold. 'The position has been *offered* but the person involved has asked for time to think about it and consult the present employer.'

'Well, he shouldn't have applied for the post in the first place, if he wasn't sure that he wanted it,' said Sidney, leaning back on his chair.

'It's far more complicated than that,' said Harold. 'There are one or two things the successful candidate wants clarifying and certain conditions to be agreed by the Education Committee before the person in question is prepared to take up the post.'

'Conditions!' spluttered Sidney. 'I hardly think a

244

candidate for a job is in a position to lay down conditions.'

'It's not that unusual,' said Gerry. 'I was once offered a job at a university and asked for more generous re-location expenses and to be higher up the salary scale. If that hadn't been agreed, I would have withdrawn. On another occasion I was offered a job and asked for time to think about it. No, it's not that unusual.'

'You aren't the mystery candidate are you, Geraldine?' asked David, peering over the top of his spectacles.

Gerry threw her head back and laughed. 'No! I think I have quite enough to do at the moment without taking on Harold's job.'

'And don't start looking at me,' I said. 'As I've told you, I didn't apply.'

'Well, I sincerely hope they make a better job of it than the last time,' said David. 'That Simon Carter was a complete and utter disaster.'

'Hear, hear,' said Sidney.

'And why weren't we involved?' asked David. 'We are always asked for our opinions when a new colleague is appointed. The interviews were at County Hall—all secretive and closeted away—instead of here at the SDC. We never had a chance to meet the candidates and you have told us precious little, Harold, about who was in for the job.'

'You should have put in for it, Gervase,' said Sidney. 'I think you would have had a strong chance this time. Just because you weren't successful before—'

'Oh, please, don't start all that again,' I told him wearily.

'Look!' said Harold, consulting his watch. 'We really must press on. You will know who it is after Christmas. Now, can we address the task in hand?'

'Christmas!' spluttered Sidney.

'The person appointed does not take over until Easter, Sidney, as you well know,' said Harold, 'so there is no massive urgency. We want to get it right this time. Now please, can we make a start? The new initiative from the Ministry of Education is called "Spirituality in the Curriculum".'

'Oh glory be,' sighed Sidney, tilting the chair back even further. 'Where do they dream these things up from? I'm sure there are better things to occupy our time than this, Harold.'

'Like it or not, Sidney,' Harold replied, shuffling a large mound of papers before him, 'we are obliged to consider this new directive when we inspect schools as from the first of January. It is not optional, it is statutory.'

'But what, pray, has it got to do with art and design?' asked Sidney, stifling a yawn.

'It has a relevance to all aspects of the curriculum,' said Harold, 'including art and design, and the whole point of this meeting today is to discuss it, decide what we have to do and go through the procedures. So, if you would bear with me?'

'And when is *she* coming?' asked Sidney, who had now taken to twisting an elastic band around his fingers.

'I have asked Miss de la Mare,' replied Harold, glancing at his watch again, 'to join our discussions when she has finished a meeting with Councillor Peterson at County Hall.'

'That will be about Hawksrill,' said Sidney.

'It's a splendid opportunity,' continued Harold, ignoring the interruption, 'while she is in the county, to pick her brains.'

'Is there any further news on Hawksrill?' I asked.

'No, no,' said Harold. 'The Sub-Committee are determined to press ahead and close the school but there's been quite a lot of pressure from so many different groups. I believe the headteacher and her deputy are now joining the fray, threatening not to resign if the school closes. The MP, the rural dean, parish councillors, parents, governors—they're all queuing up to object. It's all most unfortunate and very time-consuming.'

'Didn't I hear that your dear wife is stirring things up?' Sidney asked me, as blunt as ever.

'Let's not go into all that, Sidney,' I pleaded.

'Well, you did raise the matter.'

'No, I did not,' I said. 'You were the first to mention Hawksrill.'

'Let me know if Christine starts chaining herself to the school railings and burning her bra,' said Sidney, tipping back on his chair to a dangerous angle, 'and I shall come out and give her some support—moral, of course. I have always thought—'

'That's rather a sexist comment, Sidney—' began Gerry.

'Look, can we get on,' interrupted Harold testily. 'As I was saying, Miss de la Mare will be joining us just as soon as the meeting with Councillor Peterson has ended.'

'Well, if she's closeted with George "Gasbag" Peterson we could be here all night,' moaned David.

There was an impatient intake of breath from the Senior Inspector. 'All the more reason to make

247

a start,' said Harold. 'So, before her arrival, colleagues, I really would like to get to grips with the document which I hope everyone has read.' He looked at Sidney sceptically. 'Miss de la Mare will then, hopefully, clarify anything we are unsure about.'

I knew the formidable Winifred de la Mare, Her Majesty's Principal Divisional Inspector of Schools, pretty well. My first encounter with her had been a few months after I had been appointed as a school inspector. Dr Gore had asked me to co-ordinate the visit of the Minister of Education to the county and liaise with the HMI responsible—Miss de la Mare. Prior to meeting her, I had imagined a strapping great woman in heavy tweeds and large brogues, with savagely cropped, steely-grey hair, small severe mouth and glittery eyes. She would be entirely humourless, exceptionally critical and very short-tempered—the sort of person to put the fear of God into anyone. In the event, Miss de la Mare turned out to be the very opposite and her bark was far worse than her bite. When she had visited the county as part of the National Arts in School Survey, she had been so impressed with what she had observed, she had invited Sidney and me to contribute to a course she was directing in Oxford. So, I had seen quite a lot of Miss de la Mare over the last three years.

'I'm sorry, Harold,' said Sidney now, 'but I really do feel I have quite enough on my plate without taking on yet another cock-eyed project from London, involving another mountain of paperwork. Do we really have to do this wretched thing?'

'Look,' said Harold impatiently, 'I am not an apologist for this Ministry of Education initiative. I did not devise it and I, like all of you, have quite enough on my own plate at the moment without yet more work. But we shall be implementing it, and that is an end to the matter. We need today to get clear in our own minds what it is all about before taking it to schools, so can we please get on? You will refer to the papers I have produced and handed round.'

The initiative was called 'Spirituality in the Curriculum'. The Ministry of Education had asked inspectors to consider on each of their visits, the school's strengths and weaknesses in its provision of spiritual development in the different subjects. Inspectors were asked to evaluate how each subject area provided children with an understanding of and an insight into moral values and beliefs and how teachers equipped young people to think deeply about their experiences and feelings in such a way that it developed spiritual awareness. Each visit would be followed by a series of training courses for those teachers who it was felt needed to 'increase their awareness' and 'improve their classroom practice'.

Sidney flicked through the papers dismissively, shook his head, leaned back on his chair and yawned.

Harold ignored him. 'It says here,' he said, reading from the document before him, 'that "effective spiritual development enables young people to appreciate, through their own thoughts and emotions, something of their own life and that of others. It develops their feelings, enables them to cope with their anxieties and fears, encourages them to appreciate the diversity of cultures, religions and beliefs in society and helps them to know the difference between right and wrong."'

'But surely this is the province of religious education,' said Sidney who, having investigated the legs of his chair, had returned to an upright position. 'I can't see it has any relevance to art and design or, for that matter, to mathematics or science or music or English.'

'Would you not say, Sidney,' said Geraldine who, up to this point, had been her characteristically silent self, 'that there is more to art and design than just getting children to draw, paint and construct?'

'I am very wary of questions like that, Geraldine,' replied Sidney. 'I sense that there is some sort of trap being set.'

'Surely art is not just about producing craftsmen or competent practitioners,' she continued. 'Doesn't art also involve reflection, imagination, feeling, creativity, sensitivity? Don't you want young people to appreciate painting and sculpture and architecture? Isn't there something spiritual in the Mona Lisa, in a beautiful, carved figure by Michelangelo, in a Van Gogh canvas full of vibrant colour, in a photograph of a newborn baby or a vast panorama? What about the spirituality of the interior of York Minster or Ripon Cathedral?'

'Well,' conceded Sidney, 'I suppose, yes, there is some art which touches the soul, moves one to a sort of awe and wonder, and I would hope that youngsters come to understand and appreciate this.'

'Well, it's the same in science,' continued Gerry. 'A scientist uses his or her brain to see cause and effect, gather the available evidence, select the appropriate materials, follow a series of logical steps, reason and infer and then reach a

250

conclusion. That process has provided the means for scientists to produce serums to stop diseases, inventions to make our lives easier and happier, and medical treatments to allow childless couples to have children. It is the intellectual side of our being, to do with logic, intelligence and thought. There is no moral question here, no right or wrong in this. It is a merely a scientific process. But science doesn't end at this point. There is an ethical responsibility. To what use do we put all these advances in science? Do we use that serum to save lives or to produce a killer virus? Do we use an invention like the aeroplane to make people's lives easier and more enjoyable or to maim and kill them? Do we use our knowledge of fertility to help a desperate couple have a baby or to produce clones? That is where spirituality comes in. It helps us decide. It has more to do with the heart than the brain. It's about right and wrong, about feelings, fears, joys, loves and hates and that is why it is important to foster it in the education of young people.'

'My, my,' said Sidney, clapping his hands together silently. 'I'm most impressed, Geraldine. That was a bravura performance.'

'May I join you?' We all swivelled around on our chairs to find a plump, cheerful-looking woman with neatly bobbed silver hair. She was dressed in a coat as red as a pillar-box with black Persian lamb collar and cuffs, and sported a bright yellow scarf. Miss de la Mare was not noted for her dress sense.

*   *   *

The remainder of the afternoon was spent in lively

251

discussion. The HMI had obviously been in the room to hear Gerry's impassioned defence of spirituality in the curriculum and constantly referred to her, bringing her into the discussions on a number of occasions.

'Dr Mullarkey,' she said, 'has really got to the nub of things. I am sure you would all agree that education is not about filling empty vessels with a few arid facts. Whilst it's certainly about encouraging young people to have lively, enquiring minds and the ability to question and argue, it is also about fostering their sensitivities and emotions. Could I just ask you for a moment, colleagues, to consider the best teacher you had and the worst? What was it about those two teachers that was so different? What made one so much better than the other? Mr Pritchard, what about you? Who was your worst teacher?'

'Oh, that would have to be Mr Sewell, head of history at the Welsh grammar school I attended,' replied David. 'He had a skull-shaped head, big hooked nose, a mournful expression and a smile like a shark. Tailor-made to be an undertaker. He couldn't help the way he looked, of course, but he could help the way he treated us boys. Terrible man he was—pompous, sarcastic, cruel as well, disparaging, humourless.'

'Don't beat about the bush, David,' said Sidney, pulling a face. 'Tell us what you really think about him.'

'I hated that man, that's what,' David told us, plucking his spectacles from his nose. 'He'd make fun of our valley accents, ridicule our efforts and criticise our parents—never directly but in a sneaky, unpleasant sort of way. Very nasty piece of

252

work was "Smiler".'

'So did you dislike history?' queried the HMI, with a smile of gentle benevolence.

'Hated it. I recall him creeping into the room in his gown like a great black beetle and telling us before the history examination: "When it says on the paper, 'Use your own words', use mine! I don't want any boy trying to be clever!" Surely the whole point of education is to try and get youngsters to be clever. He gave us model answers to learn off pat. I know them to this day: "Feudalism and the manorial system cannot be said to be the main cause of The Peasants' Revolt because, by the end of the fourteenth century, feudalism was in decline. The manorial system required people to be static, but disturbing elements such as the Crusades, the incessant wars, the growth of commerce, did not make possible a static condition in society, *et cetera, et cetera.*" I could go on, but I won't bore you.'

'Thank goodness for small mercies,' mumbled Sidney.

'You talk about filling empty vessels with arid facts, Miss de la Mare,' continued David. 'Well, that is exactly what went on in Mr Sewell's room. We learnt facts off by heart like parrots. Of course, I hadn't the first idea what I was committing to memory. We learnt the Wars of the Roses, the Spanish Armada, Mary Queen of Scots, the Accession of James I and the causes of the English Civil War. Of course, nothing about Welsh history. Then surprise! surprise! All the topics we had learned came up on the paper.' David smiled wryly. 'Mind you, the fact that Mr Sewell was a Chief Examiner might have had something to do with it.'

'That, I think, is what is called the irritating

success of the wrong method,' I observed.

'What about your history teacher, Mr Clamp?' asked Miss de la Mare, inclining her head slightly in Sidney's direction.

'Very different,' said Sidney. 'He was an eccentric little man with a bald pate and a twitch. He was called Babcock, and he was a world away from David's monster. He was just an out-and-out enthusiast. Bags of energy, fired questions like a machine gun and had a great sense of humour. He loved his subject, enjoyed the company of young people and made history come alive. He used to tell the most fascinating stories, anecdotes and facts about the characters in history. I often talk about Trevor Babcock on my courses. We studied Mary Queen of Scots as well, but we looked at copies of the letters she sent, the secret codes used in the various plots, and we traced her long journey from Scotland to Fotheringay Castle where she met her end. A very complex woman. She was renowned for this wonderful head of hair, you know, but when her head was chopped off it turned out to be a wig. I always remember that.'

'My best teacher was Miss Wainwright,' I told everyone when Miss de la Mare turned to me, 'who taught me English. Actually, I studied for my "A" level English in a girls' school.'

'However did you manage to wangle that?' asked Sidney.

'Well, our English teacher at the boys' grammar was off with some sort of long-term illness and there was no one else to teach the subject. So the seven of us boys studying English went down to the girls' high.'

'Did you have to wear the uniform?' asked

Sidney mischievously. 'I bet you cut quite a dash in black stockings and a pinafore dress.'

'Of course, but it was the knicker elastic which was the worst. Cut right into the tender parts.'

Sidney and David hooted with laughter, and Miss de la Mare raised an elegant eyebrow.

'We were taught by a remarkable woman, Miss Wainwright. When we great lumbering youths arrived for the first lesson, we stood before her to be inspected. Miss Wainwright peered up at us. "I've never taught boys," she said, and then after a long pause and with a twinkle in her dark eyes added, "but I've heard of them."'

Even Miss de la Mare laughed. 'I assume she was able to teach you lads something or you wouldn't have ended up as an Inspector of English here?'

'Indeed, she did. She was warm, supportive, good-humoured, respectful and passionate about her subject. She lifted Shakespeare off the page. "He is not a novelist," she once told us. "He is a poet and a dramatist and the greatest writer that has ever lived."'

'Amen to that,' remarked Miss de la Mare. 'Well, what these good teachers had in common,' she said, 'was an enthusiasm for learning and also a desire to help their students appreciate and explore the subjects they taught, more profoundly. What this Ministry initiative is trying to do is to get teachers to consider the deeper, spiritual side of education a little more in all subjects. Just as Dr Mullarkey said earlier, it is important to teach the various skills but also to develop the spiritual and the moral elements as well. In the teaching of reading, for example, the appropriate materials are selected. The teacher follows a series of logical steps, teaching the mechanical process of how to decode those black marks on the paper. Children can then reason, infer and apply their knowledge to reading. But the teacher's job does not end there. She develops enjoyment in reading and introduces children to stories and poems which amuse, provoke, entertain, touch their feelings. In music, children learn the mechanics on the piano but use this knowledge to play or to sing to lift our spirits, make us feel happy or sad. In history lessons they can perhaps empathise with a lonely Scottish queen hated by most of her subjects and imprisoned for most of her life. That is the underlying philosophy behind this initiative. I hope I have put it in some sort of context for you.'

'Well,' said Harold, smiling widely and showing his set of tombstone teeth, 'I think we have explored this in enough depth. After a tea break we can move on to the practicalities.'

*　　　*　　　*

'You've certainly changed your tune, Sidney,' I remarked over my cup of tea and one of Connie's Garibaldi biscuits. Sidney, David and I were in the staff room; Harold and Gerry were still in deep conversation with Miss de la Mare.

'Well,' replied my colleague, stirring his tea vigorously, 'I'm nothing if not open-minded.'

'Huh,' responded David. 'The danger of being open-minded, Sidney, is that your brains might fall out.'

'I am, at heart, a very flexible thinker,' continued Sidney, undaunted. 'If an argument is put simply,

256

effectively and convincingly, as I feel it was this afternoon, I will willingly consider it. And I do have to concede that there may very well be something in this spirituality thing. It's just all the paperwork which I do so abhor.'

'Well, don't get too keen,' I warned him. 'There is nothing so fearsome as a convert. They become unbearably zealous, tiresome in the extreme and entirely single-minded. We certainly don't want you proselytising all over the office, Sidney.'

'Certainly not,' agreed David.

'I must say, though,' said Sidney, pausing to take a great gulp of tea, 'our pale Irish beauty continues to be a bit of a dark horse, doesn't she? She sits there for ages without a word but when she gets started there's no stopping her. I've never seen her so animated and vociferous. To be honest, I cannot recall having heard her speak more than a few words in the office and then this afternoon she launches into a lecture which would not have disgraced a presentation on the podium of the Royal Society of Arts.'

'She was very impressive,' I agreed.

'Do you think she *was* trying to impress?' asked David.

'I just wonder whether she did put in for Harold's job,' said Sidney.

'You may very well be right,' said David. 'She didn't sound all that convincing to me when she denied that she had applied.'

'Then there were her comments about applying for that university post,' said Sidney, 'and asking for time to think about it.'

'And why is she with Harold and that HMI now?' asked David. 'Why are they closeted together and what are they talking about?'

'Have you got a thing about closets, David?' I asked. 'That's the third occasion you've mentioned them this afternoon.'

David ignored me. 'I think she may very well be our next Senior Inspector. Everything is pointing to it.'

'I'm not sure,' I said. 'I can't imagine Gerry taking on Harold's job and all it entails. She has Jamie to look after, for one thing.'

'There's another mystery,' mused Sidney. 'She never mentioned that until it was discovered. A dark horse indeed is Dr Mullarkey. She never talks about the father of her child. Do you know any more, Gervase? Doesn't Christine sometimes look after the son?'

'Yes, but she hasn't said anything to me,' I said. 'She steers well clear of the subject.'

'He could be some politician or media personality,' mused Sidney. 'Does Jamie resemble anybody?'

'Oh, for goodness sake, Sidney, will you let it drop!' I exclaimed. 'If Geraldine wanted people to know who the father is, she'd tell them. Clearly she does not, so that's the end of the matter.'

'Mysterious, though,' persisted Sidney. 'Anyway, as I said, she was most impressive this afternoon. You might be sorry you did not put in for Harold's job, old chap. I agree with David. I think Geraldine might well be our new boss.'

'She's welcome to it,' I said.

'Geraldine wouldn't be all that bad,' said David.

'No,' agreed Sidney, raising the mug to his lips. 'I could live with it.'

'My, my,' I said, 'this must be a record. You two

agreeing for more than an hour.'

Further discussion was curtailed by Connie entering the room. She was wearing the familiar shimmering-pink overall and holding a clipboard like a game-show host. 'Good afternoon,' she said, casting a critical glance around the room to make sure everything was as it should be.

'Good afternoon, Connie,' we chorused.

'I've been doing my monthly stock check and things have gone missing.' Without waiting for a response she consulted her clipboard. 'There's someone been stealing toilet rolls from the gentlemen's lavatory. Can I ask you to keep your eyes peeled when you run your courses?'

'Yes, Connie,' we replied.

'I put four rolls in there last week and they've all gone,' she said.

'Do you want us to frisk people on their way out?' asked Sidney. 'Make certain they don't have a toilet roll concealed about their person?'

'You get worse,' she told him.

'When I was at school, you know, Connie,' remarked David, 'when we wanted to go to the toilet, we had to ask the teacher for a piece of toilet paper. He gave us a regulation two segments of that rather smelly, pale-brown, shiny variety. It certainly made sure there was no extravagant use.'

'Well, it's a thought,' said Connie, 'but I don't want to go that far.' I could see from her expression, however, that a seed of an idea had obviously been planted in her head. The very notion of teachers having to collect a toilet roll from the caretaker prior to paying a visit brought a smile to my lips. 'And have any of you seen my pair of steps—the small wooden ones which I keep in

259

the storeroom? They've gone walkabout again.'

'No, Connie,' we chorused.

'Well, somebody's got them. They don't just disappear. They haven't got legs. I need them next week when they're coming from the Parks Department to cut back that ivy what's creeping all over the place. They cut it last year but the thing's gone berserk again. If it was up to me I'd cut that creeper, whatever you call it, down.'

'Clematis,' said Sidney.

'What is?'

'The ivy that's creeping all over the place. It's called clematis.'

'Yes, well, I'm not sure if I believe you,' said Connie, waving her clipboard towards Sidney. 'I well remember you telling me that red flower what grew in the tub was a variegated flaming alopecia and then I found out that was a scalp condition.'

'It *is* a clematis, Connie,' I said.

'Well, whatever it's called, it wants pruning and I need those ladders. Are you sure you haven't had them, Mr Clamp, for when you do your mounting?'

Sidney arched an eyebrow. 'I have not, Connie, but if I had borrowed your steps, I should have made sure they were put back in the storeroom.'

'Mmmmm,' she hummed. 'What about you, Mr Pritchard? Have you been using them on your P.E. course for climbing activities?'

David rolled his eyes. 'No, Connie, I haven't touched them.'

'Mr Phinn?'

'Sorry, Connie,' I said. 'I haven't seen them.'

'Have you asked Dr Mullarkey?' asked Sidney.

'She wouldn't have them,' said Connie. 'She's the only one of you inspectors who puts everything

260

back and leaves the room as she finds it.'

'Another fan,' murmured Sidney.

'It's a mystery to me where they've gone,' moaned Connie. She scribbled on her clipboard before adding, 'Well, if they're not back next week, steps will be taken.'

'I thought that they already had been, Connie,' remarked Sidney, keeping a deadpan expression.

'What?' she snapped.

'Taken the steps, that is.'

'You might think it amusing, Mr Clamp, but I have to account for all my equipment and it's no laughing matter. You'll soon be complaining if the top surfaces are dirty because I can't reach to do my dusting because my steps have gone missing.'

'Could it be the vicar, Connie?' I asked. 'He uses the Centre, doesn't he?'

'I hardly think a man of the cloth would walk off with my stepladder. Anyway, what would the vicar be doing climbing up ladders?'

'Taking the moral high ground?' suggested Sidney, grinning at his own mirth.

'What about the pensioners who use the Centre on Fridays?' asked David.

'They have enough trouble with their zimmers, never mind clambering up a set of steps. Some of them are very dodgy on their legs. Most of them have to use the ramp to get in the Centre. Steps are too steep for them. The Council has had to remove those stiles on the Dales Walk footpath and replace them with gates because the old people just can't get their leg over.'

Sidney raised an eyebrow again. 'You don't say?'

'Anyway, I shall take up the matter of my missing steps with Dr Yeats just as soon as he's finished talking to that multi-coloured inspector. Oh, and Mr Clamp, how long are those nudes going to be up on the wall?'

'Don't you like them, Connie?' asked Sidney.

'No, I do not!' she snapped. 'I've never seen anything so horrible in all my life.'

'You will be relieved to know then, Connie,' said Sidney, 'that I shall be changing the display next week. Oh, and speaking of things going missing, have you any idea where the portrait of Mrs Osbaldiston has gone? Somebody seems to have walked off with her.'

Connie gave me a knowing look. 'No idea,' she said, before departing with the clipboard tucked under her arm.

CHAPTER SIXTEEN

The scenery was at its best the bright early December morning when I visited Shaptonhall Primary School. As Harold had asked, we were to visit a number of schools as part of the initiative on spirituality to see how teachers promoted children's spiritual development in our particular subject area. Miss de la Mare had also encouraged us to observe some school assemblies which she felt played a significant part in extending pupils' moral and ethical insights, so I had arranged a series of morning visits. Shaptonhall was top of my list.

I was a little early so I drove at a leisurely rate along twisting narrow roads, bordered by black hawthorn hedges or walls of square, deep stone, marvelling at the boundless views which stretched around me: tawny green pastures cropped by a few vagrant sheep and only interrupted by little copses and scattered farmsteads, sweeping up to the swelling contours of the distant windswept summits.

In the school assembly the headteacher, Mr Greenaway, a small man with large expressive hands and a deep resonant voice, related the parable of the Prodigal Son. 'There was once a farmer who had two sons,' he boomed. 'One day, the younger son said to him: "Father, will you give me my share of your property?" The father agreed and divided all he owned and gave half to his son. The young man sold it and left home with a bulging purse and a light heart.' The headteacher continued with the story, telling the children how the younger son had squandered all this money and then had returned home penniless, ashamed and repentant, with his head held low. He told them how the father, with great happiness in his heart and with tears of joy in his eyes, had run to meet his son and how he had put his finest robe around his shoulders, sent his servant for his best sandals and ordered the fatted calf to be killed for a splendid feast to celebrate his son's homecoming. He paused momentarily, then continued, loudly and dramatically: 'And when the elder son heard the sound of the music and laughter and the news that his brother had returned, he was not pleased and would not enter the house. His father was saddened about this but his elder son told him angrily, "I have worked like a slave all these years for you, yet you have never even offered me so much as a goat for a feast with my friends. Now my good-for-nothing brother, who has spent all your money, turns up and you kill the fatted calf for him." The father had replied, "My son, you are with me all the time and everything I have is yours. Is it wrong that we should celebrate your brother's homecoming? My son was dead but now he is alive, he was lost but now he is found." '

Mr Greenaway spread wide his arms. 'Now children,' he said, 'who do you think was the happiest of all?' There was a forest of hands. He picked a small girl in the front row.

'The father!' she cried.

'That's right, Katy, and who do you think was the saddest and most disappointed about the son's return?'

Before he could pick anyone, a large boy at the back shouted out, 'Well, I reckon t'fatted calf can't 'ave been too 'appy.'

The next school on my itinerary was St Margaret's Church of England Primary School, in the picturesque village of Hutton-with-Branston. This discrete, grey stone building with a red tiled roof stood adjacent to the old church and faced the village green. The Chairman of Governors, the Reverend Featherstone, whom I had arranged to interview, was a dour-looking individual with a large hawkish nose, grey wispy hair and heavy-lidded eyes.

'I'm afraid we live in a secular society, Mr Phinn,' he told me, stroking his long nose, 'a world of fast food, television and fancy holidays. There's precious little spirituality in the world these days. My Sunday School teacher read the story of David and Goliath last week and asked the children who beat the Philistines. One child replied that he didn't know because he didn't follow the minor leagues.' The cleric shook his head wearily. 'I am saddened that children's biblical knowledge these days leaves a lot to be desired. I've had children tell me about Moses going up Mount Cyanide to receive the Ten Commandments, and Solomon with his three hundred wives and seven hundred porcupines. Do you find this lack of biblical awareness on your travels, Mr Phinn?'

'I'm afraid so,' I told him. 'Scripture isn't taught a great deal in schools these days, unless of course it's a church school.'

'Well, this is a church school,' he reminded me. 'I cannot say that the children here are any more acquainted with the Bible than in any other school. My curate questioned a class only last week about the Garden of Eden and asked the name of the person who stole the apple from the tree and a child promptly told him that it wasn't him because he didn't like fruit. It doesn't help, of course, when parents these days take it into their heads to call their children all sorts of weird and wonderful names. Gone are the fine biblical names like Hannah and Simon. Instead, they are named after pop singers and film stars, footballers and—'

'Exotic drinks,' I added, thinking of Tequila Braithwaite.

'I've had requests for Jezebel and Salome and Delilah,' bemoaned the vicar. 'It's very difficult explaining to the parents who these women were and what their line of work was. One child very nearly went through life with the exotic name of Onacardie. I asked the parents at the christening: "And what do you name this child?" The mother replied loudly, "Onacardie." I had just begun sprinkling the water over the baby's head and intoning: "I christen this child Onacardie," only to be quickly interrupted by the irate mother. "No, no, vicar!" she hissed. "On 'er cardy. The name's written on her cardigan. We want her to be called Siobhan." '

I was reminded all too forcefully of the Reverend Featherstone and our discussion about children's lack of biblical knowledge when I visited High Ruston-cum-Riddleswade Endowed Church of England County Parochial Junior and Infant School later that week. It was there that I met Elizabeth. She was a tall girl of about eleven, with pink-framed glasses and a rather earnest expression.'

'Are you looking forward to Christmas?' I realise it was a rather inane question which I asked her but she answered pleasantly and with a small smile.

'Oh yes, it's a lovely time of year,' she said. 'I love the smells of mince pies and fir trees and all the lights twinkling. And I like the Christmas morning service, the carols and the readings. The church is always full and everyone is friendly and happy.'

'Well, Christmas is the most important time in the Christian year, isn't it?' I said casually.

'No,' she replied. 'I don't think you will find it is.'

'Pardon?'

'I said, no, it isn't. Christmas is not the most important time in the Christian year.'

'Oh.' I was quite taken aback.

'It's Easter, Mr Phinn,' she told me. 'That's when Jesus suffered on the cross, died for our sins and rose from the dead.'

'Yes, of course,' I said hurriedly. 'The only one to do so.'

'What?'

'Rise from the dead.'

'No, that's not right either.' Oh dear, I thought. A walking biblical encyclopaedia. 'There was Mary and Martha's brother.'

'Who?'

'Lazarus.'

'Oh, yes,' I said. 'I'd forgotten about Lazarus.'

'And don't forget Jairus's daughter. Jesus told him that she wasn't dead but sleeping and said, "Little maid, arise."'

'Oh yes, of course. How could I have forgotten Jairus's daughter?'

'Mr Phinn,' said the girl, scrutinising me through the pink frames of her spectacles, 'your biblical knowledge is not all that good, is it?'

Later that morning the headteacher escorted me to the door. 'I gather you had an interesting conversation with Elizabeth?'

'Very interesting,' I replied simply, not wishing to elaborate.

'She's a delightful girl and very bright. Elizabeth is the granddaughter of one of our governors. I believe you've met Reverend Braybrook, the Rural Dean.'

* * *

At Holmdale Junior and Infant School, situated deep in a secluded dale in the heart of the North York Moors and surrounded on all sides by rugged moorland, the local Baptist minister, an evangelical young man wearing a T-shirt with 'Fight truth decay—study the Bible every day' on the front, re-told the parable of The Lost Sheep. I had once recounted this story myself in an assembly at Winnery Nook Nursery and Infants School. In fact, Christine—the school's headteacher—has never let me forget and bursts into laughter every time it is mentioned. I was therefore interested to see how the young man would get on. He started well, immediately capturing the children's interest. The great majority of his audience came from farming families so at the mention of sheep all ears pricked up.

'When Jesus was alive,' he told them, 'sheep were very important in the lives of people.'

'They still are,' said one rosy-cheeked girl, sitting near the front.

'Yes, indeed,' continued the minister. 'And in those days, sheep provided meat and milk and cheese. But pasture was poor on the hills—'

'Not too good up here, either,' said the girl.

'No,' agreed the minister. 'So pasture was poor on the hills and the shepherd had to move his flock from place to place to find grass for his sheep. Unlike today, the shepherd at the time when Jesus lived, did not drive his flock in front of him but led it and he knew each of his sheep personally and they answered to his call.'

There were several sceptical looks and furrowed brows at this point. 'How many would he have in his flock, then?' asked a boy of about ten or eleven with a shock of red hair.

'Well, in the parable I'm going to tell you in a minute, the shepherd has a hundred sheep,' replied the minister.

'He's not likely to know an 'undred sheep personally,' observed the boy. 'Cows, mebbe, but not sheep.'

268

'Well, I . . . the shepherd . . . he probably would have known his sheep very well.'

'But not an 'undred!'

'Let's make a start on the story and then we can talk about it afterwards, shall we?' said the minister, looking a little uneasy. I could see from his expression that he was unused to members of his congregation shouting out and commenting at every turn. This was clearly not his usual captive audience. 'Now, if any of those sheep strayed, the shepherd would search for them until he found them.'

'He wanted a good collie-dog,' said the red-haired boy. 'Save a lot o' time and trouble.'

'Aye,' nodded a few of his companions.

The minister carried on regardless and speeded up his delivery, hoping by doing so to discourage any further interruptions. 'The shepherd protected his sheep from wild animals and thieves by using a catapult and a wooden club—'

'Shotgun would 'ave been better,' remarked a child.

'And at night,' continued the minister, ignoring the observation, 'the shepherd kept his flock in a stone-walled sheepfold topped with thorns and he would block the entrance by lying across it.'

'I can't see my dad doing that,' said the girl at the front, laughing.

'Now this parable is called The Lost Sheep and it was told by Jesus nearly two thousand years ago.' The minister took a deep breath, rubbed his hands, smiled and began. 'There was once a shepherd and he had a hundred sheep. One day he discovered that one of the sheep had strayed. He could have said, "Ah well, I have ninety-nine so why should I bother searching high and low, hither and thither, for just one sheep? If I leave the other sheep they will be at the mercy of wolves and thieves. Anyway, the lost sheep might be dead by now." But the shepherd did not say this, for every single one of his sheep was precious to him. So he went in search of the one lost sheep.'

'Hardly worth the effort, price of lamb being what it is at t'moment,' commented the rosy-faced girl.

'This was quite a long time ago,' the minister informed her, still managing to retain his smile. 'So, the shepherd left the ninety-nine and went in search of the one lost sheep.'

'What breed o' sheep were they, then?' asked the girl.

'Breed?' repeated the minister.

'Aye, what breed?'

'Well, does it make a difference?' he asked.

'It makes an 'ell of a lot o' difference. Some sheep are docile, others are reight frisky. If you're talking 'erdwicks, they never shift, they'll stop where they are till t'cows come home. We've got 'erdwicks. They may be small but they're a tough breed and eat owt that's going—grass, heather, couch grass—owt. Now, if t'shepherd left a flock of 'erdwicks, he'd still find 'em theer when he got back.'

'I see,' said the minister lamely and wrinkling his forehead into a frown. 'Well, I shouldn't imagine that the sheep were Herdwicks.'

'But if you're talking Leicesters,' continued the girl, 'they'll be leaping all ovver t'show. They'd be off as soon as shepherd's turned 'is back.'

'That's why tha needs a good collie-dog,' insisted

270

the boy with the red hair.

'So what breed were they?' asked the girl.

'Well,' said the minister, having a sudden flash of inspiration, 'these were Palestine Blues, a very lively breed.'

'Never 'eard of them,' commented the girl sulkily. 'What do they look like?'

'Oh, big and woolly and white,' began the minister feebly. He pressed on quickly to prevent any further interruptions and awkward questions. 'What joy the shepherd felt when he found his lost sheep. He put it on his shoulders and hurried back to tell everyone his good news and invite his friends to share his happiness.'

'And were his other sheep still there?' asked the boy with the red hair.

'Indeed, they were, and the shepherd was very happy. Now, in the same way, there is greater rejoicing in heaven over one sinner who turns back to God than over ninety-nine people who see no reason to repent. Remember, children, none of us is a lost sheep in the eyes of God. Did you enjoy that story?' he asked, facing the sea of little faces.

There was a long pause. Then the little boy with the red hair gave a great heaving sigh. 'It were rubbish,' he said simply. 'Nowt 'appened. I like a story wi' a bit o' action.'

'Most sheep are big and woolly and white,' started the rosy-cheeked girl sitting at the front. 'What I want to know, is this. Are these Palestine Blues—'

Without pausing, the minister clasped his hands together and said very quickly, 'Let us pray,' thus putting a stop to any more comments from the sheep experts in the hall.

271

'I think I'll pick Matthew 10 for the next assembly,' remarked the minister later in the staff-room. 'You might recall the words of Jesus about the sheep among the wolves. I was eaten alive in that assembly, wasn't I?'

'If I may offer a little advice, minister,' I said, 'to someone new to the county. Stay away from stories about sheep. When I once related the same parable, at the school where my wife is the headteacher, I asked the children the question: "Why do you think the shepherd risked losing all his other sheep just for the one which was lost?" and some bright spark replied, "'Appen it were t'tup."'

*   *   *

The last school on my programme was St Bartholomew's School. The headteacher, Sister Brendan, was most intrigued by the initiative and quizzed me unmercifully about it.

'And how does one go about assessing something as intangible as spirituality?' she asked, fixing me with her small, dark eyes. 'Surely, like a love of poetry or an appreciation of music, it is something which is impossible to evaluate.'

'Well, it is difficult, Sister, but—' I started.

'It's rather like the question on my niece's recent religious education examination: "Explain the concept of the Trinity." Theologians have argued about that for centuries. I should imagine that the Pope himself has some problems explaining that one. I'm so sorry, Mr Phinn, do go on. You were about to elucidate just how you are to inspect spirituality.'

I endeavoured to explain but felt on very shaky ground. Eventually, I extricated myself from her room, having prevailed upon her to let me sit in on the rehearsal for the school play on the life of St John the Baptist.

Sister Brendan's assistant teacher, Mrs Webb, was in full flow when I entered the hall. On stage a large, shaven-headed boy holding a paper crown and a large plastic sword was staring impassively at the teacher.

'Now, Herod,' said the teacher, 'when Salome brings on John the Baptist's head, you look very sad. You really didn't want to have him killed but had to keep your promise to Salome that she could have anything she wanted.' The teacher caught sight of a small boy at the side of the hall, holding a large papier-mâché plate. 'John,' she said irritably, 'where is the head?'

'Pardon, miss?' asked the child.

'Where is John the Baptist's head? It should be on the platter.'

'I haven't got it, miss,' replied the child. 'No one has given it to me.'

'Peter,' the teacher instructed another child, 'go to the staff room and fetch the bleeding head.'

The boy returned moments later with Sister Brendan.

'Did you wish to see me, Mrs Webb?' asked the nun.

*   *   *

Dr Sadler examined the knee. 'Quite a nasty knock,' he said. 'Whatever were you doing?' I explained. 'Have you banged this knee before?' he

273

asked.

'Yes,' I replied, 'but that was some years ago when I used to play rugby.'

'And it's been fine since?'

'Well,' I told him, 'I have had a few twinges and it aches a bit when I've been on my feet for a long time.'

My heart sank when he said, 'Well, I think I need to refer you to a specialist. The swelling should have gone down by this time. I'll give you a prescription for an elastic stocking. In the meantime, try and take the weight off it as much as you can and don't stand for long periods.'

Chance would be a fine thing. That very evening I was to speak at the Farmers' Dinner. All spruced up, I was limping for the car when I caught sight of Harry Cotton taking his terrier for her constitutional. There was an icy wind blowing in my face but I just could not wait to tell him about the chapel.

'Good evening, Harry,' I called out.

'Evenin',' he replied. He gazed up at the sky. 'Gerrin a bit nippy, in't it? When t'badgers get theer beddin' out, t'weather'll be mild. That's what my owld dad used to say. Well, they haven't got it out so I reckons we're in for a spot of cowld.'

'You know the Methodist chapel you were telling me about—' I started.

'See that holly tree,' he said, pointing at a little tree in the nearby hedge. 'No berries. If there were berries on t'holly tree, we'd be bound for a soft winter 'cos t'birds only feed off t'berries if there's cowld weather a'comin'. I'll tell thee what—'

'Harry,' I said, 'the building at the back of the cottage wasn't a Methodist chapel, after all.' I rather expected him to dispute this and then I would have the pleasure of putting him right and relating my conversation with Jasper Perkins.

'Aye, I know,' he said to my surprise.

'You know?'

'Aye, I know. I was goin' to pop up and tell thee. I got it wrong. I was talkin' to Albert Tattersall last week in t'Golden Ball and 'e put me right.'

'Well, we all make mistakes,' I said. I felt pretty smug.

'No, it weren't a Methodist chapel at all. It were Quaker. I knew it were summat of t'sooart. Built in seventeen 'undred and summat, mebbe earlier according to Harry. Them Americans I was telling you about, dropping in to t'village to 'ave a look at it, they was Quakers not Methodists. Very pacific people are your Quakers, can't be doin' wi' violence and the like. I remember in t'war they were conscientious objectors. Some of 'em were locked up in Richmond Castle, tha knaas. I allus respected 'em. Nice people they were. So, it's just as well for you that they're a peaceful lot because they'll not be dead chuffed to see what thy's gone and done to their meeting 'ouse. Anyroad, it were not Wesley what preached 'ere, it was a man called Fox and on t'anniversary of 'is death, this minister from York and not Reverend Jessop, 'eld a service up 'ere. That there building you demolished were a Quaker meeting 'ouse, even rarer than a Methodist chapel, so Albert Tattersall were telling me.' I was lost for words. 'I 'eard from yer missis that you 'ad a bit of an accident when you were demolishin' it.'

'Yes,' I sighed, 'I did.'

'Still limpin', I see.'

'Yes, still limping.'

'Could be divine providence that,' said Harry, ambling off. ' 'Ave a nice evenin'.'

*　　　*　　　*

I was really not in the mood to give an amusing after-dinner talk that evening but cheered up when I saw Jacob Bannister waiting to greet me outside The Marrick Arms, a great beaming smile on his face. He was a small, wrinkled individual with wisps of white wiry hair combed across his otherwise bald pate.

'Ee, it's grand to see thee,' he shouted at me as if I was a good distance away. 'Find us all reight, then?'

'No problem,' I said.

'Come on in an' I'll sooart thee out wi' a drink.'

I followed him through a noisy throng of largely stout, red-cheeked, healthy-looking men until we arrived at the bar where I was introduced to Jacob's cousin, 'our Barry'.

'This is t'speaker, Barry!' roared Jacob, looking up at the round red face.

'Oh aye,' replied his cousin.

I had never seen any other human being as large as 'our Barry'. He was mountainous: six foot six at least, broad as a barn door, arms like tree trunks and a huge round pudding face. The pint glass looked like a thimble in his massive hand.

'What are you 'avin', Mester Phinn?' shouted Jacob.

'Just a half of bitter, please,' I replied.

Jacob roared down the bar making the glasses rattle. ' 'Arf o' bitter 'ere, Jack, for t'speaker an' another pint for our Barry and one for me!' He then turned round, nudged me with his elbow and looked up at his cousin. ' 'E's a big bloke, in't 'e, our Barry?' he asked.

'He is,' I agreed.

' 'Is mother, mi Auntie Betty, were a big woman, wunt she, our Barry?'

'Aye,' replied the huge man.

'Wonderful woman, she were. 'Eart o' gowld, do owt for anybody, wunt she, our Barry?'

'Aye,' nodded Barry, before polishing off half the pint in one great gulp.

'She nivver missed a service at t'church. Come rain or shine she'd walk all t'way from Durdeyfield Farm up to t'village. One winter, it were thick wi' snow, drifts up to ten foot deep, rooads like icing rinks, wind that 'ud cut thee like a sharpened scythe but she made it up t'church. Cooarse, vicar were not expectin' anybody and then mi Auntie Betty turns up. Only one theer, she were, sitting in t'front pew as large as life. Anyroad, vicar asks 'er if 'e should carry on wi' service like, seeing as she were t'only one in t'church. "Look 'ere, vicar," she tells 'im, "I can't tell thee what tha should do, but if I went out of a morning to feed t'cows and only one on 'em 'ad tekken trouble to turn up, I'd feed it." He were nonplussed at this, was t'vicar. "Do you know," he says, "yer right." And he went ahead with t'service and give one of these long sermons just for mi Auntie Betty's benefit. He were pretty pleased wi' hissen afterwards. "I hope you felt it were worth the walk through all that snow, Missis Bannister," he tells 'er. "Look 'ere, vicar," she replies, "I don't reckon I know all that much about sermons and the like, but if I went out of a mornin' to feed t'cows and only one 'ad tekken trouble to

277

show up, I'd not be likely to give it t'whole lot of feed."'

'It's a nice story, that—' I began.

'She passed on a couple of years back did Auntie Betty, di'n't she, our Barry?'

'Aye, she did.'

The beer arrived, was paid for and Jacob continued. 'When she died, they 'ad to 'ave a special coffin made for 'er, she were that big, and t'grave diggers were paid extra 'cos o' size of t'hole. And it were a reight carry on at t'funeral. They'd just lowered 'er deep into t'ground and t'vicar were startin' up wi' 'is ashes to ashes bit, when one of t'undertakers pipes up. "It'll 'ave to come up, vicar." "It's just gone down," says t'vicar. "I know," says t'undertaker, "but it'll 'ave to come up. I've dropped mi glasses down t'ole and they're on top o' t'coffin." It were a job and an 'alf gerrin 'er up. Coffin were up and down like a bloody yo-yo, weren't it, our Barry?'

'Aye, it were.'

'Anyroad, later on t'vicar says to mi Uncle Stan, that's our Barry's dad, he says, "You'll miss your wife and no mistake, won't you, Mester Bannister?" "I will that," he says. "Fifty-two year o' marriage and not a cuss word. I shall miss 'er most in bed at neets tha knaas," he goes on. "Hold on," says t'vicar, "this is not t'time nor t'place to hear about that sort of thing." "Nay, vicar," says mi Uncle Stan, "I don't mean what you're a-thinkin'. On a cowld winter's neet, when wind's whistling through cracks in t'winder and there's a reight draught under t'door, she were like a bield wall, my missus, like a bield wall." Does tha follow mi drift theer, Mister Phinn? Does tha knaw what a bield

278

wall's fer?'

'I do,' I replied, laughing.

I had been told exactly what a bield wall was the previous year by a small boy. It is a short stretch of wall, starting nowhere, ending nowhere, for the sheep to shelter behind in wet and windy weather—a sort of windbreak.

'Now, mi Uncle Stan were a character and no mistake, wa'n't 'e, our Barry?' continued Jacob Bannister.

'Aye, 'e were,' replied his cousin, finishing the second pint of beer in a great gulp.

'I was just wondering—' I began.

'Once mi Uncle Stan goes and buys this tup— that's a ram, tha knaas—from Bentham market.' There was no way I was going to get a word in. 'Lovely looking creature it were. Texel. Square as a box, four solid legs, beautiful fleece. Anyroad, he puts it in t'field wi' yows—them are t'ewes—and sits back to watch 'im do what nature intended 'im to do, if you follow mi drift. Well nowt 'appens. Tup just stands theer, then does a bit o' walking, a bit o' grazin', but he's not interested in any o' yows. They stand theer waiting for 'im to mek a move but 'e's just not interested. Well, mi uncle scratches 'is 'ead and dunt know what's up. 'E's nivver seen the like afoor. So, he sends for t'vet. T'vet's puzzled an' all. "I shall tell thee what I'll do, Mester Bannister," he says, "I've got this 'ere Dutch medicine which might just do the trick. Just come on t'market." And he tells mi Uncle Stan to give t'tup one o' these pills in t'mornin'. Vet gus back on t'Thursday and 'e asks 'ow things are goin'. "Champion," says mi Uncle Stan. "I've nivver seen the like. Them theer pills certainly did t'trick. Tup's

279

gone mad. Chasing anything that moves. Sex mad 'e is. Nothing's safe in t'field wi' 'im." We were talking about it in t'pub later that day and I says to mi Uncle Stan, I says, "I wonder what was in them theer pills what t'vet give t'tup." "I don't know," says 'e, "but they taste of peppermint." ' The speaker threw his head back and roared with laughter and a smile even came to the lips of his cousin. 'It's a good un, that one, in't it, our Barry?'

'Aye, it is,' said his cousin.

Jacob put his hand on my shoulder. 'Well, it's about time to get 'em in for t'dinner. Prime beef toneet, Mester Phinn, wi' Yorkshire puddin' an' onion gravy.' As I finished the half pint, he said, 'I say, I 'opes tha's goin' to be a bit more talkative like, wi' yer after-dinner speech. You've said nobbut a few words in t'last 'alf hour.' Barry looked down at me, gave me a knowing look and winked.

CHAPTER SEVENTEEN

My favourite time in the school year is Christmas. It is then that teachers make a massive effort to create the magical atmosphere of this very special season. Schools at Christmas-time are ablaze with colour. Fat Father Christmases, their silver sleighs pulled by teams of prancing brown reindeer, gallop across the walls. Fir trees twinkle in entrance halls, and corridors are festooned with bright decorations. Each classroom has a crib crammed with little wooden figures crowding around the manger. Christmas is a time for children.

Of all the activities which take place at

280

Christmas it is the infant Nativity play to which I most look forward. Innocent children re-enacting one of the greatest stories of all time capture the essence of Christmas. To see Mary, aged six, draped in pale blue and tightly clutching Baby Jesus (usually a large plastic doll) to her chest, never fails to bring a tear to the eye. To see Joseph, a thick multicoloured towel draped over his head (usually held in place by an elastic belt with a snake clasp) and attired in a dressing gown and red socks, never fails to bring a sympathetic smile to the lips. And then there are the shepherds (usually a motley group of little boys who scratch, fidget and pick their noses throughout the performance), the Three Wise Men (who invariably forget their lines or drop the gifts), the adoring angels clad in white sheets with bits of tinsel stapled to the bottom and uncomfortable-looking cardboard wings strapped to their backs and, of course, there's the grumpy Innkeeper, who very often steals the show. There is something very special and heart-warming about the infant Nativity.

The first Nativity play this year took place at Willingforth Primary School. Willingforth was something of a showpiece school and the headteacher, the formidable Miss Pilkington, was one of the most highly regarded educationalists in the county. So I anticipated that the performance would be rather special, and indeed it was.

From the outside, the elegant grey stone building, with high leaded windows and imposing oak door, resembled a substantial, immaculately maintained private residence. Inside, there was just the one large airy classroom. It was an impressively decorated room, blue being the dominant colour—

pale blue walls, navy blue and cream ceiling beams and supports, and blue floral curtains. The Reading Corner was attractively inviting with blue carpet and cushions. I recalled thinking on my first visit that it was the first colour-co-ordinated classroom I had seen.

The school looked particularly warm and cheerful that cold December afternoon. Greens and reds, gold and silver made the room look very bright and festive. Using tissue paper of varying colours, the children had transformed the windows into the most wonderful stained glass, depicting scenes in the early life of the Holy Family. On a table in one corner there was a small crib with delicate porcelain figures. In the Reading Corner stood a modest Christmas tree.

For the Nativity play, the desks had been removed and replaced with rows of chairs. By the time I arrived the place was packed with mums and dads, grandparents and governors all facing a makeshift stage.

As I made my way to my reserved seat in the front row, a figure a few rows back stood up and waved at me. It was Connie, almost unrecognisable without her bright pink nylon overall. She had told me the week before that, since there were no courses on at the Centre that day, she was taking the afternoon off. She was determined that this year she was not going to miss the Nativity play in which one of her grandchildren, little Lucy, had a starring role.

Miss Pilkington, a tall, elegant woman, opened proceedings by welcoming everyone. Then the Chairman of Governors, Canon Shepherd, a jolly little man with ruffled hair and flabby cheeks, read in a deep sonorous voice a passage from Luke: 'The Angel Salutes the Virgin Mary'. As the children sang 'Away in a Manger', a pretty little girl playing Mary entered, accompanied by a small boy in the regulation brown dressing gown. Despite the multicoloured towel draped over his head, I recognised Terry the Terror, the boy who had almost caused a riot at the school the previous year. Forget about the miracle of Christmas! A modern miracle had been performed at the school and I was undoubtedly now looking at Terry the Tamed. Mary and Joseph knocked on the inn door, found there was no room and were shown to the stable. Things went like clockwork until the Three Kings arrived on the scene. The first little boy, carrying a golden box and dressed in a red velvet cloak made from curtains and sporting a cardboard crown which covered half his face, announced loudly:

> I am Melchior and gold I bring,
> In homage of our new born king.
> I have travelled from afar,
> Following yon twinkling star.

The second Wise Man strode onto the stage carrying a blue box. He too boomed out his words:

> I am Gaspar. Frankincense I bring,
> In homage of our new born king.
> I have travelled through the night,
> Following yon star which shines so bright.

The third Wise Man entered carrying a green box. He shuffled nervously to the centre of the stage and stared around him wide-eyed and frightened as if lost in a busy shopping street. There was a pregnant silence. The child sniffed, then his small shoulders heaved and great tears rolled down his small red cheeks. Suddenly he let out a most desperate and plaintive cry: 'I don't know who I am. Will someone tell me who I am?'

'You're Balthazar, Gavin,' Miss Pilkington said in a loud stage whisper, from the side of the room, 'and you've brought Baby Jesus a special present of myrrh.'

'I don't know who I am,' the child whimpered again. 'Will someone tell me who I am?'

'Balthazar!' the audience chorused.

'I don't want to do it!' he wailed. 'I don't want to do it.'

The headteacher moved forward, helped the little boy place the box before Mary and Joseph, gave him a cuddle and, taking his hand, led him off the stage. We all applauded loudly.

It was wonderful drama. I had watched a very similar scene when I had accompanied the teachers and students of The Lady Cavendish High School on that fateful school trip. During the production of *King Lear*, the actor playing the lead had entered just as the small child had done that afternoon, looking lost and alone and frightened. Poor, deranged Lear, he had plucked at his hair, thrown out his arms and appealed to the heavens: 'Who is it that can tell me who I am?' It is one of the saddest lines of Shakespeare. On that occasion there had been no Miss Pilkington to help out.

Every infant headteacher has a story to tell about the Christmas Nativity play. There was the time the Innkeeper, when asked if there was any room in the inn answered, 'Plenty,' and ushered the startled Holy Family inside; the occasion when Mary had dropped Baby Jesus, immediately bursting into floods of tears as the pink doll rolled off the stage; the time that the Archangel Gabriel had informed Mary that he 'had tidings of great joy to bring' but had completely forgotten what they were; the occasion when a frightened little girl decided to announce, 'Welcome to our Harvest Festival' because she was fed up with being teased because she couldn't say the word 'Nativity'; the memorable time when the large cardboard and wooden star which had been suspended on a wire above the stage, had fallen onto Joseph who, very much out of character, had rubbed his head and exclaimed, 'Bloody 'ell!'

In one school I had eavesdropped on a conversation between a parent and the teacher concerning the Nativity play. 'So what's this play about, then?' asked the mother in all seriousness. In another school I had heard a father complain that, 'You allus do t'same play every Christmas. Tha wants to do summat different.'

Infant Nativities are rarely without incident and the one at Tupton Road Primary School the following week was no exception. When I received an invitation from the headteacher to join the guests, I readily accepted.

The headteacher, Mrs Wilson, wended her way through the throng of parents and governors to greet me at the entrance.

'Rather a different reception this time, Mr Phinn,' she said, extending a long white hand and smiling broadly.

'Yes, indeed,' I replied rather sheepishly and

285

wishing she hadn't reminded me of a rather embarrassing incident the previous year when I had been apprehended by the local policeman who had been tipped off by a local resident that I was a suspicious character loitering outside the school. All I had been doing was writing up some notes prior to my visit, for which I had arrived early.

Mrs Wilson was a tall, pasty-faced woman with short, dyed black hair and heavy make-up. It had occurred to me on my previous visit, and I was reminded of it now, how very like a racoon she looked with her pale face and large dark eyes nestling in heavy black eye-shadow. Fussy Mrs Thickett, a mousy-haired, sharp-faced woman, was at her side nodding nervously.

The play opened in the traditional fashion with Mary and Joseph setting off for Bethlehem. Joseph, a confident little boy in large glasses, spoke his lines clearly and loudly. Holding Mary's hand he gently led her across the small makeshift stage. Things didn't go so well when the Innkeeper appeared. He was a sturdily built child with spiky ginger hair and his two front teeth missing. It was clear he had a number of family members present that afternoon for there were adoring 'Oohs' and 'Aahs' whenever he opened his mouth.

Before Joseph could even enquire whether there might be room at the inn, the little bruiser, arms folded tightly over his chest and chin jutting out like a miniature Mussolini, announced: 'There's no room!'

'But we have travelled far and—' began Joseph.

'There's no room,' repeated the innkeeper even louder.

'But—' started Joseph.

'Did you not hear me?' The innkeeper bellowed. 'I said there was no room. You can go round the back in the barn.'

'A barn?' repeated Mary. 'We can't go in a barn.'

'There's nowhere else,' said the innkeeper. 'Take it or leave it.'

At this point the little boy caught sight of an elderly woman in the middle of the front row. It was obviously his granny. He grinned maniacally and tinkled the air with his fingers. The old lady, rather unhelpfully, smiled and waved back. This continued for what appeared an age.

'Shane!' came the teacher's disembodied voice from offstage. 'Shane! Come off!'

The Innkeeper continued to smile and wave. The voice from the wings was now more insistent. 'Shane Merryweather, get off that stage right now!'

The child was finally prevailed upon to exit stage left but did so in a flourish, smiling and waving, like a famous actor receiving the plaudits of a smitten audience.

Things then went smoothly until the arrival of the Three Wise Men.

'I bring you gold,' said the first child, laying a small golden box at Mary's feet and bowing low.

'I bring you myrrh,' said the second, laying a coloured jar at Mary's feet and bowing low.

'And I bring you frankincense,' said the third king, laying down his gift.

'Bow!' came the disembodied voice from the wings. 'Bow!'

The third king looked perplexed. He stared around him like a rabbit caught in the headlight's glare.

'Jason!' came the voice again. 'Bow! Bow!'

The little boy looked first at the audience and then at Mary. 'Woof!' he said. 'Woof! Woof!'

*   *   *

I was still chuckling to myself when I arrived for my next appointment at St Bartholomew's School. Sister Brendan greeted me in the entrance hall and ushered me into her room. With her black habit, dark, darting eyes and a sharp little beak of a nose, she always reminded me of a hungry blackbird.

'I do so love Christmas,' she trilled. 'It's such a joyous time. Such a great festival in the Christian calendar—the birth of Our Lord.'

'But not as great as Easter, Sister?' I said mischievously, recalling my conversation with Elizabeth. 'Isn't that the greatest festival in the Christian calendar, when Jesus suffered on the cross, died for our sins and rose from the dead?'

'Why, Mr Phinn,' cried the nun, her small eyes widening in amazement, 'I never knew you were a bible scholar.'

This would be the last visit to those schools involved in the 'Spirituality in the Curriculum' initiative. During the Christmas holidays I would have a lengthy report to compose but I had seen a large number of lessons, observed countless assemblies and had had a range of lively discussions with headteachers and teachers so I had a clear idea of what I was going to write.

'Mrs Webb is all ready for you,' explained Sister Brendan, a small smile appearing on her lips. 'A little nervous, I have to say, after the last rather embarrassing occasion. This afternoon you'll be joining her for story-time, which, hopefully, will be without incident.' Even nuns, as I soon discovered, can sometimes be wrong.

The story Mrs Webb began reading that afternoon was the deeply moving account about the woodcarver. He had been a happy, good-natured man until his wife and child had died, then he ceased to smile and became bitter and unpleasant to anyone who came near him. One cold winter's day a widow and her small son called on him and asked him to carve a set of Nativity figures and that's when a Christmas miracle happened.

Mrs Webb had arrived at the most poignant part of the story, when the woodcarver, having tried again and again to carve the faces of Mary and her baby but without success, finally reaches into a drawer and takes out the charcoal sketch of a young woman sitting in a rocking chair cradling a tiny baby. It was of his wife and child. With tears streaking down his face, he carves Mary in her rough woollen shawl looking down lovingly at her precious baby. At this point Mrs Webb stopped reading and a tangible silence fell. She put her hand to her face and began to cry. I was at a loss what to do. Never, in all the years I had been observing teachers, had I ever seen a teacher break down like this in front of her class. She took a handkerchief from her handbag, dabbed her eyes and continued to weep.

'I'm sorry,' she sobbed. 'I'm sorry, I just can't read any more.'

I felt a lump come into my throat and my eyes began to fill up too. Then Peter, the small boy who had been instructed to go to the staff room and get 'the bleeding head', stood up and strode to the front of the class. He took the book from the teacher's hand, gently patted her on the arm and said gently, 'You sit down, miss, I'll finish the story.'

Mrs Webb was not alone in crying that afternoon. I had witnessed exactly what the 'Spirituality in the Curriculum' initiative was all about. I had seen awe and wonder in Mrs Webb's classroom that cold December day.

At break-time I sought out the boy. He was in the playground sliding with his friends on the icy surface. 'What you did today,' I told him, 'was a noble deed.'

He looked up at me seriously. 'Pardon, sir?'

'It was a very kind and thoughtful thing to do, helping Mrs Webb out like that.'

His smile stretched from one ear to the other. 'Oh, that,' he told me cheerfully, 'I often have to do it.'

*   *   *

I called in at Crompton Primary School a few days later, just prior to the school breaking up for the Christmas holidays. Mrs Gardiner's room was so crammed full of brightly-wrapped Christmas packages that there was hardly any room for me to get in.

'Sorry about this, Mr Phinn,' apologised the headteacher, clambering around the piles of parcels. 'We don't want the children to see them and my room is the safest place.'

'Are these all for the children?' I asked, amazed by the spectacle before me.

'Indeed, they are,' the headteacher replied. 'We like to give each child a small gift at Christmas.

Always a book. Nursery rhymes or fairy tales for the infants, a poetry anthology or children's novel for the older ones.'

'What a lovely idea,' I said. 'But however can you afford it?'

'Well, the Rotary Club and the Lions help out,' explained Mrs Gardiner, 'and we have raffles during the year, bingo sessions and other fund-raising activities. It raises just about enough. You see, some of our children might have wonderful televisions at home but no books at all, not a one. They get lots of toys and sweets and bicycles on Christmas morning but seldom a book. They never visit the library and are rarely seen in a bookshop. So I think it's important for them to have a reading book. Then there are other children in the school who will get precious little at all for Christmas. Our book might be one of the few things they get. Little Matty, for example. You remember Matty, the boy who stole the pound coin? Well, his mother told him last year that Father Christmas had run out of presents when he got to him. Sad, isn't it?'

'It is,' I agreed. 'You're passionate about reading, aren't you, Mrs Gardiner?'

'Yes, I suppose I am,' she replied. 'I always have been. I get it from my parents. My father used to say that books are the architecture of a civilised society and reading the most important tool of learning.'

'He was a wise man,' I said.

'Taught for forty years, did my father,' said Mrs Gardiner proudly. 'My mother read to me every night until I was well into my teens, and she bought me a book every birthday and every Christmas and always inscribed it with a little message. Those

291

books are my treasured possessions. I remember when I first became headteacher here at Crompton and asked a child what books he had at home. I have to admit I was shocked by the answer. After thinking a bit, he replied that they did have one—a big, thick, yellow book which they kept underneath the telephone. I feel that children should own books and build up a little personal library, so we buy them one each Christmas and put a bookplate in the front with their name and the date. Reading is so important. If parents would just spend fifteen minutes each evening with their children, talking about the words and the pictures and making reading enjoyable, what a difference it would make to their learning.'

'I couldn't agree more,' I told her.

'And do you know, some of the children coming into this school at five have never had a story read to them at bedtime or heard a nursery rhyme. Some parents just don't seem to bother these days. The children know all the pop song lyrics, of course, but few of the traditional rhymes. We have to teach them about Jack and Jill and Humpty Dumpty and Little Jack Horner.'

'Well, I think it's a splendid idea to buy the children books, I really do.'

'There's only one problem,' said the headteacher.

'Oh?'

'Father Christmas.'

'Why?' I asked. 'What has Father Christmas done?'

'He hasn't done anything,' said Mrs Gardiner. 'It's just that we haven't got one. The crossing patrol warden took on the part last year but ended up nearly having a nervous breakdown. He said he'd rather face a roadful of careering traffic than the hall full of excited children again. I have to say they did give him a bit of a hard time. Tequila interrogated him as to why she hadn't received the presents she had asked for the previous year, another child told him he wasn't the real Father Christmas and one little girl got completely carried away, fastened onto him like a Whitby limpet and just would not let go. She screamed and yelled and when we finally managed to prise her off she threw a most disgraceful tantrum. Then Father Christmas's beard kept slipping and he forgot the names of the reindeers.' The headteacher paused for a moment and gave me a sly sort of look. 'Now, I've just had a thought. Mr Phinn. You don't fancy—'

I cut her off, throwing up my hands as though to fend her off. 'No, no, Mrs Gardiner, I've played Father Christmas before and it is not false modesty when I tell you that I was an unmitigated disaster.'

'Ah well,' she said, 'I shall just have to twist my husband's arm.' At that moment there was a loud rap on the door. 'Excuse me, Mr Phinn,' said the headteacher.

Outside she was confronted by a round, shapeless woman with bright frizzy blonde hair, an impressive set of double chins and immense hips. She had a ruddy complexion, heavy sleepy eyes and a mouth which turned downwards as if in perpetual hostility.

'Can I 'ave a word, Mrs Gardiner,' she said angrily.

'I am a little busy at the minute, Mrs Braithwaite,' replied the headteacher.

'Yes, well you might be, but this is himportant.'

'It always is, Mrs Braithwaite,' sighed Mrs Gardiner.

'Eh?'

'What seems to be the problem this time?'

'Our Tequila came 'ome yesterday wi'out 'er Christmas bobbles. She had 'em in 'er 'air yesterday morning when she come to school and she come 'ome wi'out 'em. Somebody's gone an' nicked 'em off of 'er.'

'We can't be certain about that,' replied the headteacher. 'They might have fallen out when she was running around in the playground.'

'No, they didn't!' snapped Tequila's mother. 'I tied 'em on right tight. She come 'me wi'out 'em, rooarin' 'er eyes out. They was new, them bobbles. Just bought 'em from t'market.'

'And what do these Christmas bobbles look like?' enquired Mrs Gardiner.

'Well, they was red Father Christmases wi' winking eyes. I didn't shell out good money to 'ave 'em nicked.'

'We will have a good look round for them, Mrs Braithwaite, and now if you will excuse me, I am rather busy.'

'No!' cried Tequila's mother. 'That won't do. It won't do at all. Somebody's nicked 'er bobbles and I want 'em findin'. It's 'appened before. My Tequila's come 'ome without other things which 'ave gone missing like her Mickey Mouse knickers for one thing.'

'Mrs Braithwaite,' said the headteacher sharply. 'Leave the matter with me and I will make inquiries. Now I really must ask you—'

The woman was not to be put off. 'Well, I wants

to know what you are going to do.'

'Well, let me see,' said Mrs Gardiner calmly. 'Tomorrow, I shall get the teachers, the classroom assistants, the dinner ladies, the mid-day supervisors, the cleaners, the lollipop lady, the caretaker and all the children to search for Tequila's Christmas bobbles which must have cost you all of two pounds. We will stop all the lessons to look high and low and we will leave no stone unturned until we have found them.'

Mrs Braithwaite paused for a moment before replying, 'Are you taking the piss?'

*   *   *

In the infant classroom the children were busy colouring in Christmas cards.

'Just put your pencils down for a moment please, children,' said the teacher, 'and look this way. Now, do any of you remember Mr Phinn? He came into our school earlier this year.' Amidst the sea of faces I noticed Matty observing me from his desk in the corner of the room, a truculent expression on his little face. I felt certain he remembered me. I certainly remembered him.

'I know who 'e is,' said a large and very voluble infant with a plump face, frizzy hair in huge bunches (minus the Christmas bobbles) and great wide eyes. I knew it wouldn't be long before Tequila made her presence felt. 'It were 'im what told us about that cat.'

'That's right,' I said. 'Lazy Tom.'

'We might be gettin' another cat for Christmas,' Tequila told me.

'I thought your granny didn't like cats,' I said.

295

'She dunt, but she dunt live wi' us any more. She's in an 'ome.'

'Well, I am very sorry to hear it,' I said.

'My dad's not,' said the child. 'He said it were t'best place for 'er. Mi granny dribbles in 'er knickers and she—'

'Yes, you told me before,' I said.

'That's enough now, Tequila,' said the teacher.

'But I were tellin' 'im about mi granny.'

'Yes, I know you were,' said the teacher sharply, 'and we've heard quite enough. Now, I'm sure Mr Phinn would like to see our crib.'

'Very much,' I said.

The crib was a large but extremely sorry-looking affair with dull strips of wood stuck together haphazardly, scraps of faded hay and huge figures which had clearly seen better days. The white paint had flaked off the Baby Jesus giving Him an unhealthy grey appearance. Joseph had lost an arm and the angels their haloes, the three kings looked like down-and-outs and the ox and the ass were chipped beyond recognition. Someone had tried to brighten up the Virgin Mary by re-painting her with long yellow tresses, bright red lips, crimson cheeks and an electric blue cape. She had a strange, rather alluring smile on her face. Looking at her, the adjective 'virgin' was the last word that came to mind.

'They've gorra much nicer one in Fettlesham,' Tequila informed me. 'Ours is really tatty.'

'But that's what it probably would have looked like,' I told her. 'Baby Jesus was born in a stable, a cattle shed, and he had a manger for a bed. It wouldn't have been nice and clean and bright like the crib in Fettlesham. The stable Baby Jesus was born in would have been full of rather smelly animals and dirty hay. There was no room in the inn, you see, so Mary and Joseph had to stay in the stable and it didn't have lovely furniture and carpets and central heating.'

'Well, they should 'ave booked in advance,' pronounced Tequila. 'It allus gets busy at Christmas.'

'Mary had to have her baby in a cold, dark barn,' I continued. 'He had no nice new clothes, no toys, no cot. He came into the world with nothing. He was one of the poor and mean and lowly.'

Matty, who had been watching with eyes like saucers, shook his head slowly and said quietly but with feeling, 'Poor little bugger.'

CHAPTER EIGHTEEN

One evening, just after the schools had broken up for Christmas, Christine and I were snuggled up on the sofa in front of a blazing fire.

'I can't remember when we last did this,' she said.

'Well, we've both been so busy,' I replied. 'This has been such a hectic term, not one I would care to repeat.'

'I hope I shall see more of you when the baby arrives,' Christine said. 'When our child starts to talk, I don't want him or her asking who that strange man is who disappears early in the morning and arrives home late at night with his big black bag.'

'You make me sound like Dr Crippen,' I said.

'Well, we'll want to see more of you. You'll have family commitments.'

'You will,' I said. 'I'm determined to have more nights in and try to get home earlier. I want to snuggle up with my little girl and read to her every night.'

'And what about the baby?' asked Christine mischievously.

'I'll read to her as well.'

I was thinking of Mrs Gardiner and her remarkable father. She was right, of course: one of the most important things parents can do for their children is read with them—not to them or at them, but *with* them, making reading a pleasure.

'You are really certain it's going to be a girl, aren't you?' asked Christine.

'Of course, I am,' I said. 'The eldest child in every Phinn family as far as we can remember has been a girl and it's been the same with the Bentleys on your side. Little Lizzie will be blonde, blue-eyed and beautiful, just like her mother. And she'll be clever, too. Elizabeth Gaskell, Elizabeth Barrett Browning, Elizabeth Phinn—it's the name of a great writer. And if it's a boy he'll be called Fred and play cricket for Yorkshire.'

'I thought we had decided on Matthew,' said Christine.

'I think Matthew for son number two. A first born son should have his father's names.'

'Certainly not!' exclaimed Christine. 'One Gervase in the family is more than enough.'

'If it's a boy, what about naming him Richard, then, after my father?'

'Or Leslie, after mine?'

'Or Richard Leslie?'

'Or Leslie Richard?'

'This is all academic, Christine,' I said, 'because it will be a girl—little Lizzie Phinn.'

We sat in silence for a while, watching the flickering flames and feeling the warmth of the open fire.

'This is the life,' I said at last.

I was well and truly in the Christmas spirit. The main reason I was feeling particularly pleased with life concerned Harold's job and my decision not to apply. It was as if a huge weight had been lifted from my shoulders. Had I been elevated to the Senior Inspector's position, I would have had even less time to spend with my family and when I *was* at home I'd no doubt be as grumpy as a bulldog with toothache. It had crossed my mind that Geraldine might have put in for the job. With the usual veil of secrecy that she wrapped herself in she had given nothing away, but whoever had been offered the job was taking a very long time to make up his or her mind. The office would close for Christmas the following week and we were still in the dark as to who Harold's successor would be. Secret meetings had taken place at County Hall which even Julie and her network of informants could not penetrate. It all seemed very mysterious.

Another reason for my good humour was the Quaker meeting house. The nightmare scenario of my standing at the gate of Peewit Cottage facing a coachload of American Quakers who had come to see the famous historic building had faded like the bad dream that it was. In fact, Harry had not referred to the subject on any of his frequent visits, nor had it been mentioned by anyone in the village. It was a great weight off my mind.

There was reason to feel a little optimistic concerning the proposed closure of Hawksrill School as well. Everything had gone uncharacteristically quiet at County Hall but Julie's informants had told her that, largely due to the fuss the Action Group had caused, the plans for closure had apparently been delayed. Of course, she was told, she mustn't breathe a word. So that was something else to make me feel happy about.

Then there was the gammy knee. Although it still ached after a long day, it was feeling a whole lot better. Christine was not enamoured by the flesh-coloured elastic stocking which I permanently wore, but it had certainly helped relieve the pain. Dr Sadler had arranged, within a week, for me to see a specialist at Fettlesham Royal Infirmary.

'I'm very impressed with the speed with which you've been able to see me,' I had told the Senior Registrar, as he prodded and poked my kneecap. 'I thought I'd have to wait weeks to see a specialist.'

He had smiled like a hungry vampire. 'We see patients pretty promptly, Mr Phinn,' he had told me, 'but you will probably have to wait some time until we can operate. Months, rather than weeks, I'm afraid.'

'Pardon?'

'You'll be on the waiting list for an operation. Your knee problem is not life-threatening, you see, so it may be quite some time before we get around to sorting it out.'

'Well, I guess I can live with that,' I had said.

'I'm afraid you'll have to,' he had replied, not letting the smile slip.

'What are you thinking about?' Christine asked now.

'Oh, just how lucky I am.'

We sat there just enjoying the warmth and closeness of each other.

'You know what this room needs?' she said suddenly.

'What?'

'The ticking of a clock.'

'A clock?'

'Yes, and I don't just mean a clock on the mantelpiece, but a grandfather clock. My grandparents had one, and on its face was an old-fashioned sailing ship—you know, fully rigged—which went up and down on the waves as the clock tick-tocked. I used to watch it for hours. A grandfather clock would look just right in the corner. It would tick away reassuringly.'

'And strike in the middle of the night and wake up little Lizzie,' I added.

'No, our baby will sleep like a top.'

'I don't think we can afford a grandfather clock at the moment, darling,' I told her. 'Maybe in a couple of years.'

'Yes,' she sighed. 'It was just a thought.'

It was a thought, however, which firmly planted itself in my head. I, too, liked the idea of a grandfather clock but I wasn't going to admit it to Christine. It would be a surprise. She would wake up on Christmas morning with a grandfather clock tick-tocking and chiming in the corner.

*　　　*　　　*

The following Saturday, on the pretext of completing an urgent report at the office, I set off for Roper's Salesroom in Collington to look for a

301

grandfather clock. I always enjoyed browsing around auction houses, running my hand along the smooth oak tables and mahogany chests of drawers, sitting in beautifully-carved balloon-back chairs, breathing in the smell of old furniture and beeswax, and watching the dealers pricing up the furniture and bargain hunters rootling through the boxes of bric-à-brac. Sometimes I just sat there, being buoyed up by watching other people bid against each other. I never bought anything expensive—just a box of old letters, some faded photographs, a dusty book given as a prize on some speech day in the dim and distant past, a couple of old-fashioned fountain pens, a handsome inkwell (damaged).

Once I bought, for a pound, a dog-eared exercise book with hard black covers, written by a soldier fighting in the trenches in the First World War. There are tender poems, vivid accounts and horrific descriptions. It is a gem. Books such as this, of no real value in itself, tells the story of a soldier now dead and gone and probably forgotten. There is no name, no details of his regiment, just page after page of copperplate handwriting. One would have thought that such a poignant record of his experiences would have been treasured by his family instead of ending up as part of a job lot at an auction house. As I turn the yellowing pages of the book, I think with sadness of that young man and of the horrors he had experienced, and I wonder if he ever did return home to the young woman in his poems, the girl he loved.

I had another reason for being rather sentimental about Roper's Salesroom, of course. It was where, three years earlier, I had caught sight of the person I would come to love—the stunning young woman with soft blonde hair and dazzling blue eyes who was now my wife.

The salesroom now was full of prospective buyers hoping to buy one or more of the pieces of the elegant and expensive-looking furniture on display. Perhaps someone had the wall-space for one of the huge oil paintings of solemn-faced individuals or dark landscapes in ornate gold frames: some were as big as the end wall in our sitting-room. There were sculptured bronzes, shimmering crystal and delicate porcelain but none of that interested me this time. My eye was immediately caught by two grandfather clocks which looked as if they had come straight out of the palace at Versailles. I read the catalogue description of the first:

'A Georgian eight-day long-case clock in exquisite condition, the twelve-inch brass arched dial having a silvered chapter ring with subsidiary seconds ring and calendar aperture incorporated into the unusual matted centre. The arched top is centred by a convex silvered plaque inscribed by the master craftsman Wilfred Dowson of Tickhill and flanked by scrolling dolphin mounts with ornate spandrels to the corners and engraved bands of imbricated leaves to the borders. The pagoda hood, surmounted by globe finials, has fluted columns . . .'

And so it went on for another three paragraphs. It was all gobbledegook to me. I just wanted a plain grandfather clock that worked.

'It's a beautiful piece, isn't it?' said a distinguished-looking man standing next to me. He wore an expensive woollen overcoat hanging from

303

his shoulders; beneath I could see an equally expensive black-stripe suit and a red-and-white spotted silk bow tie. 'Interested are you?'

'Yes,' I replied.

'What age do you think it is?'

'I'm afraid I've no idea,' I replied. 'I'm no expert on clocks, but it *is* splendid.'

The man, who was obviously interested in the piece himself, clearly thought that I was intending to make a bid for the clock. He realised now that I posed no threat. 'I should say *circa* 1775,' he informed me. 'More late Georgian than early. I'm looking for a companion for my flame mahogany long-case. The one I have has a painted moon roller with phases of the moon.'

'You don't say!'

'With Rococo scroll spandrels and dentil moulded hood.'

My companion obviously knew his clocks and was intent on demonstrating as much to me.

'How much do you think this clock will fetch?' I asked him.

He sucked in his breath. 'Oh, anything between two and three, I should think.'

'Hundred?'

He wagged his index finger at me and chortled. 'You're a tease.'

'You mean thousands?'

'Of course,' he replied.

'It's way beyond my pocket,' I told him. 'I just want a plain, ordinary grandfather clock.'

'They're called long-case clocks, to be correct, and I think you will find there are very, very few which are plain and ordinary. Each one is unique. They didn't come off a production line, you know.

However, you might try the new shop that's just opened in Station Parade in Brindcliffe. I bought a very attractive oak-cased bracket clock from there only last week. Very reasonable prices. The chap deals mostly in mantel clocks but I did notice he has a long-case, a little the worse for wear but it might be the thing you're looking for. Might have gone by now, of course. If it *is* still for sale, just make sure it's not been cobbled together. You know, the top of one, the bottom of another, the workings of a third. He seemed a decent enough sort, helpful and all that, but just make sure.'

'Thank you, thank you very much,' I said, 'I'll pop along there now.'

As I made my way out of the crowded showroom I heard an unmistakably strident voice. A woman with a florid face and bright copper-coloured perm was haranguing the poor young man behind the counter, who was trying to deal with prospective bidders. It was Connie, and I stopped to listen.

'What I want to know is why these medals are so small?' Connie demanded. 'Why didn't my father get big ones like everybody else?'

'He would have done, madam,' the young man told her. 'These are miniatures.'

'Well, why are they miniatures?' snapped Connie. 'Why aren't they full size?'

'If I might explain,' sighed the man. 'Your father will have been awarded the medals full size but he would wear the miniature versions for formal occasions, like regimental dinners and such.'

'Oh, I see,' said Connie, mollified. 'So they're not his proper medals?'

'No, madam, just smaller versions.'

'Now I come to think of it,' said Connie, 'he did

have some others, bigger ones. I think they're in a drawer at home. I must look them out.'

'I see here he was awarded the Military Medal,' said the young man.

'He was a brave man, my father,' said Connie. 'He lived in a cellar for a week at Dunkirk with nothing but a pound of sugar and rain water.'

'Really?' said the young man. 'And are you interested in selling the medals, madam?'

'What?'

'Put them in the auction?'

'I most certainly am not!' cried Connie. 'Sell my father's medals! Over my dead body.' With that she scooped up the items in question and headed for the door.

'Hello, Connie,' I said, coming up behind her.

'Oh, it's you. Did you hear what he said about me selling my father's medals? I only came in to see what they were and how much they might be worth and he nearly had them out of my hand.'

'Some people have to sell them,' I said. 'It's sad, but they need the money.'

'I'd sooner live on bread and water than part with Dad's medals,' she replied. 'The very thought!'

'Can I give you a lift?' I asked. 'I have to go through the town centre to get to Brindcliffe. I'm looking for a clock for Christine.'

She clearly wasn't listening. 'Sell my father's medals indeed!' she mumbled to herself, and I had to repeat my offer. 'Oh well, thanks, if I'm not putting you out.' Then, as we walked to the car park, she said, 'I'm glad I've bumped into you.'

'Not in trouble, am I?' I asked.

'No, it's me what's got problems,' she told me. She tried not to look concerned but she clearly was.

306

'I wasn't going to say anything but my Ted said I ought to mention it. It's been on my mind for quite some time now.'

'Whatever is it, Connie?' I asked.

'Serious allegations have been made about me,' she said.

'I beg your pardon?'

'Allegations that I went swanning off on holiday to France and had not got proper permission. I got back after trying to scatter Dad's ashes, in my highly peturberant state of mind, to find this very unpleasant letter waiting for me. Some nasty piece of work had words down at the Education Office, making allegations, and I got this written warning from them in Personnel.'

'But that's over two months ago!' I exclaimed, knowing all too well who was behind it. 'Why didn't you say anything earlier?'

'As I've said, I've been thinking things over. Brooding, my Ted says. Dealing with Dad's medals just now has brought it all back. I reckon it's about time I packed in the caretaking at the Centre. I'm not getting any younger and receiving nasty letters like that, after all I do, is very upsetting.'

'Don't be too hasty about packing in the job, Connie,' I said. 'We'll get it sorted out. I'm sure that when Dr Gore knows why you went to France and—'

'Oh, I've written to him. After brooding about it for a bit, I sent a letter just this last week. Speak to the organ-grinder not the monkey is what Dad always used to say. I've told him that they can stick the job. They just don't appreciate the hours I put in at the Centre.'

'But we do, Connie,' I said reassuringly. 'We

think you do a brilliant job.'

'Not so sure about that,' she said through tight lips. 'I reckon it was Mr Clamp what reported me after all that carry-on with the nudes.'

'No, Connie,' I said. 'Mr Clamp might be difficult and untidy, and lots of other things besides, but he wouldn't do such a mean-minded thing as reporting you.'

'Well, somebody's been making serious allegations about me,' said Connie, 'and I'll tell you this, when I find out who the alligator is I shall give them a real piece of my mind.'

* * *

Just Clocks was sandwiched between a health food shop and a dry cleaners on Station Parade. Its newly painted front, dark green with gold lettering above the door, stood out from the rest of the shops in the arcade. In the window a single clock was displayed—a large and impressive gilt metal mantel clock, inlaid with mother-of-pearl and standing on a black marble base. As I turned the door handle, I resigned myself to the fact that the long-case clock I had come to view would be way out of my price range. But I had come all this way, so nothing ventured . . .

The bell tinkled discreetly as I entered and then a voice came from the back. 'I'll be with you in one moment.' I stopped in my tracks. I had heard that voice before. It was distinctive: deep, resonant, authoritative. Before I could escape, a lean, sallow-complexioned man with heavy-lidded eyes and black, carefully-parted hair emerged from behind the red velvet curtain which separated the

308

showroom from the back of the shop. It was like the entrance of the villain at a pantomime.

'Mr Frobisher!' I gasped.

'Mr Phinn,' he said calmly.

We stood staring at each other for a moment and then we spoke together.

'I was—' I started.

'I hope—' he started.

We were saved further embarrassment by the bell as another customer entered, a small woman in a bright headscarf and large furry boots. 'I'm looking for a clock?' she said.

'I'll just have a look round,' I said to Mr Frobisher, relieved by the interruption. 'Please go ahead and deal with this customer.' The thought entered my head that I could wander casually to the door, pretending to look at the nearby clocks and exit quietly, but that would be cowardly, so I crossed the room to peer at the fine selection of timepieces on display. There were bronze mantel clocks, intricately inlaid bracket clocks, portico clocks under glass domes, enamelled table clocks, mahogany-cased clocks, chiming bracket clocks, round wooden wall clocks, small brass carriage clocks, lantern clocks, clocks of every size and shape and colour. Despite my genuine interest, my mind was buzzing with wondering what I would say to the man who I had driven out of teaching.

'I want a clock for my niece who's getting married,' the woman said. 'Wedding present. Something a bit different but nothing too big and certainly not too pricey. That pink and gold one in the window is a bit too fancy for my taste but I like the shape.'

'Ah, yes, the French mantel clock,' said Mr

Frobisher, smiling slightly. 'Yes, it is rather ornate and not to everyone's taste. Perhaps a trifle expensive, too.'

The woman pointed to an exquisite bronze and marble timepiece. 'That's quite nice. How much is that one?' she asked.

'Four hundred and twenty pounds.'

'What?' she gasped. 'Four hundred and twenty pounds?'

'You will find, madam,' said Mr Frobisher, 'that these are fine quality antique timepieces and, as such, are expensive.'

'I'll try the Co-op,' she said bluntly and left.

Mr Frobisher then turned his attention to me. 'Now then,' he said, looking me straight in the eye.

'How are you?' I asked. It sounded so feeble.

'Well, as you see, I'm pretty well.'

'It's a lovely shop.'

'Yes, it is.'

I coughed nervously. This was a nightmare. 'I did ring the school a couple of times to have a word with you, but you were not available. I meant to say—'

'Please, please, Mr Phinn, don't look so abashed. You really don't need to say anything.'

'I wanted to explain—'

'Your visit to King Henry's College was quite possibly one of the best things that could have happened to me.'

'Really?'

'In a strange and rather unexpected sort of way, that is,' he added. 'No teacher likes to be told he is not up to scratch. I have to admit at first I was hurt, very hurt by your report and by what I considered to be some quite unfounded comments. Then I

310

thought to myself, it was only the judgement of one person who had observed just one lesson, one person who has not had a great deal of experience in school inspection. Then I became angry, particularly when Mr Nelson seemed to accept without question what you had said. He had spoken to me a few times about my work but nothing of any consequence. I rather thought that he would spring to my defence but, sadly, he did not, no more than members of the English Faculty or my union representative. I found that the hardest. You really come to know who your friends are in situations like that. I know I was not the best teacher in the world, Mr Phinn, and, I have to admit that over the past few years I have been ground down, like many teachers, I expect, by the incessant paperwork, the interference of so-called experts, negative media reports, objectionable parents and the deteriorating behaviour of the pupils. However, I always thought I did a decent enough job. But that's by the by. Water under the bridge, so to speak.' Mr Frobisher took out a large blue handkerchief and blew his nose noisily. 'When I was offered early retirement with a pension enhancement and a lump sum, I got to thinking that perhaps all this was for the best. Did I really want to go on for a few more years quite demoralised and depressed? I had toyed with the idea of opening a shop for some time. My father was a great collector of timepieces and I, too, am fascinated by them. Indeed, the prospect of clearing out all the clocks from the house was very attractive, not least to my wife.' He paused for a moment and took a long, deep breath. 'My wife is not a well woman, and retiring early meant I could

311

spend more time with her. Time is very precious for one who has a limited amount. So why, I thought, should I not do something I really wanted to do and spend more time at home? The bank manager was most helpful, the premises came up for rent and, as you see, here I am and I have never felt more contented.'

'Well, I'm very pleased it has worked out for you, Mr Frobisher,' I said, and meant it.

'And here you are,' he said. 'Not here to inspect me again, I hope.'

'No, no,' I said hastily. 'I'm looking for a clock and I think I've seen just the one.' I turned in the direction of the grandfather clock in the corner.

'Ah, the long-case clock. Not very old. Nineteenth century. Quite plain but no less attractive for all that. Unusual painted dial, eight-day movement and signed Percy Farrington of Fettlesham. Some superficial damage to the case and at the top but the piece is all original, I can vouch for that.'

'I was at Roper's Salesroom earlier today looking at the clocks but they were a bit too expensive and, to be honest, rather too fancy for my taste.'

'Ah, you like plain things, Mr Phinn?' asked Mr Frobisher. 'This clock, in fact, came from Roper's. I bought it a couple of years ago and it's been standing in my lounge ticking away as regular as clockwork, if you will excuse the cliché. Actually, it's not been in the shop long. I have the provenance which is always of interest to buyers. It was a young man who sold it. Apparently he used to keep his cricket bats in it.' He looked at it almost lovingly. 'You would have thought he would have

312

wanted to keep the clock, wouldn't you. It was a part of his life, his boyhood. It has memories. But there's no accounting for people, is there?'

'No,' I replied. 'There isn't.'

'Now, I expect you wish to know the price. Let me see.' Mr Frobisher consulted a ledger on the counter and ran a long finger down the page. 'Five hundred and fifty pounds. If you purchase it, I would, of course, deliver the clock and ensure that it works well in its new home. Long-case clocks are a trifle temperamental, you know. Rather like people. All different, all with their own personalities.' He stroked the side gently as he might a treasured pet. 'They have to be positioned correctly, standing perfectly upright. They have to be looked after. If they are cared for, they will go on and on. I'll be sorry to see this clock go. It has a very companionable presence.'

The man had become animated as he talked about his clocks. He gestured with his hands. His eyes shone. He smiled. Had he only shown the same enthusiasm with his pupils that he showed for his clocks, I thought sadly, he would still be teaching.

CHAPTER NINETEEN

It was a bitterly cold January afternoon when I visited Mertonbeck Primary School. The overnight frost was still white on the ground. I drove deep into the dale along a narrow twisting road with a great rolling frosty expanse stretching out before me, and upwards to the curving shadowy woods

313

and bare distant fells. As I approached the village, the road rose steeply and took a sharp turn by an old stone farmhouse drenched in a great mass of twisting ivy. I had just negotiated the bend when an ancient tractor trundled out through the farm gate, right into my path. I skidded to a halt and we ended up almost alongside each other.

The farmer, a man with a red-roughened complexion and heavy grey stubble, surveyed me for a moment, before shaking his head. I had seen that face countless times before, a face seasoned by the weather, lined like leather and full of character. I could imagine this man striding out for miles across fields and moors, negotiating walls and crossing becks, living in the open, rain or shine. Here was the archetypal Dales farmer—craggy-faced, tough as old boots, with a bluntness, integrity and cheerful good humour. That day, however, the good humour was absent.

''Ast there been a deeath, then?' he asked, leaning forward and resting his arms on the steering wheel. His dog, a lean black and white collie which was perched beside him, fixed me with dark intelligent eyes.

'Pardon?'

'Is t'somebody deead?'

'Not that I know of,' I replied.

'Well, tha wants to slow down, otherwise there will be. Rooads are treacherous at this time o'year. It's like a bloody ice rink. Wherever tha're off to, it'll still be theer when tha gets theer. Tha not driving round Piccadilly bloody Circus, tha knaas.'

'Yes, I'm sorry, I *was* driving too fast.'

'Too fast!' he cackled. 'Tha came round that corner like a jack rabbit wi' t'runs. It's a bad bend is

314

that, an' icy an' all. There's sheep on these rooads and cattle and dogs. They don't use zebra crossings, tha knaas.'

I felt like a naughty schoolboy being reprimanded by the headteacher. It did occur to me that the farmer could have considered the possibility that there just might be someone else on the road and that he could have sounded his horn as a warning to other road users or even stopped to check that the road was clear before pulling out, but I did not wish to prolong the conversation. 'Yes, I'm sorry. I'll take more care in future.'

The farmer, scratching his stubble, was clearly not going to let me off so lightly. 'Mi dog were killed on this rooad a couple o' years back,' he announced grimly. 'Trying to get t'sheep into yonder field. She went back for a lazy yow and were knocked ovver by one of you speedin' motorists.' The collie beside him cocked an ear as if listening. 'Aye, and she were a champion dog were Meg.'

'I'm very sorry,' I replied feebly. 'Er . . . I wonder if you might move your tractor. I do have an appointment and I'm running a little late.'

'Better late than deead,' he observed.

'Yes,' I agreed.

'Well, tek it easy down t'hill or tha'll end up in t'watter.'

He reversed the tractor slowly and laboriously back into the farm entrance, and man and dog watched me as I drove off, at a snail's pace, down the hill and towards the village.

I knew what he meant by ending up 'in t'watter'. Ahead of me lay the clustered village, beyond which a great blue expanse shimmered in the cold afternoon sunlight. The reservoir was bounded by

315

high fells clothed in dark pine woods. What a place to live, I thought.

I had visited Mertonbeck Primary School three years before to test the children's reading as part of a survey on standards of literacy. The infant children had joined me one by one to talk a little about their reading interests, read a couple of pages from their books and to complete some word recognition tests. Standards had been exceptionally high and the subsequent report had been glowing.

That afternoon I was there to see if these standards had been maintained. I had informed the headteacher, a bright and enthusiastic young woman called Jean Potter, that I was particularly interested in the children's speaking and listening skills.

Mertonbeck Primary School lay in the very heart of the village, a small stone building with a dark grey slate roof, and enclosed by shiny iron railings. The interior was typical of many small Dales schools: one large square room, a floor of well-worn, polished wooden blocks, a high beamed ceiling and long mullioned windows. Mrs Potter was watching for my arrival and came down the path to greet me.

'I'm sorry I'm a bit late, Mrs Potter,' I said. 'I had to go slowly because of the treacherous road conditions.'

As the words came out, I remembered the farmer's remonstrations and felt a guilty flush creep up my face. Luckily Mrs Potter didn't notice as she was leading the way into the classroom. 'I thought that by the afternoon the frost would have gone.'

'Oh, Mr Phinn,' chuckled the headteacher, 'you

316

still have a lot to learn about the weather in the Dales, you really do.'

Sitting quietly with folded arms and straight backs was a class of healthy-looking, bright-eyed children.

'We've had quite a few changes since you were last here,' explained the headteacher. 'If you recall, we were then all in the one room, infants and juniors together, but our little number has increased so much in the last couple of years that we now have a separate classroom, only temporary, at the back. You won't know Mrs Cooper. She was appointed last September, on a temporary contract, to teach the infants this year. She came with excellent references and apparently has had a great deal of experience. You'll be seeing her later.' I could tell by a slight edge in her voice that the headteacher was not overly impressed with her new colleague.

Mrs Potter turned to the children who were still sitting motionless and silent, and said in a loud and cheerful voice, 'Shall we all say a nice big "Good afternoon" to Mr Phinn, children, and make him feel really welcome.'

'Good afternoon, Mr Phinn,' chanted the boys and girls. This seemed to be a sort of signal for them to relax, for they unfolded their arms and shuffled in their chairs.

'Good afternoon,' I replied, smiling at them.

'Well, Mr Phinn,' said Mrs Potter, 'if you would care to make yourself comfortable on my chair, we'll get started.' She put her hand on the shoulder of a gangly boy with ears like cup handles, who was twirling his pencil between his thumb and forefinger. 'Pencil down, please, Darren,' she said, fixing him with a face which said 'Beware'. The teacher's voice was a little sharper in tone. 'You might like to tell Mr Phinn what we have been doing.'

The boy turned and gave me a tired look. 'Legends,' he announced somewhat unenthusiastically. 'We've been writing about local legends and folklore.'

'Sounds very interesting,' I said.

'Aye,' said the boy laconically.

'And today we're reading out our final drafts to the whole class,' added Mrs Potter, smiling broadly, 'in a confident, clear and interesting way.'

The first speaker, a plump girl with a pale, heart-shaped face and large, round spectacles, came to the front clutching a wodge of paper and announced with great assurance, 'I'm going to tell you about the legend of "The Lost Village". It is a famous story told to me by my Nanna Harrison.' Here was a future teacher in the making, I thought, as she looked over the top of her spectacles, cleared her throat, paused for effect and then began.

'Many, many years ago, there was a beautiful village near here. It was set deep in the dale, and all around were rolling green hills. The village had little stone houses, a shop, an old church with a tall, tall spire, and a cobbled market place with a fountain. One day, a beggar came into the village. He had walked a long way and was hungry and thirsty. He went from house to house, asking for something to eat and drink, and shoes for his poor swollen feet. But everyone slammed their doors against him. When the beggar went to drink from the fountain, the people set their dogs on him.

318

'Just outside the village, halfway up the hill, was an old stone cottage and here a woman called Sarah Merton lived. She took pity on the beggar when she saw him lean over to drink from the muddy stream which ran outside her house, and gave him food and clothes. He thanked her, but before setting off again he turned and pointed down the hill to the beautiful little village.

"Not one cup of water,
Not one crust of bread,
Not one pair of tattered shoes,
Nor a cot to rest my head.
I place my curse upon that town;
Ye waters rise, ye people drown."

'The next day it began to rain, and for forty days and forty nights rain poured down. Streams burst their banks, gardens were swept away, fields became swamps and the road became a foaming river. When the rain stopped, the beautiful little village had disappeared and in its place was a great lake. The only house for miles around was Sarah Merton's cottage, and it is still there today.'

The girl paused for a moment, peered through the large spectacles and said, 'You may not think that is a true story, but sometimes at dusk, if you listen carefully, you will hear the distant moaning and groaning of the drowned people. Sometimes when it has been very hot, and the streams have shrivelled to a trickle, you might see the top of the church spire rising above the water. And my Nanna says she once heard the muffled clanging of the church bell.' There was total silence in the classroom. 'That's it,' she said, before folding her sheets of paper and returning to her desk.

'I think a round of applause is in order for that wonderful story,' said Mrs Potter, vigorously smacking her hands together. 'Well done, Sandra, that was a splendid effort.'

The teacher pointed to a sturdy-looking boy with shiny dark hair and large pale eyes. 'Now, James, your turn next. Let us hear your legend.'

The boy rather reluctantly made his way to the front of the room and turned to face the class. He shuffled, huffed and puffed and began. 'This is t'legend of Brave Bess. Mi granddad told me this story and I wrote it down.' He sniffed, rubbed his chin and, with brow furrowed in concentration, began to read.

'It was t'year of t'Great Winter. T'snow began to fall and soon t'land were like a white blanket. Billy Goodwin, who were a bit owlder than me at t'time, set off early one raw morning in a wuthering wind, with 'is father who were t'shepherd. 'Is father was a reight big sturdy man, used to t'bitter winters but that winter were one o' t'worst. Course 'e didn't like goin' out on such a day but 'e 'ad to get 'is sheep in. They took with 'em Billy's dog, Bess.'

'I've heard this story, miss,' cried a girl in the front desk. 'It's really good.'

'Well, let James finish it, Jade,' said the teacher. 'No more interruptions, please.'

'Shall I go on, miss?' asked the boy. The teacher nodded. 'Snow was falling fast and t'icy wind began to blow more fiercely. They wanted t'sheep in safely afore a blizzard set in. By lunchtime they 'ad gathered all t'flock and were 'eading for 'ome when a swirling mist come down. As they got lower down t'fell out o' t'mist, they noticed some sheep 'ad

320

strayed. Billy whistled for Bess and sent 'er back up t'fell into t'mist after t'lost sheep. After a short while, some sheep could be seen joining t'flock, but there were no sign of Bess. Billy whistled and whistled but Bess were nowhere to be seen. They carried on down t'fellside until they were back at t'farm. When they counted t'flock, they 'ad every last sheep, but there were still no Bess. "'Ow can this be?" asked t'shepherd. They waited and waited for Bess but she nivver did come back. Nivver! That were t'last Billy Goodwin's father saw of 'er.'

The child paused dramatically and from the back of the classroom came a faint sob. 'But that's not t'end of t'story,' said James hurriedly. 'Not by a long chalk. Many years later, and I'm talkin' ovver fifty or sixty, Billy Goodwin was again up on t'fell on a raw winter's day just like t'one before, when t'snow was falling thick and fast and an icy wind were blowing. Anyroad, 'e told 'is son to hurry on down wi' t'sheep and 'e'd follow on behind as fast as 'e could, but 'e were an old man now and couldn't move so fast across t'rough ground. Before 'e 'ad gone far, a thick mist suddenly come down just like it'd done when 'e were a lad. 'E got completely lost, not knowing whether to go right nor left. Soon, very cold and shiverin', 'e 'uddled into a little rocky hollow out of t'bitter wind and decided to wait for t'mist to clear. 'E 'ad 'ardly been crouched there for a minute when 'e saw 'er. It were Bess, 'is sheepdog from long ago. 'E stood up and went towards 'er but she moved away from 'im. "'Ere, girl," 'e called to 'er but she kept moving on, just ahead of 'im. Following 'er through t'thick mist, 'e made 'is way down t'fell. When 'e dropped below t'mist, Billy found 'imself just above t'farm

321

but there were no sign of Bess. She 'ad disappeared again. Billy realised that she'd come to show 'im t'way 'ome, that she 'ad saved 'im. And does tha know what?'

'No,' chorused the class, transfixed.

'When 'e looked into snow, there were 'is footprints, as big as owt, but there weren't a sign of any paw prints, not one.'

*　　*　　*

Later, I found the opportunity to speak to James.

'That was a remarkable legend,' I told him.

'Aye, it's not bad, is it?' he said.

'Do you live on a farm?'

'I do.'

'With lots of sheep?'

'Aye.'

'I reckon you know quite a lot about sheep.'

'Aye, I reckon I do.'

'And sheepdogs.'

'Aye.'

Not a very chatty lad, I thought, but I persevered. 'And have you got a dog, like the boy in the legend?'

'No, but mi dad 'as.'

'And what's his name?'

'Mi dad or t'dog's?'

'The dog's name. What's he called?'

'She. It's a bitch called Jess. Five-year-old. Won quite a few trials afore she were two-year.' I was about to ask another question when James continued. 'Bitches are better than dogs, tha knaas, when it comes to managing sheep, that is.'

'Really?'

'Oh, aye.'

'Why is that, then?' I asked, staring into the large pale eyes.

'They listen better, work harder and are quieter. Mi grandma reckons it's t'same with 'umans but mi granddad wunt agree.'

The boy chewed his thumb for a moment and stared out of the window. He was in no hurry to continue. I remembered what Harold had said to me early on in my career about giving children breathing space, not being too quick to come in with another question, so I paused and took in the view. We sat there together staring at the expanse of frosted greens, the distant hills capped in grey clouds.

'Grand i'n't it?' observed the boy. 'Aye, you need a quiet dog. Can't 'ave an animal that goes snappin' and yappin' and barkin' and chasin' after t'sheep, otherwise they spook 'em. You need a dog who can see well and listen well and be able to "eye" t'sheep.'

'What does that mean?' I asked. 'To "eye" a sheep?'

'Well, keep 'em together, not let 'em wander off. Now, mi dad's dog, Jess, she can "eye" champion. She can manage a large flock or a few strays and pick out a sheep belonging to another farm as easy as owt. Aye, there's not much she can't fettle. She can find a sheep buried deep down in t'snow.'

'How does she do that then?'

'Well, she stops dead still as soon as she scents owt. It's called "settin"'. She just freezes, yelps a little bit, and then we dig. Sheep can be as much as ten or fifteen feet down but a good dog will find it.'

'She sounds a remarkable animal,' I said.

'Aye, took after 'er mother. Meg were just t'same. Killed she was at top o'rooad by a right stupid speedin' driver.'

*　　　*　　　*

Later I joined Mrs Cooper in the temporary infant classroom at the back of the little school. The classroom was an unattractive barn of a place and entirely out of keeping with the rest of the neat stone building. Perched on six large concrete blocks and constructed of dark panelled wood the colour of gravy, it looked like an old shed. The only difference was that this ugly construction had huge square windows on all sides.

Mrs Cooper, a good-looking, middle-aged woman with a hennish bosom and brassy blonde hair, had made little effort to make the interior of the hut bright and cheerful. There were no displays of large, coloured paintings, no glossy posters, no children's work on the wall space that existed, just a few lists of words and rules of the classroom.

'I wish you could do something about this hut, Mr Phinn,' she told me as we waited for the children to come in after afternoon playtime. 'It's like a furnace in summer and a freezer in winter. What we need is a proper extension in keeping with the character of the school.'

'I agree, Mrs Cooper,' I said, 'but, as in most things, it comes down to money. The county has to make big cuts in the budget next year. For some schools that means closure. With your increase in numbers there's no threat of that hanging over you but, you are right, an extension is needed.' I looked out of the window. 'And at least you've got the

324

view.'

She glanced fleetingly at the magnificent landscape which lay beyond. At this point, I noticed that her desk was positioned so it faced not the awesome panorama but a muddy track leading to some dilapidated farm building which effectively blocked out any view.

'Why don't you have your desk facing the fells?' I asked.

The teacher seemed rather taken aback. 'Well . . . because I prefer it where it is.'

'But you could look out on such beauty every day,' I foolishly continued, 'rather than onto a somewhat depressing scene.'

'I really don't think it's part of my job, Mr Phinn, to stare idly at the view all day. I have children to teach. I like my desk where it is. Now, I believe this afternoon you are particularly interested in the children's speaking and listening skills. Well, I think you'll find we have no problems in the speaking area. The listening is quite another matter. It's sometimes difficult to shut them up. I might be old-fashioned, Mr Phinn, but I think there is a time for children to speak and a time for them to sit still and be quiet.'

I spent the first part of the lesson listening to the children read, talking to them and looking at their books and I was not impressed. When the teacher announced it was time for the story, I positioned myself in the corner to watch the lesson. Mrs Cooper introduced me without any fuss and then settled the children down in a circle before her on a square of carpet.

'It's story-time, Mr Phinn,' she told me. 'I feel it is important that children learn to sit still, concentrate and listen, don't you agree? David, will you stop wriggling about as if you have ants in your pants and, Gemma, use your handkerchief, please. It's not very ladylike to wipe your nose where you are wiping it. You haven't got a handkerchief? Well, get a tissue from my desk. As I was saying, Mr Phinn, story-time develops the children's concentration and listening skills and, of course, introduces them to new words and interesting phrases.'

I felt that Mrs Cooper should get on with the story and leave the justification of what she was doing until later. The children were getting restless. David had shuffled off the carpet and was polishing the floor with his bottom. Gemma had returned to wiping her nose on the sleeve of her cardigan. 'Now, before I start,' said Mrs Cooper, 'can we all sit up nicely. Straight backs, please. All eyes this way. Onto the carpet, please, David. Gemma, I won't tell you again! Have you got a tissue? Well, will you use it, please? John, I did not say lie on your back as if you're sunbathing. Sit up. Right, I think we are all ready.' The teacher paused for effect and began to read the story from a rather shabby-looking picture book. 'Once upon a time, children, long long ago there lived a—'

'Big ugly monster, miss?'

It was David, the wriggler, who was waving his hand madly in the air like a palm tree in a tornado.

'No, David, not a big ugly monster. It was a beautiful princess called Imelda. Princess Imelda had eyes as bright and as green as sparkling emeralds. She had hair which fell down her back like a golden waterfall. Her hands were long and thin and her skin was as white as—'

'A ghost's, miss?' volunteered David.

'No, not a ghost's, David,' replied the teacher, putting on an overly patient voice. 'Her skin was as white as the snow which covered the fields. Her lips were as red as—'

'Blood, miss!' piped up the child.

'David! *Will* you listen, please? You are spoiling our story with your interruptions. It was not blood. Princess Imelda's lips were as red as the cherries which covered the trees in her garden.'

Gemma ceased her nose-wiping for a moment to observe, 'Miss, there wouldn't be cherries on the trees if it was winter.'

'There would in this country, Gemma,' replied the teacher firmly. 'It was a magic country where fruit grew all the year round. But Princess Imelda was lonely. How she longed for someone with whom to play. Great tears rolled down her soft skin. "Ah me, ah me," she sighed sadly, "if only I had someone to play with and be my friend. It's so lonely being a princess."'

'Miss, I'd like to be a princess,' Gemma informed the class.

'I'm sure you would, but princesses don't wipe their noses on the sleeves of their cardigans. Get another tissue, will you, please.'

The child scurried to the front, plucked a tissue from the box on the teacher's desk and returned to her position on the carpet.

'Give your nose a good blow, Gemma. Now, where were we? Ah, yes. But the days passed and Princess Imelda grew sadder and sadder, sitting all alone watching from her tall tower. Then one day something happened—'

'Did she fall out, miss?' asked David.

The teacher closed her eyes for a moment then took another breath. 'No, she did not fall out, David. She saw in the distance a great cloud of smoke.'

'A fire-eating dragon come to eat her up!'

'David!' snapped the teacher. 'Come down here and sit at the front and listen! Thank you. You know, Mr Phinn,' observed Mrs Cooper, looking over the children's heads in my direction, 'sometimes the children get so involved in the story that they can't contain themselves.'

I could not imagine anyone getting excited about the insipid Princess Imelda sitting at the top of her castle feeling sorry for herself all day. What a tiresome story compared to the legends I had heard the older children read that afternoon.

*   *   *

I stayed for a while after school to talk to the two teachers individually and give an overview of what I had seen. In the first meeting with Mrs Potter I was able to reassure the headteacher that standards in the junior department were still very high and the subsequent report would be positive. The second interview, with the stony-faced Mrs Cooper, proved to be much more difficult. I began by informing the teacher in question that the standard of work and the quality of the teaching in the infants were just about satisfactory but that there was room for major improvements. If the look Mrs Cooper gave me could maim, I would have left the school on crutches. Before I could continue she launched into a diatribe. 'In fact,' she concluded, 'I suggest you have a go at teaching them, Mr Phinn. It's all very well making all these critical comments. You don't have the children, day in and day out. These farming children can be very difficult and demanding. They have far too much to say for themselves, in my opinion. Yes, indeed, you want to try teaching them. As my husband, who happens to be a headteacher, always says about school inspectors, they are like eunuchs. They would like to do it, but they can't. They are just good with the advice. And now I have a home to go to.' She stood, brushed the creases out of her skirt and made for the door.

'Excuse me, Mrs Cooper,' I said, as pleasantly as possible, 'I have done you the courtesy of listening to what you have had to say. Please allow me the same consideration.' She looked startled and then plonked herself back down on the chair and stared malevolently in my direction. 'Thank you,' I said and continued with the report.

As Mrs Potter and I walked to my car a little while later, the headteacher said, 'Mrs Cooper won't be with us much longer. I think I mentioned she is on a temporary contract, thank goodness, and it will not be renewed.'

'I think I got off on the wrong foot with her,' I said. 'I quite innocently mentioned that I thought it was a shame to have her desk where she can't see the magnificent view of the fells, but she bit my head off.'

Mrs Potter raised a hand to suppress a smile, chuckled to herself and then looked behind her. 'She has the desk there for a reason,' she whispered. 'Mrs Cooper doesn't think anyone knows, but she's having a bit of a fling with a local farmer. He drives his tractor up and down that track during the day and if it's on for the evening, he gives her the thumbs up. I should think everybody in the village knows about the romance, well . . . except for Mr Cooper and the farmer's wife.'

CHAPTER TWENTY

The Royal Infirmary was a square, featureless, redbrick building on the outskirts of Fettlesham. From the reception desk, I was directed to Men's Surgical. There were four tubular metal beds in Room 15 of Ward 6, three of which were occupied. By the window, an extremely large and heavily-tattooed man with a bullet-shaped bald head and a neck as thick as a pit bull terrier's, sat propped up, reading a newspaper. He nodded in my direction as I entered. Across from him lay an emaciated individual with a deathly pallor, pained expression and closed eyes. He looked for all the world like a corpse. In the third bed was a round-faced man with cheeks so red and shiny they looked as if they had just been scrubbed. I had never seen anyone look quite as healthy. He watched me critically as I made my way to the bed opposite and started to put my various personal items in the small bedside cabinet.

'How do,' he said.

'Oh, hello,' I replied.

'Another for the butcher's knife then?'

'Yes.'

'What you in for?'

'An operation on my leg,' I told him.

330

'Varicose veins?'

'No, knee.'

'I've had varicose veins—in both legs, mind. Stripped 'em out, they did, a couple of year back. Thick as ropes, they were. My legs looked like a road map of London, there were so many blue lines. Doctor said it was a miracle I could walk before the operation. Twenty-three stitches in each leg, I had, not counting the ones around the groin. What's up with your knee, then?'

'An old rugby accident.'

'Very tricky things are knees. I've heard it's a bit of a hit and miss with knees. My cousin, Stan, had an operation on his knee and limped for the rest of his life. Had to give up his ballroom dancing. Never climbed a ladder again. Like hips are knees. Tricky. They'll probably put a plastic kneecap in. You see, your joints can be very problematical.'

'Really.'

'I'm in with haemorrhoids myself. By the heck, you know what pain is with haemorrhoids. Do you know, fifty per cent of the population have had haemorrhoids by the age of fifty.'

'Really.'

'It's a fact. Haemorrhoids are enlarged blood vessels in your anal passage.'

'Yes, I know.'

'Do you know why they're called piles?'

'I have no idea,' I said, 'but I expect you're going to tell me.'

'Because the Latin word *pila* means ball,' he explained, miming a huge ball with his hands. 'I like to go into my medical condition in some detail before I comes into hospital. Read up on it, know the facts. They pays more attention to you if they

331

think you're in the know, you know. I find the doctors are very surprised when they realise I'm genned up about my condition.'

'Fascinating,' I said.

'I've tried everything for my haemorrhoids but they are unusually stubborn, as my doctor said. In fact, in all his years of practising medicine he's never seen anything like them. I may very well be in a medical textbook. I've tried creams, suppositories, ice packs. Have you had 'em?'

'No, I haven't,' I said.

'The itching's indescribable and when you go to the toilet it's like passing glass.'

'Why don't you put a bleeding sock in it!' said the bullet-headed individual. 'You've been going on and on about your bleeding haemorrhoids all morning. You're like a bleeding gramophone record.'

'Who rattled your cage then?' asked the haemorrhoids.

'I'll come and rattle your bleeding haemorrhoids in a minute. And as for pain, you don't know what pain is. You have an 'ernia, mate, then you'll know what pain is.'

I climbed into bed. The visit to Fettlesham Royal Infirmary was going to be an experience and no mistake.

'Hernia!' snorted the haemorrhoids. 'I've had a hernia. Not one, but two, mind, and they were both strangulated. Double hernia. Twice the pain. And as for the operation, piece of cake, it's over in a minute. Now, you take the operation for haemorrhoids, I can't begin to describe—'

'Well don't,' retorted the hernia.

The haemorrhoids carried on regardless. 'They

tied rubber bands around my haemorrhoids to cut off the blood supply but that didn't work. Then they injected 'em and that didn't work, neither. Now I'm having 'em removed surgically. They put a laser gun up your backside and zap 'em. Mind you, when it's over you can kiss your haemorrhoids goodbye.'

'Could we change the record?' asked the hernia loudly. 'You're like a bleeding medical dictionary.'

At this point the emaciated individual with the pained expression opened his eyes and yawned widely.

'The Sleeping Beauty awakes,' remarked the haemorrhoids.

'I just nodded off,' he said.

'Never mind, "nodded off",' remarked the haemorrhoids, 'we thought you'd popped off!'

'Did I miss the tea trolley?'

'You look as if you need an undertaker's trolley, state you're in, squire.'

'Do you know,' said the hernia slowly and with malice, 'you really are a pain in the arse.'

'You never did say what you was in for,' said the haemorrhoids, addressing the prone figure next to him.

'No, I didn't,' replied the man, sitting up.

'Well, come on then, what's your problem?'

'I'd rather not say,' replied the man in a deeply mournful tone of voice.

'Come on,' urged the haemorrhoids, 'you're among friends.'

'It's of a very personal nature.'

'Vasectomy?'

'No.'

'Circumcision?'

'No, nothing like that.'

'Look, you can't get much more personal than haemorrhoids or more painful.'

'Oh, yes you can,' replied the man. 'Oh, yes you can.'

'For God's sake tell him,' snapped the hernia, 'and shut the bugger up.'

'I've got an anal ulcer,' announced the man without any gloss.

The haemorrhoids sucked in his breath noisily. 'Oooooh,' he groaned. 'Nasty.' He didn't open his mouth again for the next ten minutes. During the welcome period of quiet, I managed to get on with some work.

After the consultation with the specialist, I had expected to wait for quite some time for the operation but a cancellation meant I was called into hospital at short notice, which suited me fine. The sooner the knee was sorted out the better. When I had informed Harold that I was to go into hospital for the operation, he had asked me, rather tentatively, if it would be at all possible for me to check the reports I had written over Christmas for the 'Spirituality in the Curriculum' initiative before they were despatched to schools.

'If my memory serves me correctly,' he had said, 'you have a day prior to the surgery when they carry out various tests—blood pressure, cholesterol level, that sort of thing. It's a time to settle in, to relax and prepare for the operation. I was just wondering if you might be able to glance through the reports you have written. It might take your mind off the big event.'

'Of course,' I had replied and had arrived at the hospital with a large red folder with the words

334

'STRICTLY CONFIDENTIAL' and 'THE INSPECTORS' DIVISION' written in bold black letters on the cover. It was the papers in the folder that I now began reading. I soon sensed that I was being watched and, looking up, found the haemorrhoids staring intently at me.

'You're an inspector then?' he remarked.

'That's right,' I replied.

'Police?'

'No.'

'Tax?'

'No, not a tax inspector.'

'Public health?'

'No.'

'VAT?'

'No.'

'Come on, it's not a bloody quiz show. What sort of inspector are you?'

'I'm not allowed to say,' I told him, putting a finger to my lips.

'Why not?'

'It's strictly confidential.'

'Come on, what sort of inspector are you?' he persisted.

'I really can't tell you,' I said. 'It's more than my job's worth.'

'Suit yourself,' he said peevishly. Then addressing himself, he observed, 'You try and be friendly and that's all the thanks you get.'

'All right,' I said in a hushed voice, 'I'll tell you, but you must promise me not to breathe a word to anyone in the hospital.'

'Come on, then.'

'I can't shout it across the ward,' I said. 'It's strictly confidential.'

The haemorrhoids clambered out of bed and, considering his medical condition, moved with remarkable speed to my side. 'Well—' I began. At this point the tea trolley arrived. 'I'll tell you later,' I whispered.

The tea trolley had barely left the room than the haemorrhoids was at my side again, leaning over the bed, his ear in my face.

'Come on, then,' he said, 'spill the beans. What sort of inspector are you?'

'You really have to keep it to yourself,' I told him.

'Course I will,' he agreed.

'It's very hush-hush.'

'All right, all right.'

At this point, a nurse, in a dark blue uniform with pristine white collar and cuffs, entered. 'I'll tell you later,' I whispered.

'Mr Prout!' exclaimed the nurse. 'Whatever are you doing out of bed? Do you want to end up in here for another week?'

The haemorrhoids shuffled back to his bed sheepishly and clambered in. But as soon as the nurse had departed he was back at my side.

'You're like a bleeding shuttlecock,' remarked the hernia. 'Backwards and forwards.'

'I'm a hospital inspector,' I whispered conspiratorially in the haemorrhoids' ear, 'but you mustn't say anything. I wish to remain incognito, sort of under-cover.'

'Hospital inspector?' said the haemorrhoids for all to hear. 'What's that when it's at home?'

'He inspects hospitals,' said the hernia. 'What do you think it means?'

'But you're here for an operation, aren't you?'

336

'That's right,' I said. 'Strictly speaking, I'm off duty. I do need this operation, of course, and it's only a minor one, but it will give me the opportunity of gaining an inside picture of how the hospital is performing. But I am sure you understand that I would rather no one knows my identity so could we keep things to ourselves.'

'You might as well have given him a bleeding megaphone,' said the hernia.

'You see,' I continued, keeping a straight face, 'it's a chance to experience things at first hand, see the whole of the process from beginning to end.'

'Get on,' snorted the haemorrhoids, shuffling back to his bed. 'You must think my brains are made of porridge. Hospital inspector. Huh.'

'Well you did ask,' I said, returning to the reports.

*   *   *

'You're causing quite a stir,' said the nurse later that morning when she came to take my blood pressure.

'Really?' I replied innocently.

'Telling them you're a hospital inspector indeed.'

'People will believe anything, nurse,' I said, smiling.

She caught sight of the red folder on my bedside cabinet. 'So, what sort of inspector are you then?' she asked casually.

'I'm afraid I'm not at liberty to say, nurse,' I replied. 'It's strictly confidential.' As she leaned over to attach the flap of black material to my arm to take my blood pressure, I scrutinised the badge pinned to her bosom. 'Staff Nurse R. Leach,' I said.

337

'That's right.'

'A rather appropriate name for someone taking blood pressure.'

'Pardon?'

'Leach, although your name is spelt with an *a*, isn't it?'

She began to pump the machine. 'That's right.'

'Is that Rowena?'

'Pardon?'

'Your first name?'

'Robyn.'

'With an *i*?'

'With a *y*.'

'Lovely name. And how long have you worked at Fettlesham Royal Infirmary, Nurse Leach?'

She stopped pumping. 'You do ask a lot of questions.'

'It's the nature of my job.'

'So what sort of inspector are you?' she asked again.

'I'm afraid I'm not at liberty to say,' I replied. 'It's strictly confidential.'

Just before lunch, which was the highlight of the day for my three companions, Mr Todd, the surgeon, arrived, accompanied by the ward sister in a smart blue uniform complete with black belt and silver buckle, and a group of medical students in white coats and the obligatory stethoscopes draped around their necks. Mr Todd was a distinguished-looking man of about sixty with steel grey hair and a spotted bow tie.

'And how are we, today, Mr Siddall?' he asked the hernia.

'We're not too bad, thank you, Mr Todd,' replied the hernia.

'Excellent.' The surgeon turned to the students who were watching his every move. 'Hernia,' he remarked dismissively, 'very straightforward case, no complications,' and he swiftly moved on. 'And how are you, Mr Prout?' he asked the haemorrhoids.

'Mustn't grumble,' replied the rosy-cheeked chatterer.

'Chance'd be a fine thing,' commented the hernia, not quite under his breath.

'But now you ask, Mr Todd—' began the haemorrhoids, sitting upright quickly and becoming very animated.

'Haemorrhoids,' interrupted the surgeon, turning to his young colleagues. 'I will save you the ordeal of an examination. Again straightforward. Simple case, no complications. Have you back on your bicycle in no time, Mr Prout.'

'I was about to say—' started the haemorrhoids.

Mr Todd was now at the bottom of the anal ulcer's bed. The patient was sleeping peacefully. 'Little point in disturbing Mr Quayle. Anal ulcer.' He then turned on his heel, looked me full in the face and smiled rather disconcertingly. 'And that brings us to Mr Phinn.' All eyes settled on me. 'Mr Phinn, who has a most interesting, not to say intriguing, condition, the result of a rugby accident when he was a youth. Do you play rugby, gentlemen?' he asked two young male students. Before they could respond he continued. 'If you do, be aware that the injuries come back to haunt you when you get older.' He made me feel ancient. 'Screens please, sister,' he said. 'I would like these would-be medics to give me their considered opinions of Mr Phinn's condition.' The screens

339

were hastily pulled around my bed and all the white coats gathered round like dogs with a bone. 'It is the ankle, isn't it, Mr Phinn?' observed the surgeon mischievously.

'No, no,' I spluttered, 'the knee.'

'Ah yes. The right knee, isn't it?'

'The left, it's the left knee,' I emphasised.

'Quite so. Just wanted to be sure of the facts. It's always important to be aware of the facts. Now, what is all this I have been hearing from Nurse Leach about you being a hospital inspector?'

'I'm a school inspector,' I told him, smiling pathetically like a naughty child caught out by a teacher. 'Your wife will vouch for me. I believe I inspected her earlier this year.'

'Did you, by God?' he exclaimed, laughing loudly.

'Professionally speaking,' I said. Then I added deferentially, 'I know nothing about hospitals, but I must say that I'm getting five-star treatment.'

'I am so glad to hear it,' said Mr Todd, smiling like Dracula about to sink his teeth into a victim. 'We aim to please. Now, let us look at this troublesome knee of yours.'

*   *   *

'I don't know what's so special about a knee,' said the haemorrhoids after the specialist and his entourage had left. I could tell by his tone of voice and his demeanour that he was none too pleased about the attention I had received earlier. 'We've all got knees. There's nothing unusual about knees, but only a chosen few have haemorrhoids and I've got piles of them. Didn't even exchange the time of

340

day with me, that Mr Todd. Just sailed past me as if—'

'Will you put a bleeding sock in it!' exclaimed the hernia. 'I'm sick and tired of hearing about your bleeding haemorrhoids.'

'Well, Inspector Clouseau over there had half the medical staff at the hospital around *his* bed: Sweeney Todd, the demon surgeon of Fleet Street, Sister Enema and all the trainee sawbones. That screen was pulled round for a good ten minutes. Laughing away they were. Preferential treatment, that's what he got. I bet they all knew he was a hospital inspector.'

'And how would they know that?' I asked. 'I never mentioned it, did I? And you didn't, did you?'

'No, no,' said the haemorrhoids hastily. 'Never breathed a word.'

At visiting time, Christine arrived with an immense bunch of purple grapes which she placed in a bowl on the bedside cabinet. The haemorrhoids' visitor, a small wizened woman with a world-weary expression, sat glumly in silence, listening. I could hear the key words of his monologue: 'pain', 'excruciating', 'toilet', 'suffering', 'ache', 'discomfort', 'agony', 'misery', 'torment'. Poor woman, I thought.

'Sidney phoned earlier this evening to wish you well for tomorrow,' said Christine. 'He said word is out that the Education Committee is at last going to announce the appointment of the person to replace Harold.'

'It's about time,' I said. 'It's dragged on for months.'

'Do you think it *might* be Geraldine?'

341

'Well, if it is,' I replied, 'she wants her head examining, that's all I can say. How can she bring up Jamie as a single parent and hold *that* job down?'

'Some women hold down very demanding jobs,' said Christine, 'and bring up a family and manage very well. You underestimate us.'

'Well, let's not talk about it,' I said, 'but I have to say at once that I hope this is not your way of telling me that you want to go back to work once little Lizzie is born. I hope we are still agreed that you'll give up your job in February. You are not now wanting to take maternity leave and go back to work afterwards, are you?'

'No,' said Christine. 'I want to watch our child grow up and be there for him . . . or her.'

'Phew! That's a relief! So what else did Sidney say?'

'He said it was a great pity you didn't put in for Harold's job.' She waited for a response before continuing. 'You're not regretting it now, are you?'

'Not at all. It's a poisoned chalice,' I said. 'I'm much better off as I am.'

She smiled. 'I'm glad.'

'And how are *you* feeling?' I asked.

'Mother and baby doing fine. No swollen ankles, no mad cravings. It was quiet without you last night. I'll be glad when you're home.'

'You've got the clock to keep you company,' I said.

Christine had been over the moon when she saw the long-case clock on Christmas Day in pride of place in the sitting room. I had had the devil's own job keeping it a surprise—collecting it from Mr Frobisher at Just Clocks, hiding it in Harry

Cotton's outbuilding, creeping out late on Christmas Eve after Christine had gone to bed to collect it, then trying to put it together and set the pendulum going without waking her. Of course, I had forgotten about the chiming. Christine saw her Christmas present fifteen seconds after midnight when the clock had struck the hour. There was nothing I could do to stop its chiming. Instead, I had intense pleasure watching Christine, tousled from sleep, come down the stairs to find out whether the noise had been in her dreams. She loved the clock on the spot.

At breakfast on Christmas morning, when I was telling her the story about my buying the clock from Mr Frobisher and how he would be coming out in the New Year to make final adjustments to it, Christine had gazed across at the clock. 'It is simply perfect there,' she had said. 'It looks absolutely at home in that corner.'

This turned out to be not very surprising. On Boxing Day, Harry Cotton had come in for a glass of sherry with us and, seeing the clock in its corner, had suddenly realised that it had belonged to old Mrs Olleranshaw, the previous owner of Peewit Cottage. He recognised the maker's name, Percy Farrington of Fettlesham, on the clock's face. It had been sold at Roper's Salesroom by Mrs Olleranshaw's nephew, along with the old woman's other possessions when she had died. At that point, I had remembered the provenance which Mr Frobisher had given me in an envelope. I fetched it from my desk and it indeed confirmed that the clock had returned home to where it had previously stood for over a hundred years.

'Oh, the clock's lovely,' Christine said now, 'but I

343

think we are going to have to ask Mr Frobisher to come back because just after you left for the hospital it stopped. It was really strange. I asked Harry Cotton to have a look but he couldn't get it going. I had to laugh. He said the last time it had stopped without any reason was the night before old Mrs Olleranshaw died.'

'Thanks a bundle,' I said. 'Let's change the subject. Any other news?'

'Indeed there is!' replied Christine, beaming. 'I heard just before coming out to see you that they're definitely deferring the closure of the school. It doesn't mean that the school won't close, of course, but it's really positive news. We'll go on campaigning and maybe we'll overturn the decision officially.'

'You've done a magnificent job,' I told her. 'It wouldn't have happened if you hadn't got involved.'

'Well, I don't know about that,' she said. 'Anyway, I must be off, darling. I've got so much to do before I leave Winnery Nook. Good luck tomorrow. I'll be saying a prayer and I'll be thinking of you.' She gave me a great big hug and a kiss and left.

'Nice-looking young woman, your daughter,' observed the haemorrhoids as he watched Christine leave the ward. 'Is she expecting?'

'She's my wife actually and, yes, she is.'

'It's a known fact that women suffer from piles during pregnancy, you know, when the baby puts pressure on the circulatory system. Has she had problems in that direction?'

'They'll be a bleeding problem in your direction in a minute,' said the hernia, stabbing the air with a finger. 'I'll come over there and sort out them bleeding haemorrhoids for you and save the surgeon a job.'

It was five minutes after visiting time had finished when Harold breezed in, carrying a large bunch of purple grapes. He was looking very distinguished in a charcoal-grey suit and gleaming white shirt with his old college tie. He was also looking particularly pleased with himself.

'However did you manage to get past the ward sister?' I asked, when he reached my bed. 'I'm told she's a stickler for people keeping to the visiting hours.'

'Charm, dear boy, charm,' said Harold, 'and a little help from this.' He tapped the badge on his chest which said in bold black lettering: 'Dr Harold J. Yeats'. 'I think the good sister assumed I was one of the medical fraternity and I didn't disabuse her. You know, having a PhD sometimes comes in very useful.' He put down the fruit. 'You seem to have a surfeit of grapes.'

The haemorrhoids, who must have had telescopic vision, had caught sight of the badge and made the same assumption as the ward sister. He shouted across the room, 'Evening, doctor.'

'Oh, good evening,' replied Harold, smiling and showing his set of tombstone teeth.

'Doing your rounds, are you?' asked the haemorrhoids.

Harold clearly misunderstood, for he nodded. 'Yes, indeed.' Then he turned his attention back to me. 'I've spent the day with Dr Gore and the person who will take over from me in April, and I now have the go-ahead to release the name of the new Senior Inspector. I've just come from telling your colleagues but I wanted you to know as soon as possible who we've appointed.'

'Yes, I heard the news was imminent, and am on tenterhooks to know,' I said.

'Well, I think you will be somewhat surprised but, I hope, extremely pleased when you hear whom we've appointed.'

'When you've got a moment, doctor,' shouted the haemorrhoids, 'could you pop over? I'd like to have a word.'

'Yes, of course,' said Harold. 'Now, Gervase—'

'It's just that I'd like to discuss one or two things with you,' continued the haemorrhoids.

'Ignore him, Harold,' I said. 'He's a pain in the . . . the backside. So who is he?'

'I'm sorry?'

'The new Senior Inspector, who is he? What's he like?'

'She,' replied Harold. 'It's a she.'

'A she?' I repeated.

'That's right,' said Harold, smiling widely and showing his set of great tombstone teeth.

'It's not Geraldine, is it?'

'No, no, not Geraldine,' replied Harold. 'She hasn't quite got the experience. Geraldine might make a Senior Inspector in the not too distant future, but she told me back in the autumn that she wasn't planning to apply because she puts young Jamie before her job—and quite right too.'

'Who is it, then, Harold?' I urged.

'Miss de la Mare.'

'What?!' I cried.

'Winifred de la Mare.'

'But she's an HMI,' I spluttered.

'Yes, I know.'

'Why on earth would she want the job?'

'She's become wearied with the hectic life in London,' Harold told me. 'All the paper pushing, bureaucracy, constant new initiatives, travelling on the Tube every morning and evening has taken its toll. She's ready for a different sort of challenge. Of course, Dr Gore was very keen to appoint her. None of the other candidates could hold a candle to a senior HMI. However, as you know, she's a forceful character and, before accepting the position, there were certain conditions she wanted the Education Committee to agree to, including that it would support certain innovations she would wish to put in place.'

'But why has it taken so long, Harold?' I asked.

'Ah well, as soon as the mandarins at the Ministry of Education got wind of her possible move, they exerted considerable pressure for her to stay. It was agreed that she could have Christmas to think things over. So, she gets to live in Yorkshire, which can't be bad, and has the opportunity of leading a team of colleagues whom she genuinely likes and respects. I think she'll be excellent.'

'That's wonderful,' I said. I shook Harold's hand enthusiastically. 'Wonderful!'

'Good news, is it?' came the voice of the haemorrhoids. 'He doesn't have to have the leg off then?'

'No,' said Harold over his shoulder. 'So,' he said to me, 'things have worked out pretty well. David and Geraldine are, of course, delighted and Sidney made some typical comment about "well, the devil you know". I feel I shall be leaving the department in very good hands. She's just right for the job and has masses of experience.'

347

'And Christine tells me the Education Sub-Committee is holding fire with the Hawksrill School closure.'

'That's right,' said Harold, 'and I have a feeling nothing will happen in that direction for quite some time now. Councillor Peterson has just about thrown in the towel, by all accounts. He was unusually quiet at the last meeting and, thank goodness for small mercies, wasn't at the appointment for my replacement. Pressure of work, I was told. Now, I must let you get some rest. I promised the ward sister five minutes and no more. She'll be having my guts for garters if I stay any longer. Oh, did you manage to finish reading through the reports?'

'Yes, they're here,' I said, reaching into my bedside cabinet.

'Splendid. I'll take them with me. Well, Gervase, good luck for tomorrow. And don't think of coming back to work until you are fully fit again.'

'Thanks for calling in, Harold. I can't tell you how pleased I am with the appointment. Oh, and thanks for the grapes.'

As Harold made for the door he was verbally waylaid by the haemorrhoids. 'If I could have a word, doctor,' he said.

'Well, I am in a bit of a hurry,' Harold told him pleasantly.

'I thought you might want a quick look at my haemorrhoids.'

'Pardon?' gasped Harold.

'To have a look at my haemorrhoids.'

'No, no!' spluttered Harold. 'Thank you kindly for the offer but I really must decline.' With that he shot out of the door.

'Well, what about that!' cried the haemorrhoids, addressing no one in particular. 'Not so much as a glance at my condition. He shot out of that door like a rat up a drainpipe.' He looked across at me angrily. 'They'll be laying a red carpet down to the operating theatre for you. You mark my words, you'll be in your own personal private room tomorrow with coloured telly and Jacuzzi. Well, I'm complaining. It's not right, hospital inspectors getting preferential treatment.'

I held up the big bunch of purple grapes and smiled sweetly. 'Would you care for a grape?' I asked.

*　　　*　　　*

The following morning, the anaesthetist arrived at seven-thirty prompt to give me an injection. As I was wheeled out of the ward, feeling pleasantly drowsy, the haemorrhoids got his own back, breaking into a loud and cheerful rendering of 'You May Never Walk This Way Again'.

CHAPTER TWENTY-ONE

'I'm looking for a man!'

I recognised immediately the aristocratic tones of the Honourable Mrs Cleaver-Canning at the end of the line. The previous year I had received a telephone call from the said 'honourable' lady inviting me, on the strength of a friend's recommendation, to speak at the Totterdale and Clearwell Golf Club Christmas Ladies' Night

Dinner. First, however, she had wanted to meet me—to look me over.

So I had duly presented myself at the imposing Georgian residence in Prince Regent Row, Fettlesham, to be 'vetted'. The elderly stooped figure with wisps of sandy hair and an extravagant handlebar moustache who answered the door, I had taken to be an old family retainer. It turned out that the man in question was Mrs Cleaver-Canning's long-suffering husband. Everyone called him Winco.

Much to my relief, my talk about my experiences as a school inspector was well received. The audience, no doubt buoyed up by good food and wine, had been extremely warm and receptive and I had left with a generous cheque to swell Sister Brendan's charity appeal. Now, here was Mrs Cleaver-Canning on the telephone again, no doubt wanting me to do a repeat performance somewhere or other.

'Good morning, Mrs Cleaver-Canning,' I said brightly. 'And how are you?'

'I'm extremely well, thank you, Mr Phinn,' she replied, 'but I am desperate for a man.'

'Really?'

'And you fit the bill. You are exactly what I am looking for.'

'I am certainly flattered,' I told her, 'but what about Winco?'

'Oh, you are a one,' she chortled down the line. 'No, no, I want a man for our musical drama. You may be aware that I am a leading light in the Fettlesham Literary Players and next month we will be staging *The Sound of Music* at the Civic Theatre in town. Unfortunately, one of the cast, Mr Dutton

350

of "Dutton's Carpets of Distinction"—you probably know his emporium in the High Street—has dropped out. Literally, as a matter of fact. The poor man fell off the stage at Castlesnelling High School where we hold our rehearsals, and is in traction at the Royal Infirmary. He tripped over a sign which warned of projecting stage sets and just dropped off the stage like a sack of potatoes. You may have heard the theatrical expression "break a leg". Well, Mr Dutton actually did. So, how about it?'

'How about what?' I asked.

'Standing in for him.'

'You mean take his part?'

'If you would. We only have six weeks to go and, as I said, I'm desperate.'

'I fear not,' I said hastily. 'I'm so very busy at the moment, Mrs Cleaver-Canning, and I've not long been out of hospital myself. I really couldn't commit myself to—'

'Hospital? Oh dear, I trust it wasn't serious?'

'No, no, a minor operation on the knee.'

'I'm very pleased to hear it. Well, the exercise will do it good. It's only a small walk-on part.'

'Nevertheless—'

'You would come on stage in the last act, say a couple of lines and walk off. You would only need to attend a few rehearsals, and on the nights of the performance you would not be needed until 8.30 at the earliest.'

'Yes, I appreciate that, but—'

'As I mentioned, I don't think you have got above two or three lines. It's the part of the SS Lieutenant who is pursuing Captain von Trapp. He only appears at the very end when the family are

351

making their escape across the mountains. There's no singing or dancing involved. It really wouldn't be at all onerous.'

'I am flattered to be asked, Mrs Cleaver-Canning,' I began, 'but—'

'After your bravura performance at The Totterdale and Clearwell Christmas Ladies' Night Dinner, I think you would be ideal. Clear, strong voice, excellent timing, confidence and that air of authority. As I said to Raymond, our producer, you would be just perfect for the part.' As an SS officer, I thought, smiling to myself. I assumed she meant her comments about me to be complimentary. 'We are really desperate,' she continued. 'It's so hard to get men these days. All I ask is that you glance through the libretto before you give a definite thumbs down. Will you do that?'

'Well—'

'Excellent! Winco will pop it in the post today.'

With that the line went dead.

*   *   *

'Why do you let yourself be dragged into things?' Christine appeared not at all pleased when I related the conversation I had had with Mrs Cleaver-Canning. We were sitting having a coffee after dinner that evening. 'You are just out of hospital, you have work to catch up on in the office, there are things to do in the house and you get dragooned into being in a play. I should have thought that you had quite enough on your plate at the moment.'

'I haven't actually agreed,' I said feebly.

'You've as good as. Why didn't you just say no

352

and put the phone down. I reckon you've got enough amateur dramatics at the inspectors' office with Sidney and David without looking for any more.'

'She's a very persuasive woman,' I began.

'And I'm not?'

'Of course you are, but she just wouldn't let me get a word in. Every time I made an objection, she had an answer. Anyway, it's only a few lines, not a major role. It might be quite fun.'

'And what about the rehearsals?'

'She said I only have to attend a few and appear on the nights of the performance, of course. I simply need to arrive for my bit at the end of the play. I walk on, say a couple of lines and walk off.'

'You really are infuriating at times, Gervase Phinn,' she said good-humouredly. 'You take all these things on without a thought for the commitment. Haven't you forgotten what's happening in March, which is next month, for heaven's sake?'

'Of course not, but the baby isn't due until the end of the month.'

'Suppose it comes early while you are goose-stepping across the stage with the Fettlesham Literary Players, singing "Edelweiss" and climbing up mountains.'

'I couldn't be goose-stepping and climbing up mountains at the same time, could I, and certainly not with this knee. Anyway, as I told you, I don't have any singing or dancing. It's just a walk-on part.'

'You'll get this coffee over your head in a minute.'

'Anyway, if little Lizzie does arrive early, I'll just

have to goose-step it down to the hospital. The Civic Theatre isn't that far. I could be there in ten minutes. Look, Christine, if you are dead set against it, I'll tell her I won't do it. I really don't want to argue with you about it.'

Christine put down her coffee, leaned over to me, smiled and gave me a peck on the cheek. 'Neither do I. Actually, you might look rather dishy in the uniform.'

The letter from Mrs Cleaver-Canning, which accompanied the libretto of *The Sound of Music*, arrived through the letterbox that weekend. It was clear from her comments that she assumed I had already agreed to take on the part and had sent a list of rehearsal dates with the ones I needed to attend—the first being the following Tuesday. I passed the letter over the breakfast table to Christine.

'What did I say,' she said, shaking her head.

*　　*　　*

On the next Tuesday, I made my way through the main school entrance of Castlesnelling High School at the prescribed time. I was greeted (hardly the right word) by the caretaker, an extremely thin man with a baleful countenance. He was attired in grey overalls, sported a rather greasy flat cap and was accompanied by a fat, vicious looking dog. As I approached, he jangled an enormous set of keys noisily.

'I'm looking for the—' I began.

'They're in the hall,' he said in a voice as dry as sawdust. 'And watch the floor on the corridor. I've just buffed it.' Perhaps he had trained at the same

College for Would-be Caretakers as Connie, I mused.

In the hall, a group of people was standing just below the stage, one small man waving his hands around and talking excitedly. When I reached the gathering, I coughed quietly.

The small man—who wore a pair of extremely tight jeans and a T-shirt emblazoned on the back with the motif 'Wrinkled Was Not One of the Things I Wanted to be When I Grew Up!' spun round. 'Ah, and you must be Gervase Phinn!' I nodded. 'Welcome, welcome!' he cried, grasping my hand and shaking it vigorously. 'I'm Raymond, but everyone calls me Ray. I'm your original drop of golden sun.'

'I'm sorry?' I said.

'You know,' he replied, breaking into song: "Doe a deer, a female deer. Ray a drop of golden sun."'

'Ah, indeed.' I smiled weakly.

'Oh ye-es!' said Ray, scrutinising me as an art expert might an old master. 'I can just see you in black boots. You're ideal. Margot does have a knack of picking the right people. She said you'd be perfect and she was right. I feel sure you'll be a natural for the part. And I don't expect you'll need much direction since I suppose that being a school inspector is not that far removed from that of an SS officer, is it?' He swung back to the group of people waiting patiently. 'This is our little troupe of thespians. As per usual, we have a surfeit of nuns, an abundance of children wanting to play the parts of the little von Trapps but we are, like all amateur dramatic productions these days, bereft of young men.' He smiled and took my arm. 'Do you know, I spend so much time looking for young men,' he

355

added.

'Really?' I said.

'And this,' announced Ray with a dramatic flourish of his hands, 'is our replacement stormtrooper, Gervase.' There was a ripple of applause.

'Not the most convincing name for a stormtrooper, is it?' observed a large bearded individual sitting on the stage.

'Bernard, really!' said Ray before turning to me and taking my arm. 'You'll get to know us all in the course of the evening, Gervase, so I will dispense with introductions. Just take a pew and I'll let you know when I want you on stage. Now, let us make a start, so a bit of hush everyone. I want to go through the scene with Liesl and Rolf again. It's still not quite right.'

I watched Liesl and Rolf going though their paces with a sinking feeling in the pit of my stomach. Why on earth had I let myself be press-ganged into this? I asked myself. I recognised the woman playing the part of Liesl, Captain von Trapp's eldest child. She was the Head of Food Technology at the school in whose hall we were rehearsing. She was an extremely thin and intense-looking woman with large staring eyes and long straggly hair. I had last seen her trip the boards two years before in Castlesnelling High School's production of *Oliver!* when she had played the part of Nancy and had had a rather unfortunate confrontation with the fearsome dog playing Bullseye. Now, here she was, taking on an entirely different role as the teenage von Trapp.

'Look, darling,' Ray told her now, 'it says in the libretto that Liesl in this scene is "awkward, naïve and generally unknowing in the ways of sophistication". Do you think we could have a bit more of the innocence and naïvety. Imagine you are one of the girls you teach.'

'I think the last words to come to mind when I think of the girls I teach are "innocence" and "naïvety",' said the Head of Food Technology, raising her eyebrows. 'Judging by the conversations I hear in the cookery room, most of them could tell us all a thing or two.'

'Well, just try, darling, to be more unworldly,' said Ray. 'And Rolf, you are supposed to be completely bowled over by this beautiful young woman in the first bloom of her youth. Could you look a little more enamoured with Liesl. You look as if you have acute constipation.'

I took a seat next to an elderly man in a black suit.

'I'm Zeller,' he told me, without taking his eyes off the stage.

'I'm Gervase,' I replied.

'No, no! I'm Zeller in the play. Herr Zeller, the Gauleiter. I come to arrest Captain von Trapp. I'm really George Furnival of Furnival's Funeral Parlour in Collington. We've been established since 1887.' He rootled in his pocket and produced a black-edged card which he thrust into my hand. 'Here, in case there's a death in the family. You'll find us very discreet and respectful.'

'Thank you.'

'I supplied the coffins for the school's production of *Oliver!* the other year, you know,' he continued. 'There were quite a few favourable comments about them.' The man was tailor-made for the part of a Gestapo official: long despondent face, short black hair parted down the middle, cold eyes as grey as the autumn sky and a vulpine mouth. His voice was wonderfully whispery and unnerving. I could just imagine him turning up at two o'clock in the morning in a long black leather coat.

'I don't know why I agreed to do this,' he said.

'Neither do I,' I agreed.

'I suppose it's good for business,' he told me.

'Good for business?' I repeated.

'Aye, getting your face known in the community, networking, making contacts, chance to promote your business. Pity there are no coffins in this production. I did suggest to Raymond that perhaps one of the nuns could cop it and I could provide a coffin or maybe have the last scene in a crypt, but he's not one to be open to suggestions. These artistic types are very unpredictable. I had a tidy little acknowledgement about my coffins in the programme when they did *Oliver!*' He paused and looked round at me. 'We very nearly had a fatality, you know. Old Mr Dutton of "Dutton's Carpets of Distinction", him who had your part, fell off the stage and broke a leg. Could have broken his neck. Yes, it could have been very nasty.' He sounded almost disappointed.

The Head of Food Technology had now launched into song with: 'I am sixteen going on seventeen, innocent as a rose—'

'More like thirty going on forty, if you ask me,' commented Mr Furnival. 'Mind you, with a bit of stage make-up, a long blonde wig and subdued stage lights she should be all right. It's amazing what a bit of make-up can do. I do a lot of embalming, you know. It's quite an art form.'

358

It soon came to what Ray described as 'Gervase's little spot'. I sounded like the acne of the production.

'Watch your step,' warned Mr Furnival, as I went forward to climb the steps to the stage. 'We don't want another person breaking a leg.'

'Now,' said the producer, 'this is the dramatic climax of the drama. We are in the garden of Nonnberg Abbey. A gaggle of nuns is standing anxiously by the door.' Ray paused in his narration. 'I'm not sure what the collective noun is for nuns. Anyway, the nuns are standing anxiously by the door. Could we look anxious, please, nuns? You're not waiting for a number 9 bus. The von Trapps enter nervously, clutching their cases. They hear a noise and hide in the shadows. Do try and look as if you're frightened, von Trapps. Cluster, don't queue. Rolf enters. Gone are his *lederhosen* and Tyrolean hat. He is now dressed in SS uniform. He swaggers onto the stage. The light from his torch sweeps before him. It picks out Maria. She gasps. Then it lights up the Captain. He scowls. Don't overdo the scowl, please, Bernard. The Captain walks towards Rolf. Rolf flashes. Flash, please, Rolf. Now draw your pistol. Just use your fingers for the time being, please, Fraser. He calls: "Lieutenant!" Then he sees Liesl. She looks appealingly at him. We hear the lieutenant's footsteps approaching. Rolf clicks off the light. The sound draws nearer and nearer. The lieutenant struts onto the stage. This is you, Gervase.' I limped onto the stage. 'He looks around arrogantly,' continued the producer. 'He should have with him two or three stormtroopers,' Ray explained, 'but we haven't got enough men for the stormtroopers and, anyway, we can't afford to hire all those uniforms, so it'll just have to be you, Gervase, looking nasty and threatening.' His voice became suddenly dramatic again. 'Then Rolf changes his mind and decides not to betray the von Trapps after all. He calls: "No one out here, sir!" "All right!" snarls the lieutenant. "Come along." '

We tried the scene a couple of times and Ray seemed well satisfied. 'Oh, I could feel the tension,' he said. 'My heart was in my mouth. However, Gervase, I'm not so sure that that limp quite works. I was wanting more of a *braggadocio*.'

'Braga-what-o?' I asked, quite perplexed.

'A strut. Can you strut or swagger, onto the stage?'

'Difficult, really. I've just had a knee operation,' I told him. 'It's a real limp, I'm afraid.'

'Oh well, we'll have to keep the limp in then.'

'But I have a limp!' called Mr Furnival, who had been watching proceedings intently. 'There can't be two of us with limps.'

'No, you are quite right, George,' said Ray. 'Dispense with yours.'

'Dispense with mine!' he retorted. 'I've taken ages perfecting that limp.'

'Yes, I know,' sighed Ray, 'but yours is an artificial limp, Gervase's is a real one.'

At nine o'clock prompt the caretaker arrived. 'Let's be having you,' he bellowed from the back of the hall, 'I want to lock up.'

'Right, everyone,' announced Ray. 'Let's call it a day. Next Tuesday, please, for those in the ball scene.'

'And stack the chairs before you leave!' shouted the caretaker.

'Stacking chairs,' retorted Ray.

'And put your litter in the bins. There were plastic cups all over my floor last week.'

'Picking up litter,' Ray trilled back, retrieving a crisp packet from the floor.

'And somebody's been tampering with the electrics back stage so whoever it is, can stop it.'

'And no tampering with the caretaker's electrics back stage,' said the producer, giving the sticklike fellow an immense smile. 'Is that everything covered?' he asked.

'I'm sure there'll be other things,' grumbled the caretaker. 'There always are.'

'Oh, I'm certain of it,' replied the producer.

It occurred to me, as I observed the caretaker stomping around the hall, that there was someone infinitely more suitable than I to take on the role of the SS stormtrooper. It was clear no one was going to argue with this man, especially since he was accompanied by the fat brute of a dog with a body like a barrel and cold, grey eyes. I had immediately recognised the creature when I had set eyes on it in the school entrance. It had been Bill Sikes's dog, Bullseye, in the production of *Oliver!* but had ended up terrorizing Nancy, alias the Head of Food Technology, and I noticed that the woman was now giving the dog a wide berth as she edged for the door.

'Are you the new recruit then?' asked the caretaker, jangling his keys noisily, as he followed me to the exit. The dog followed behind us, rumbling like a distant train.

'Yes, I am.'

'Well, I hope you know what you're letting yourself in for.'

'It's only a small part,' I told him.

'It is this year, mate,' he said, 'but you'll be the leading man in the next production, you mark my words. They suck you in. That's what they do. That big woman, the fat nun with the plummy accent, takes no prisoners. She won't take no for an answer. Nobody argues with her. I don't know what she said to the Headmaster but she got round him to let them rehearse here in the school hall. And no one bothered to ask me, and it's all extra work for me, you know—keeping the heating on, cleaning up afterwards, stopping late to lock up.'

At that moment the woman we had been discussing could be heard coming down the corridor behind us, singing a snatch of 'Climb Every Mountain'.

'Hold up,' said the caretaker, 'here she comes.'

His dog stopped, turned, curled a lip, showed an impressive set of sharp teeth and moved towards her, growling menacingly.

'Shut up, you silly creature!' ordered Mrs Cleaver-Canning. The dog stuck its tail between its legs and lowered its head. It had met its match.

'You were excellent, Gervase,' said Mrs C-C as she sailed past. 'I think you're in for a much bigger role in the next production.'

'See what I mean,' said the caretaker, tapping the side of his nose.

*   *   *

'How did it go?' asked Christine when I limped through the door of Peewit Cottage later that evening.

'Fine. I only need to attend a couple more times

and the dress rehearsal, of course. I told you it wouldn't involve much.' I flopped into the nearest chair.

'I don't understand why they were so desperate for you to do this part if it's such a small one. Couldn't the producer or somebody have done it?'

'If you had met the producer, Christine,' I told her, 'you would see why he would be the last person to play the part of a nasty SS officer.'

'Too nice?'

'Far too nice.'

'I'll put the kettle on,' Christine said. 'I'm sure you could do with a cup of tea after all that goose-stepping. You can have a piece of cake as well.'

'Oh, you've been baking?'

Christine called from the kitchen. 'No, Mrs Poskitt called round with it. You should try a piece of her sponge cake. It's delicious—"as light as a nun's kiss" as my father would say.'

'That depends on the nun,' I muttered to myself, thinking of Mrs Cleaver-Canning. 'What did Mrs Poskitt want? I hope it wasn't to give us one of her kittens.'

'She's invited me to the next WI meeting.'

'You are not thinking of joining the Women's Institute, are you?'

'Why not? It sounds good fun. When I give up work, I don't intend sitting around all day by myself, knitting, with no one to talk to. I know I've got the garden at the front to sort out and some decorating and I need to put up some shelves in the nursery and—'

'Not in your condition, you're not,' I told her. 'Digging and hammering and climbing up ladders—'

363

'I'm joking,' she said. 'But I do want to keep occupied.'

'I should think that school closure group you're involved with will take up most of your time.'

'Aah, that is where you are wrong,' she said. 'You've had a phone call.'

'Go on.'

'From Harold. He had just come out of one of his late meetings about the school closures and he rang here straightaway. He wanted us to be the first to know. He said he would ring you back. I don't suppose he should have told me, but he was so pleased with himself.'

'Well, go on,' I said. 'Don't keep it to yourself.'

'The meeting was for the Education Sub-Committee to consider the response from the Ministry of Education about the school closures. You will never guess. They've reversed the decision to close Hawskrill School.'

'What?'

'Isn't it fantastic! Evidently the Ministry, which has to make the final decision, has blocked it. It's marvellous news.' She put her arms around me. 'So you see, all our little efforts on the Action Committee have paid off. I'll get the tea.'

I didn't say anything to Christine, but I thought to myself that there was far more here than a pressure group's efforts. I just wondered if our Senior Inspector designate had a hand in the decision. Miss de la Mare had been the HMI sent from London to look into the matter and report back. Did she delay her acceptance of the post until she had seen this through? I wondered.

Christine interrupted my thoughts. 'He said he'd phone back about ten.'

364

'Who?'

'Harold.' At that very moment the telephone rang 'That'll be him now.'

'Hello, Harold—' I began.

'Beg pardon?' came an American voice down the line.

'Oh, I am sorry,' I said. 'I was expecting another call.'

'Is this an inconvenient time?'

'No no, go ahead.'

'Is that Mr Gervase Phinn?'

'It is.'

'The owner of Peewit Cottage?'

'That's right.'

'I'm truly sorry to disturb you so late, Mr Phinn,' said the man, 'but your lady secretary at the office in Fettlesham did say I might phone you at home, bearing in mind the nature of my business. I do hope it's not inconvenient.'

'No, it's fine,' I told him.

'You're a seriously busy guy, from what your secretary said. Let me introduce myself. My name is Brewster—John K. Brewster—and I'm with the US delegation of The Society of Friends.'

'Quakers?'

'That is correct. I and a group of colleagues are over for the International Convention at York. I wanted to get in touch straight away, to tell you the good news—'

'I'm sorry, Mr er, Brewster,' I interrupted, 'but I am pretty certain in my own beliefs and—'

'No, no, I'm not proselytising.'

'Well, how may I help you?' I asked.

'The thing is,' he said, 'my colleague, Dr James L. Bradford of the University of Irvine, California,

Department of Comparative Theology and Christology, came out to your village of Hawskrill a couple of years back to visit the Quaker meeting house which I understand is on your land.'

My heart sank. 'The meeting house?' I murmured.

'That is correct, the unique eighteenth-century meeting house which is on your land. Just a shell, I believe, but of such great historical significance, particularly for we Quakers. James Fox himself preached there, but I am sure you know that. I understand the delightful old lady who owned the land prior to you was so very kind and allowed my colleague, Dr James L. Bradford, and some friends to visit the site. I am told it was quite a moving event. The elderly lady did not have the financial resources to restore the building but it always had a special place in her heart, as I'm sure it does for you. To have something so steeped in history is truly, truly awe-inspiring. When he returned to the States, Dr James L. Bradford was quite fired up and suggested we try to restore the building.'

'Restore it?' I whispered.

'Re-build it. Now, I want to make a proposition. We are prepared, my American Quaker colleagues and I, to restore the vitally important and unique meeting house to its former glory. We shall cover all costs. Now, what do you think of that, sir?'

I was stuck for words. How could I tell him the vitally important and unique eighteenth-century Quaker meeting house was now a lowly wall. 'I'm speechless,' I managed to say.

'I guess this news must have come as quite a surprise to you?'

'That's an understatement,' I replied under my

366

breath.

'Look, it's late and I can tell from the sound of your voice, you're tired and a bit emotional. With your permission, I'll ring back later in the week and maybe arrange for me and my colleagues to come over next weekend to discuss the re-building plans. I have an appointment with a Mr J. Perkins of the County Architects' Department in Fettlesham tomorrow morning. I understand there's all sorts of planning permission, listed building regulations, that sort of thing to sort out. I'm so excited,' he said, 'and I guess you are too! God bless you, and goodnight.' Before I could reply, the phone went dead.

'I need a whisky, a very large one,' I told a bemused Christine.

CHAPTER TWENTY-TWO

Mrs Savage sat stiffly behind her impressive desk, enthroned in her large swivel chair, looking haughtier than ever. This was, I sincerely hoped, the final meeting with her to go over the details for the forthcoming visit of the foreign school inspectors.

Since October I had met with her twice to discuss the Ministry of Education initiative and both times she had sent me away with a thick dossier of papers 'to peruse'.

The CEO's personal assistant was dressed in an elegant chartreuse-coloured suit and plain cream silk blouse and was adorned in her usual assortment of heavy silver jewellery. As Sidney often remarked, Mrs Savage was never knowingly underdressed and that morning she had really gone to town. Her make-up appeared flawless, her long nails, as red as blood, were impeccably manicured and not a hair on her head was out of place. She had adopted the Eva Peron style, with hair scraped back and gathered immaculately behind her head. I had to admit she looked quite magnificent.

'Good morning, Mr Phinn,' said Mrs Savage, looking up from the papers before her and giving me a small forced smile. 'Do take a seat.'

'Good morning, Mrs Savage,' I replied, sitting on the hard wooden chair in front of her and placing my briefcase on the floor beside me. 'I see your buzzer is working all right now.'

'I beg your pardon?' There was an explosive look in her eyes.

'The buzzer on your door. There was a point when all your little lights lit up.'

The small forced smile disappeared. 'It is working perfectly well, thank you, and it has been for some time. You might recall you asked me about the buzzer the last time we had a meeting in my room. Now, shall we make a start? I have a briefing with Dr Gore later this morning, so we do need to knock on. The CEO wants to touch base and go through a few items with me regarding the new Senior Inspector.' She fluttered an eyelid. I knew, of course, that it wouldn't be long before she mentioned the Senior Inspector's post. 'You are, of course, acquainted with Miss de la Mare.'

'Yes,' I replied simply.

'It's about time they had more women in senior positions in the Authority,' she observed, shuffling the papers on her desk.

'Yes.'

'I have to prepare a detailed dossier for Miss de la Mare to acquaint her with the workings of the department.'

'You have such a big remit, Mrs Savage,' I remarked, taking some papers from my briefcase.

'I beg your pardon, Mr Phinn?' she said sourly.

'I was observing that you seem to have more and more responsibilities thrust upon your shoulders these days. Personnel issues, secretarial duties, the "Health and Safety" initiative, the EIEI. It's a wonder you have the time to fit everything in.'

'Oh,' she said, oblivious of the sarcasm, 'I see what you mean. Yes, I am indeed kept extremely busy and that is why we need to expedite the business of the EIEI.'

'So, shall we do that?' I suggested.

She flicked open a file on her desk and tapped a red nail at the document inside. 'I have received from you the names of some suitable schools for the foreign inspectors to visit but these need to be ratified, of course, by Dr Gore. He would, I'm sure, only want them to visit our flagship schools. The inspectors will, no doubt, wish to observe some lessons and talk with teachers to compare our system of education with that in their own country. I am told that they speak very good English.'

'Yes, I know that, Mrs Savage,' I told her wearily, 'and all has been prepared. If you remember, we went through what they would be doing when we met at the SDC early last term, the morning you were mistaken for Mr Clamp's nude model.'

Her mouth tightened. 'The least said about that the better, Mr Phinn,' she said. Her voice was hard and clipped. 'I did have a word with Dr Gore about that whole incident. I imagine he spoke to Mr Clamp.'

'Not to my knowledge,' I informed her.

'And I also contacted Personnel about the janitor taking time off to holiday in France without seeking the required permission.'

'Yes, you said you would,' I replied. 'Actually, Mrs Savage, Connie went to scatter her father's ashes. I believe Dr Gore very kindly wrote to her expressing his condolences. Connie *was* considering resigning after receiving a rather unpleasant letter from Personnel containing a written warning, but Dr Gore persuaded her to stay on.'

'I do not recall seeing any letter from Dr Gore and I deal with all his correspondence.'

'Being a letter of condolence and therefore personal, I expect it was hand-written,' I said. 'Now since, as you have pointed out, we need to expedite the business of the EIEI, Mrs Savage, shall we do that? The schools have been identified, the arrangements made, the visits organised, which leaves little to be dealt with.'

'It does no harm to recap, Mr Phinn,' she said in a patronising voice. 'Then we don't get crossed wires. Dr Gore wishes you to set up a meeting at the SDC with invited headteachers and governors to talk about the education system over here. He, of course, will address them. If I might suggest—'

'That, too, has all been taken care of, Mrs Savage,' I assured her in a deliberately impatient tone of voice.

She was rather taken aback. 'Really?'

'Yes, I've arranged all that as well.'

'Oh, then we can move on.'

370

'If we might.'

'Now, if two of your colleagues and yourself,' she suggested, 'accompany one of these foreign inspectors each for the two days and look after him or her, it would mean that they would see a range of different subjects in a variety of schools.'

'I have taken care of that, too, Mrs Savage,' I told her, gritting my teeth. 'Mr Clamp and Mr Pritchard are only too happy to be involved.'

There was a long silence before she said, 'I take it, then, that Dr Yeats and Dr Mullarkey are not available?' Her voice was laconic.

'I don't know whether Dr Yeats and Dr Mullarkey are available or not,' I told her, my voice again taking on an exasperated edge. 'I didn't ask them.' Actually I had had a word with Geraldine but she was extremely busy running a course at that time as well as attending appointment panels during the week of the visit. Harold, too, had said he had far too much on. After the change of heart with regard to the closure of the small schools, a series of meetings had been arranged to see where else money could be saved from the education budget. Harold, of course, was required to attend. 'I have spoken with both Mr Clamp and Mr Pritchard and explained what will be required, and they would be very pleased to take part in the initiative.'

'Do you think that those two colleagues are the most suitable for this endeavour?' Mrs Savage asked.

'Eminently.'

'I see,' she said curtly, after another long pause. 'Well that, of course, is your decision.'

'Yes, it is,' I agreed.

371

'But it is imperative, Mr Phinn,' she announced, snapping shut the file in front of her and giving me an icy glare, 'that you liaise with me at all times. I need to be kept fully informed.'

'Of course,' I replied, wishing that this totally unnecessary meeting would end. 'Surely that is the point of this meeting?'

'It makes my life so much easier if I am kept fully up to speed,' she continued. 'I will, of course, deal with all the administration, send the foreign inspectors the relevant documentation, arrange their travel, send them a detailed itinerary and programme of events and so forth, but there is one thing I would like you to do as a matter of some urgency. I would appreciate it if you could have a word, sooner rather than later, with that janitor at the Staff Development Centre—that woman in the pink overall.'

'Connie,' I reminded her.

'I have to say that I find her quite abrasive and difficult. Sometimes I don't think she knows who I am and what position I hold at County Hall. She has a most offhand manner. You will recall that when we held the interviews for the Senior Inspector's post, when that Mr Carter, he who gave back-word, was appointed, the woman was most rude, very unhelpful and quite obstructive. I merely asked her for more tea and biscuits and one would have thought that I had asked her to lay down her life.'

'So what's this matter of some urgency that you wish me to deal with?' I asked irritably.

'The matter of the catering,' she replied.

'The catering?' I asked.

'As we agreed, there will be a reception for our

foreign visitors at the SDC. There will be nibbles and drinks, that sort of thing.' She cleared her throat. 'I can see problems with . . . with that woman.'

'Connie?'

'Yes. If she is unable to provide tea and biscuits, how will she cope with a buffet? I really do not feel inclined to liaise with her over the provision of the food and drink. As I said, she can be very difficult.'

That's ripe coming from her, I thought.

'Well, this really is part of *your* remit,' I said.

'Not necessarily,' she replied. There was a softer tone to her voice now. 'You spend far more time at the SDC. It occurred to me that you might like to deal with that side of things.'

I was beginning to enjoy this. 'No, not really,' I replied. 'I have quite enough on. I think the catering is best dealt with by you.'

'Mr Phinn, do you want our European colleagues to return to their respective countries with an unfavourable impression of English hospitality?'

'Of course not,' I replied, stuffing the papers back in my briefcase and getting to my feet. 'Well, Mrs Savage, everything seems to have been dealt with. I will let you get to your briefing with Dr Gore and compile your detailed dossier. I'll give you a ring next week to check on final details before the foreign inspectors' visit.'

Mrs Savage twisted a ring around on her long finger. 'Mr Phinn,' she said, 'I would be very grateful if you could see fit to arrange the catering. I would find it very helpful.' There was another long pause, then, 'Please.'

'I don't recall your being particularly helpful,

373

Mrs Savage,' I told her, 'when I wanted that report back. In fact you were most unhelpful.'

'That was an entirely different matter,' she told me. 'It was—'

'More than your job was worth? Yes, I recall you telling me.' I then added, 'Very well, Mrs Savage, I will arrange the catering.'

'Thank you,' she said simply.

On my way out of County Hall, I kept a sharp eye open for a party of American Quakers heading for the County Architects' Department.

* * *

'I'm sorry, Sidney, but it is a well-known fact that other Europeans speak their own language much better than the English speak theirs.' David was in one of his more serious moods and was holding forth about the visit of the foreign inspectors. 'And furthermore, they are far more likely to speak English than we are to speak their language. These three inspectors coming here, for example, are all apparently fluent in English. How many of us are fluent in Italian or Spanish or French? You see, they make the effort and the English do not. Indeed, the Englishman abroad expects the foreigners to speak English. If no one understands him, he then goes up an octave and starts shouting. And, I would go further than that. The foreigner very often has a better command of the English language than the English have themselves.'

'And upon what do you base these observations about the state of our language?' enquired Sidney. 'Have you done some sort of detailed research?'

'I don't need to do any detailed research,'

374

replied David. 'You only have to look around to see how the use of English has declined. People don't seem able to spell or punctuate or express themselves any more. Julie, for example, is forever misplacing a participle.'

'She always was very forgetful,' remarked Sidney. 'I do hope she found it.'

'And splitting her infinitives,' continued David.

'Oooh, that sounds painful,' said Sidney, screwing up his face dramatically.

David was in full flow by this time and not to be stopped. 'And when we had young Frank doing the letters, his spellings were patently bizarre. He was a nice enough young man, but his English! I really don't know what they will make of him in Financial Services. I hope he's better with numbers than he is with words. Julie tries her best and I know she is overworked but I have to check everything she writes.'

'Come on, David,' I said. 'It's not that bad.'

'Then there's Connie,' continued my colleague.

'Don't mention that woman,' spluttered Sidney.

'She is a prime example of how not to use English. She mangles and murders the language with malapropisms and *non sequiturs*. I arrived at the SDC last week and there was a notice outside the Gents: "Attention! Wet floor! This is not an instruction!" I mean, what do visitors think?'

'Oh, for goodness sake, David,' I said. 'Connie is a cleaner, and a damn good cleaner as well, not a professor of linguistics. She doesn't need to have a perfect command of the English language to polish and dust and clean the toilets.'

'And that is exactly what she should do,' said Sidney, 'polish and dust and clean the toilets. I

375

couldn't care less how she speaks, it's what she says that makes my blood boil.' He thought for a moment. 'I say, does that make sense? Anyway, you know what I mean—it's her attitude.'

'Then there's Mrs Savage with her management gobbledegook,' David continued, unabashed. 'Let's hope these foreign inspectors don't meet either of them. They'll be utterly confused by the one and totally confounded by the other. At that wretched "Health and Safety" meeting, it was as if Mrs Savage was—were,' he hastily corrected himself, 'speaking a foreign language, flagging things up, getting up to speed, thinking outside the box, climbing aboard, having thought showers, finding windows in diaries. Even Dr Gore is not guiltless. "The Education Committee have decided . . ." he wrote in the last memorandum. It should be, "The Education Committee *has* decided".'

'Does it really matter?' sighed Sidney. 'I mean, aren't there more important things to occupy your time than spotting the odd split infinitive and misplaced participle? In the whole scheme of things, does it really, really matter?'

'Of course it matters!' snapped David. 'It's just a sloppy use of the language. It's part and parcel of the decline in standards. I was in a school last week and a teacher had not only misspelt "parallelogram" on the mathematics examination paper but had informed the students that "This option is compulsory". I mean, how can an option be compulsory?'

'Oh, don't be so pedantic, David,' said Sidney. 'You are an old misery-guts, moaning and complaining. You should be rejoicing. Miss de la Mare is taking over. Surely that should bring a

376

smile to that little wizened Welsh face of yours.'

'I am trying to have a serious discussion here, Sidney,' said David. 'I think Gervase might run a few courses for education employees on the effective use of English.'

'No chance!' I spluttered. 'I have enough on at the moment, thank you very much.'

'Well, I despair at the flagrant misuse of the language,' said David.

'We all make mistakes,' I said. 'Are you telling us, David, that you never ever make an error with your own writing?'

'Of course not, but not in every other word.'

'English is a very tricky and troublesome language,' I commented. 'It is full of minefields. You tell me a rule of spelling, David, and I'll find you an exception. Anyway, I find those double meanings are rather amusing. I remember a history essay we were asked to do at school: "Trace the events leading up to the birth of Henry VIII".'

'I reckon your history teacher received some very interesting answers to that question,' smirked Sidney. 'And talking of *double entendres*, have you seen that priceless sign outside the new Dales Visitors' Centre: "Please Leave Heather For All To Enjoy". I suggested to the man at the desk that poor Heather must have been feeling rather the worse for wear. He didn't appreciate the witticism, I'm afraid.'

'Christine found some priceless advertisements for jobs last week in the *Fettlesham Gazette*,' I said. 'She always cuts them out for me.' I extracted the little clippings from my notebook. 'One said: "An opportunity to join an expanding contracting company". Another, "Are you going places in

377

aluminium foil?" Then there was "Street lighting engineers—two posts".'

'Quite a little treasure trove you have there,' remarked Sidney. 'What on earth do you keep them for?'

'They are very useful to lighten the atmosphere at some of the dinners I am asked to speak at,' I replied. 'Or should I say, at which I am asked to speak.' I glanced over in David's direction. 'Here's a headline from a couple of weeks ago,' I said, reading from another clipping: ' "Man battered in fish shop".'

'Ah, well they do that deliberately,' said Sidney, laughing. 'The secret of a catchy headline is to convey the greatest ambiguity in the fewest words. Here's some more that you can add to your collection, Gervase: "General Montgomery flies back to front". "Captain Fuchs off to Antarctica". "Body in garden is a plant, says woman".'

'You are making my point precisely,' said David. 'Newspapers are some of the worst offenders. The *Fettlesham Gazette* is a prime example of sloppy English. They should be setting a good example. It is something I feel very strongly about.'

'About which I feel very strongly,' said Sidney and then, ignoring David's angry glare, continued: 'I've told Julie to go very carefully with that lipstick she's using at present. She could be severely incapacitated should she follow the instructions printed on the side.'

'What does it say?' I asked, intrigued.

' "Take off cap and push up bottom".'

Sidney and I cackled with laughter.

David gave us a pitying look. 'It's no use trying to have a serious conversation with you two

378

schoolboys. I could have predicted your response, Sidney, but I have to say, Gervase, I rather expected a little more support from the English inspector. Well, I'm off.'

'Yes, I thought I could detect a strange, rather fishy smell,' remarked Sidney as David strode for the door.

'You know,' said David, pausing at the door, 'things will change when Miss de la Mare takes over, I can tell you. I bet she's a stickler for correct English.'

When David had gone I turned to Sidney. 'You shouldn't rib him so much.'

'Well, he's so serious these days. I should have thought with the appointment of Miss de la Mare, he would be walking on clouds. We could have been landed with that odious Mr Carter and his management speak.' As was his wont, Sidney leaned back expansively on his chair. 'Yes, indeed, I'm so much looking forward to working with dear Winifred. I love Harold dearly and will miss him greatly, but Winifred will bring a breath of fresh air with her. We have so much in common.' He caught sight of the expression on my face. 'What are you grinning at?'

So much in common, I thought: the one a totally unpredictable, larger than life, mercurial bear of a man; the other, a precise, highly-organised woman with a mind as sharp as a razor. It would be very interesting to see what our new Senior Inspector made of the Inspector for Creative and Visual Arts.

'Nothing, Sidney,' I said. 'Nothing at all.'

We worked on our reports and correspondence for the next hour in relative silence. When the clock on the County Hall tower struck six o'clock,

379

Sidney stretched and sighed. 'Governors' meeting for me tonight at High Ruston-cum-Riddleswade Junior and Infant School, right out in the sticks. I do hope it doesn't go on and on. That Mrs Dingle-Smith and her side-kick, the tiresome Mrs Powell (pronounced Pole), never shut up. Like chattering monkeys. Of course, they'll be delighted that their school, which was on the list for closure, has been reprieved. I suppose that will be high on the agenda and it will be after ten before I get home. This is the third late night this week. Oh, by the way, your Christine needs to be congratulated on her efforts to keep the small schools from closing.'

'Yes,' I replied, 'she caused a few waves.'

'Waves!' exclaimed Sidney. 'It was a veritable tidal deluge.'

'She did very well,' I said.

'Wonderful woman. You're a lucky man, Gervase.'

'I know.'

'So, where are you tonight then?' Sidney asked.

'It's Christine's leaving do at Winnery Nook. You were invited but—'

'Governors' meeting,' he sighed. 'I know. In fact,' he exclaimed, swinging his chair back into an upright position with a clatter, 'that will be a perfect excuse to leave early, and then I will come on to the party.'

'Excellent! She'd love to see you. Anyway, I must make tracks,' I told him. 'I said I'd pick Connie up before seven.'

'Connie's going?'

'Of course she's going. She's not that bad, you know, Sidney. Her heart is in the right place, and she's always had a soft spot for Christine.'

380

'The right place for Connie's heart is on a kebab,' said Sidney, violently jabbing a pile of paper on his desk with his paper-knife. 'The woman's an interfering, bad-tempered, entirely unreasonable menace. I shall be having words with our new Senior Inspector. She's just the person to put Connie in her place. She forgets that I am a senior member of the Education Department. Connie speaks to me as if I were a naughty schoolboy.'

'You sound just like Mrs Savage, Sidney,' I said. 'Apparently she doesn't think Connie knows who *she* is. I also remember her saying to Mrs Osbaldiston, the time she was mistaken for your nude model, "Do you know who I am?"'

'Oh, well, I would never say that,' protested Sidney. 'In fact, I cannot abide people who say that. "Do you know who I am?" No, no, I would never say that. I remember reading once about this extremely rude and aggressive individual dressed in a bright checked jacket and dangling camera who pushed his way to the front of the queue at the airport and demanded attention. He informed the airline attendant that he had to be checked through first since he was on the next flight. The attendant asked him very politely to wait his turn. No doubt, she told him, he could see there was a long queue of other passengers ahead of him. Anyway, the man banged his fist on the counter, waved his business class ticket in front of her face and shouted for all to hear, those ridiculous words: "Do you know who I am?" The attendant stared at him for a moment before picking up the public address microphone and announcing calmly: "May I have your attention, please. There is a passenger in a rather

381

loud jacket who does not know who he is. Could anyone who may be able to identify him please come to desk 9."'

'I remember the occasion when I was sitting for my finals,' I said, reminded of an incident similar to Sidney's. 'The invigilator was insistent that we stop writing immediately when he told us to do so. He made a point of repeating a number of times that if anyone still had a pen in his hand after he had told us "Pens down", then the paper would be invalidated. Anyhow, this pal of mine, Dermot Monaghan his name was, was writing his name on the top of his paper when the invigilator, or perhaps more appropriately as it turned out, the invalidator, called "Pens down". Dermot carried on writing and when he came to hand in his paper he was told it wouldn't be accepted.'

'That was rather petty and mean-minded,' said Sidney. 'He sounds like a male version of Mrs Savage with her rules and procedures.'

'So Dermot explained he was only writing his name, but the invigilator still would not accept the paper and started stacking this massive pile of examination papers on his desk. Dermot pleaded with him but to no avail. "You heard what I said," the invigilator told him. "I cannot accept it." Dermot drew himself up and looked the invigilator straight in the eye. "Do you know who I am?" he asked in a really pompous tone of voice. "No," said the invigilator, "I have no idea who you are and telling me anyway will not have the slightest effect." "So you don't know who I am?" Dermot asked again. "No," replied the invigilator. "That's good," said Dermot and, as fast as lightning, stuffed the paper right into the centre of the pile.'

'I never know whether to believe your stories, Gervase,' said Sidney, laughing.

'That's ripe coming from you,' I said.

'It's good that you *can* laugh,' said Sidney. 'I would have thought that you had little to find amusing at the moment.'

'Why's that?'

'You must be feeling pretty awful about demolishing that old Quaker meeting house, the one those Americans want to restore.'

'Who told you about the American Quakers?' I asked.

'I took a call for you yesterday. Delightful man. What was his name? Brewster, was it? He was wanting to get in touch with you again. He said he'll ring you at home tonight. He wants to discuss the plans for the restoration.'

'Oh heavens! You didn't tell him I'd knocked it down, did you?'

'Of course not.'

'This is a nightmare,' I said. 'Perhaps I ought to go and see Jasper Perkins. Get his advice.'

'Old Perkins is on holiday. The Americans tried to see him but they were told he won't be back for a week. There's a stroke of luck for you.'

'Oh dear me,' I sighed. 'Whatever am I going to do?'

'I've told you, old boy,' said Sidney, patting me on the shoulder, 'blame it on the vandals.'

CHAPTER TWENTY-THREE

Señor Carlos Itturiaga was a small, plump, jolly man with typically dark Spanish eyes, a friendly face and black lustrous hair slicked back in rippling waves. Wearing a crumpled linen suit and clutching a giant multicoloured umbrella, he was waiting with his companions in the hotel lobby. With him were Signor Toria, a very tall and thin inspector from Florence, most amiable-looking and, her curves somewhere between the two, a stunning Brigitte Bardot look-alike from Tours called Simone.

The foreign inspectors had arrived late the previous evening and gone straight to the hotel where they were staying. Sidney, David and I now arrived early the next morning at the hotel to collect them and take them round the selected schools. Over the next two days, they would observe some teaching, talk to teachers and learn a little about the English education system. Of course, it was Sidney who made a bee-line for the divine Simone and whisked her off before we could discuss who was accompanying whom. It ended up with David Pritchard taking tall, thin Signor Toria, and me with the plump, little Spaniard.

Carlos Itturiaga talked all the way to the car like a revolving door: round and round he went, chattering, commenting, laughing and asking questions and all the while shrugging, gesticulating, rolling his eyes and waving his plump-fingered hands in every direction. I had imagined that the initial conversations with our foreign visitors would be rather stilted and formal and therefore I was greatly relieved to find such a bubbly and uninhibited companion. By the time we arrived at the first school on our itinerary I had learnt all about Vigo, the city where he lived, his family, his interests, and I was pretty well conversant with the whole of the Spanish education system and his own views on teaching and learning.

From Fettlesham, I took the scenic route to the first school and wound my way, in low gear, up a track which twisted and turned like a coiled spring. I had travelled this narrow road many times before and knew what an amazing panorama we would see when we reached the brow of the very steepest hill. Presently, I pulled over into a small lay-by so my companion could view the serene beauty of the scene which lay below the bare lonely hills, largely treeless and austere, the craggy outcrops of rock sticking up out of the dead bracken.

Señor Itturiaga immediately ceased his constant chatter and stared out of the car window. 'It ees very beautiful,' he said. 'Not at all as I expected. I was told England ees very green, very flat, lots of trees and plenty of water.'

'You are in Yorkshire, Carlos,' I told him. 'There is nothing quite like Yorkshire. It's called God's own country.'

'And it ees cold,' he observed. 'It ees very cold for me at thees time of the year.'

'Now in Yorkshire we would say you were "nesh".'

'Nesh?' He tilted his head quizzically.

'Rather sensitive to the cold.'

'Nesh,' he repeated. 'Nesh. Very interesting.'

Below us stretched a vast canvas of empty grey moorland, scattered with great jags of rock. It was a rugged and primitive landscape, naked save for a few hardy, grubby-looking sheep which were foraging for food, and a small copse of skeletal trees clawing for the sky. In the far distance, pale purple hills shrouded in a smoky mist rose majestically to a pale blue sky. It was an awesome sight. Returning to the car, we dropped down into the village huddled round the old church in the bottom of the valley.

Loxley Chase was typical of a Dales village school: a square and solid stone building enclosed by low, craggy, limestone walls. While we were waiting for the headteacher, Mr Leatherboy, Carlos stood looking out of a window at the magnificent view up to the fells beyond.

Following a tour of the school with Mr Leatherboy, Carlos and I joined a junior class and a group of twenty or so seven- to eleven-year-olds. It was one of the healthiest groups of youngsters I had ever seen: sturdy bodies, rosy-red cheeks, bright eyes and clear complexions. The children obviously came from good farming stock and spent a great deal of the time outdoors.

'Why do the sheep on the hills have a red colour on their backs?' asked Carlos of a stocky boy.

'Tha knaas.'

'Pardon?' asked Carlos.

'I said tha knaas.'

'Tha knaas?' repeated my colleague, appearing completely flummoxed. He looked appealingly in my direction. 'Translate, plees.'

'He is sure you already know,' I replied. 'I'm afraid my friend doesn't know,' I told the boy, 'and, for that matter, I don't either.'

'Tha does,' chuckled the boy.

'No, no, I don't.'

'Gerron wi' thee! Tha does.'

'Really,' I laughed. 'I don't know.'

The boy looked at me with a wry smile on his face and a twinkle in his brown eyes which were strangely speckled. He then glanced out of the window at the sheep lazily cropping the grass on the hillside beyond. Many of the sheep were splashed with red at the end of their backs. 'Are tha 'avin' me on,' he asked, 'or dunt tha reeally knaa?'

'I'm not joking,' I told him. 'I really don't know. Is it to tell which shepherd they belong to?'

'Nay,' said the lad. 'They all belong to t'same shepherd. They're ruddled.'

'Ruddled?' I repeated.

'Aye, in some dales they say "raddled" but up 'ere we says "ruddled".'

Carlos looked at me and repeated the word slowly, 'Ruddled. Very interesting.'

I shrugged and turned back to the boy. 'I'm still in the dark,' I told him.

'Well, tha sees,' began the boy, 'on yer fells yonder is a goodly number of "yows"—them's ewes—female sheep, and one or two "tups"—rams, male sheep. Are tha wi' me so far?'

'I am.'

'Reight then. Tha dunt need many tups. Does tha know why?'

'Yes, I'm still with you. Go on.'

'Reight then, t'shepherd puts an 'arness under yer tup's belly, sooart o' leather strap affair wi' a sooart of big red wax crayon in it. It 'angs down under 'im. Are tha still wi' me?'

The scales were falling from my eyes. 'Yes. I've got the picture now, thank you very much. I think I can work the rest out for myself. Shall we have a look at your writing book?'

'Naa then.' The boy was not going to be stopped half way through his explanation, so carried on regardless. 'When 'e's served a yow—does tha—'

'Yes, I know what that means,' I interrupted.

'Well, when 'e's served a yow, t'tup leaves 'is mark on 'er back which means she's been ruddled. Does tha follow mi drift?'

'Yes, I've got the idea,' I said.

'Cooarse, if there's no colour on 'er back at all, then tha knaas t'tup's not been doin' what Nature's intended 'im to do, and 'e needs a bit o' encouragin' like. T'shepherd knaas, tha sees, that she's not been seen to.'

'Fascinating,' I said quickly. 'So, shall we look at your book?'

'What language ees thees boy speaking?' asked Carlos, looking completely dumbfounded. 'I thought my Engleesh was quite good, but I have not understood a seengle word.'

'It's "Yorkshire"—a variation of English,' I told him. 'Dialect.'

'Thees "seen to",' he asked, still with a puzzled expression on his round face. 'Could you explain thees "seen to" for me, plees?'

'It's rather complicated,' I told him. 'I'll explain it later.'

'Now then, during some parts o' year,' continued the boy, 'you don't want your tup bothering t'yows, so you put 'er in 'er winter clouts. They're sort of triangles of jute sacking which you stitch to your yow's back end to stop your tup from—'

'Yes, I've got the idea,' I interrupted. 'But why doesn't the shepherd just put the ram in a different field if he wants him away from the ewes?'

The boy shook his head. 'We're talkin' Swaledales, mester. Your hardy, black-faced Swaledales are at hooam on t'fells and moorland. You don't fence 'em in. They dooan't stop in t'fields all year round, tha knaas. They wander free and yer yows are only brought down to t'valley at lambing time to give birth in t'fields near t'farm buildings. Then they're driven back on t'hills. Now, with yer winter clouts—'

I thought it appropriate at this point to try and change the subject again. 'Do you do much poetry in class?' I asked.

'Poetry?' repeated the boy. 'Aye, we do some poetry. But I was tellin' you about t'winter clouts.'

'Perhaps another time,' I said.

'Waay,' said the boy, a flash of anger in his eyes, 'it were your pal what brought it up. I were only anwerin' 'im, when 'e asked about sheep bein' "ruddled".' With that, he shook his head again and got on with his work.

*   *   *

At morning break, while Carlos quizzed Mr Leatherboy about the English education system, I strolled around the front of the school, breathing in the fresh air and marvelling at the panorama before me.

'Admirin' t'view?'

I turned to find a small man with a huge hawk-like nose and the small down-turned mouth of a peevish child. He was attired in a grey overall and carried two long-handled spades.

'Yes, it's beautiful,' I said. 'Are you the school

389

caretaker?'

'Site manager,' he corrected me.

'Doing a bit of gardening?'

'I'm bloody not!' he exclaimed. 'I've got enough on looking after t'building wi'out goin' searchin' for work. I'm after t'rabbits this mornin'. There's 'undreds of 'em. I trap 'em, net 'em, gas 'em, poison 'em, block up their warrens. I've 'ad mi ferrets down their 'oles, mi Jack Russell catching 'em but they go on breedin' like . . . like . . .'

'Rabbits?' I ventured.

'Aye, they do. I'm after t'diseased uns today, them wi' myxomytosis. I don't like rabbits, but it's a terrible sight to see 'em all deformed and crippled. I wait until t'kiddies are in school, then come out wi' mi spades to dispose of 'em.' He lowered his voice to a whisper. 'Look, there's a couple of 'em ovver by t'wall. Can you see 'em?' The creatures he pointed out looked pathetic indeed, hunched up with their pale grey eyes seeing nothing. 'Only 'umane thing to do is to put 'em out of their misery. One short, sharp smack wi' mi spade and then I bury 'em in t'field yonder. If you leave 'em, they die a long and lingering death. Terrible disease is myxomytosis. I wouldn't wish it on any creature, even on rabbits.' He looked around conspiratorially. 'Of course, I 'ave to be very discreet about it. I don't want t'children peering out of t'classroom windows to see me flattening a rabbit wi' a spade. It'd give 'em nightmares. So I wait till they're all in t'playground at t'other side of t'school and then I do what 'as to be done. You see, if I don't dispose of 'em, kiddies might go up and touch 'em and we can't be 'avin' that, now can we?'

'No, we can't,' I agreed.

390

Then, before I could protest, he thrust a spade into my hand. 'Come on,' he said. 'You can 'elp me.'

'No, no,' I said, 'I really couldn't.'

'I'll do t'disposin', you just make sure they don't go back to their 'oles. Not that they look as if they're goin' anywhere.'

I followed him charily towards the poor creatures and watched the executioner raise his instrument of death high above his head. He took a deep breath and was about to bring the spade down with a sickening thud onto a shivering little creature, when Carlos and a group of chattering children appeared from around the side of the school. The small group froze in amazement.

With great presence of mind, the caretaker skipped towards me and tapped my spade handle with his. 'Pretend we're morris dancin',' he said, out of the corner of his mouth.

*　　　*　　　*

I was dismayed to learn from the headteacher later that morning that Mrs Savage was to make an appearance. No doubt she wanted to check up on things and make her presence felt.

'There's a very nice little pub in the village,' Mr Leatherboy told me. 'I expect the three of you will want to go out for something to eat so you can discuss things.'

Under no circumstances was I having lunch with Mrs Savage. 'Oh no,' I said. 'I always eat with the children when I visit schools. It's an excellent opportunity to meet them informally and I always find they are far more relaxed and talkative over the dinner table. We'll have school lunch here, if that is all right.'

'Of course,' replied the headteacher, 'it's fish fingers today.'

Mrs Savage, resplendent in her early spring ensemble—a pale cream suit and matching accessories—was all smiles and jangling jewellery when she sailed past the school secretary and through the headteacher's door.

'*Buenos días*,' she said, holding out a manicured hand to the Spanish inspector.

'*Ah, buenos días, señora*,' replied Carlos.

'I'm afraid "*Buenos días*" is about the extent of my Spanish, Señor Itturiaga,' said Mrs Savage, giving him the most charming of smiles. 'I do so love Spain. The sunshine, the colours, the people, the wine. I am Brenda Savage, Personal Assistant to Dr Gore, the Chief Education Officer, by the way. You'll be meeting the CEO tomorrow evening, Señor Itturiaga, at our little reception.'

'Carlos, plees.'

'Carlos,' she said somewhat breathlessly.

If was as if the headteacher and I were invisible.

'This is Mr Leatherboy, the headteacher,' I said stiffly. 'This is Mrs Savage.'

'Good morning,' said the headteacher. I could see he was rather put out by this woman swanning into his office without a word to him.

'I've just popped in to see how things are going,' said Mrs Savage, as if she were in complete charge of the whole undertaking.

'Things are going very well,' I said. 'You needn't have troubled yourself.'

'Oh, it's really no trouble. As you are aware, Dr Gore is particularly keen that this visit from our

European friends should go well.'

'Well, things are going extremely well,' said the headteacher. 'In fact—'

'I'm very pleased to hear it.' She looked at me. 'And have you lunched?' she asked.

'We were just about to eat,' I said, 'if you would care to join us.'

'Very much,' she trilled. 'There's a very quaint and typically English country inn in the village, The Marquis of Granby, quite famous for its seafood, I hear.'

I cut her short. 'We're eating with the children, Mrs Savage,' I said. 'We always do when we visit schools. I'm sure you have no objection.'

'Oh,' she replied, making a face. 'Actually eating with the children?'

'Yes, that's right,' I said, suppressing a smile.

'That would be very nice,' she lied.

'And, as it so happens, it's a seafood delicacy today,' I told her, giving the headteacher a sideways glance.

'Really?'

'Yes, fish fingers.'

I very much enjoyed watching Mrs Savage's discomfiture as she sat on a long wooden bench designed for small children, sandwiched between two rather messy little infant eaters who chattered without pausing, liberally spitting out food. Mrs Savage managed to force down half a fish finger and two chips before placing her knife and fork together.

'Are you 'avin' them fish fingers?' asked the little girl on her right.

'No, dear, I'm not,' replied Mrs Savage.

'Can I have 'em?'

'Please do.'

'Are you 'avin' yer chips?'

'No, dear.'

'Can I 'ave them, an' all?'

'Yes, you may.'

'Are you 'avin' your yoghurt?' asked the child on her left.

'No.'

'Can I 'ave it?'

'Please do.' The fish fingers, chips and the yoghurt were quickly commandeered. 'Well,' said Mrs Savage, 'if you will excuse me, I need to freshen up.' She turned to the child who had just scooped out a great spoonful of pink yoghurt. 'Could you tell me, dear, where the staff toilets are?'

'Over theer,' replied the child, waving the spoon in front of her and, in the process, spattering Mrs Savage with strawberry yoghurt.

Mrs Savage rose solemnly from the bench with surprising equanimity, stared for a moment at the thin pink line which ran across her pale cream suit with matching accessories, and took a deep breath. 'Thank you, dear,' she said, with a sour smile. 'Thank you so very much.'

*   *   *

Carlos and I visited four schools during the two days and my colleague seemed immensely impressed with the high standard of work, the excellent teaching, the rich and challenging environments and the friendly children, but he had some reservations when it came to the education of the small children.

394

'You know, Gervase,' he said to me as we drove back to Fettlesham at the end of the second afternoon, 'I do have to say that I think the children start their formal education in England too early. Small children should be allowed to play. Everything in the world ees new and exciting for small children. We should let them enjoy. Of course, reading and writing and the mathematics are important, but so are art and music and drama and playing with sand and water and everything that little ones so love to do. I just wonder whether thees young children ever get those little hands of theirs red with paint or covered in sticky clay, or if they ever build castles in the sand and fill up jars with water and go fishing for leetle feeshes. It ees just a thought.'

Carlos's thoughts about early education stayed with me many weeks after he had returned to Spain.

One thing that greatly impressed Carlos was the quality of the education in the small schools. He had expected the curriculum to be rather narrow and unadventurous and that the standards would be lower than in the larger schools. In fact, he found the opposite and became very animated.

'The small schools are quite *excepciónal*,' he told me on the way back to Fettlesham. 'I am very much in favour of the small schools. They are like families.'

I thought immediately of Hawksrill. 'You might share your observations with Dr Gore at the reception this evening,' I said. 'I am sure he would be very interested to hear your views on the quality of small rural schools.'

The Staff Development Centre was at its

burnished best the evening of the reception for the foreign inspectors. Connie had surpassed herself and the whole place sparkled. For the guests' arrival, she had abandoned the pink overall and feather duster in favour of a bright floral print dress and lemon-coloured cardigan, enhanced by a rope of large orange beads and an extremely colourful brooch in the shape of a parrot. Her hair had been recently permed and coloured bright copper.

'I didn't recognise you without your feather duster, Connie,' remarked Sidney as he walked with David and me into the entrance where she was standing sentinel.

'To what are you alluring?' asked Connie.

'I was merely observing how very nice you look this evening,' burbled Sidney.

'That's as may be. Anyway, there's that Semen woman looking for you,' she told him.

'I *beg* your pardon?'

'The French inspector, Semen.'

'Her name, Connie, is Simone,' Sidney informed her.

'Semen, Simone, whatever. I don't know why these foreigners have such funny names.' She huffed and turned to me. 'I've put the food in the lounge area as per instructed but there's no frogs' legs, snails, smelly French cheeses and the like and there's no fancy bagatelles, just plain Yorkshire baps. It's good simple English food what I've done. As I say, nothing fancy.'

'Spotted Dick?' enquired David mischievously.

'What?' asked Connie.

'Good plain English fare. Spotted Dick? Jam roly-poly? Yorkshire pudding? Tripe and onions?

Fish and chips?'

'It's a buffet,' Connie told him, pronouncing it 'buff-it', 'not a five-course meal.' Then, scowling at David, she said, 'You're getting as bad as him.'

'Ignore them, Connie,' I said. 'It sounds splendid.'

At this point Dr Gore, accompanied by Mrs Savage, joined us. Mrs Savage had certainly gone to town with her outfit. She wore a close-fitting mulberry-coloured wool suit, pale lilac chemise and matching silk scarf and court shoes. The heavy silver jewellery she was wont to wear had been abandoned in favour of delicate peridot earrings and matching pendant. She also wore a spectacular ring set with the pale green stones. She was, as always, impeccably made up.

'Good evening, good evening, everyone,' said the CEO, smiling and rubbing his hands together.

Connie, who had treated everyone in the same blunt manner, moved forward to welcome him. He was now on her territory and she did the greetings here.

'Hello, Brian,' she said.

I saw Mrs Savage wince. No one in the office referred to the Chief Education Officer by his first name. It just was not done. It was always Dr Gore or 'sir'.

However, Connie's familiarity never seemed to bother Dr Gore. He continued smiling and rubbing his hands. 'And a good evening to you, Connie,' he said pleasantly. 'I was very sorry to have heard about the death of your father.'

'Yes, well, he had a good life. By the way, thank you for your letter of convalescence. It was much appreciated.'

I cast Mrs Savage a sideways glance. She had pulled a familiar disapproving face.

'And how are you, Connie?' asked the CEO. 'No more thoughts of leaving us, I hope?' Before she could answer, he said, to no one in particular, 'Connie here used to clean my office down in the Annexe, when I was an education officer. Always left it spotless, did Connie.'

'Well, it's nice to be appreciated,' she said, looking knowingly in Sidney's direction.

'And we were an untidy lot, were we not, Connie?' continued Dr Gore.

'Not as untidy as some I could mention,' she said, looking at Sidney again.

'Well, Connie, the Centre is looking splendid as usual,' said the CEO, 'and I much appreciate that you have been able to arrange the refreshments and have given up an evening to help out.'

'It was my bingo tonight,' Connie told him.

'I am indeed most grateful.'

'As I was saying to Mr Phinn, Brian, there's nothing fancy.' It was Mrs Savage's turn now to receive the knowing look. 'Nothing fancy at all. I can't be doing with fancy things.'

'I am sure that the repast you have provided, Connie, will be first class. Now shall we go in and have a pre-prandial drink with the others?'

'Oh dear, I've none of that,' said Connie quickly. 'Just wine, orange juice or tea. Nobody said anything to me about prandials.'

The evening was a success. Dr Gore's address to the foreign inspectors and the invited headteachers went down well, Connie's plain English food was consumed with gusto, a good quantity of wine was drunk and the atmosphere was most convivial.

398

'Splendid evening,' enthused Dr Gore as he made ready to depart. 'Many thanks, Gervase, for all your hard work and for your sterling efforts, too, Brenda. You make a formidable team.' I kept a deliberately straight face. Mrs Savage raised an eyebrow. 'Our visitors have been most complimentary and will return to their respective countries, I am sure, suitably impressed.'

At this point, Connie materialised. She had put on her pink overall when she had served the food—and it clashed horribly with her new copper hair-do.

'Many thanks, Connie, for your help,' said Dr Gore. 'As efficient as ever.'

As Connie blushed prettily and preened a little, I could see out of the corner of my eye that Mrs Savage was looking thunderous.

'Sorry to butt in,' said Connie, 'but I was just coming to tell Mr Phinn that my steps what'd gone missing last autumn have suddenly turned up. You were right, Mr Phinn, the vicar had them. He kept them to put up the Christmas decorations in the church, and someone else tidied them away into the back of the vestry.'

'That's good news, Connie,' I said. 'But a bit late for that creeper to be pruned now.'

'No, it's all right. The chap from the Parks Department came ages ago with his own set of steps, and he cut that clitoris right back.'

*   *   *

'Well, the EIEI visit seemed to go very well,' said Sidney. It was Saturday morning and we were sitting in the lounge at the Staff Development

Centre having just said our farewells to the three inspectors.

'Signor Toria was delightful,' said David, who looked a whole lot happier than he had done for weeks. 'He's invited me over to Italy, you know, to see the schools there. Florence. *Firenze!*' he said expansively, waving his arms in the air. 'He said the standard of numeracy was higher in our county schools than in Italy. I must say I felt quite vindicated. Yes, he was absolutely delightful and spoke perfect English. After Welsh, I think that Italian is the most mellifluous of languages. They don't have a problem with spelling in Italy because Italian, based on Latin, of course, is a very logical and phonetic language. Very much like Welsh, you know. Why can't English be like that, Gervase?'

'Oh, let's not go down that road again, please,' begged Sidney.

'Actually, he felt very much at home, did Mario,' said David. 'I took him to Willingforth Primary and he thought he had arrived at an Italian school. There was a child shouting out at the gate: "*Mama mia! Mama mia!*" I had some difficulty in explaining to him that the boy was not, in fact, speaking Italian but trying to get his mother's attention on the other side of the road where she had just arrived. "Mum, I'm 'ere! Mum, I'm 'ere!" We did laugh,' chuckled David.

'I am delighted that you are back to your cheerful old self, David,' remarked Sidney. 'You have been as miserable as a jockey with haemorrhoids, lately.'

'Please, please don't mention haemorrhoids,' I said, thinking of my stay in hospital.

'You haven't got what my dear old Welsh

400

grandmother called "problems in your parts of dishonour", have you, Gervase?' asked David.

'No, I haven't,' I said quickly.

'Terribly painful are haemorrhoids,' said Sidney.

I changed the subject. 'And how was Simone?' I asked him. 'She seemed very amiable.'

'Amiable? Amiable?' scoffed Sidney. 'Hardly the most appropriate adjective to describe a woman of such outstanding beauty and composure. Simone was *ex*quisite.'

'And how did she cope with the Yorkshire dialect?' I asked.

'I had to translate a great deal of what the teachers said to her, let alone what the children said,' Sidney told us, leaning back on his chair. 'There were a number of little gems, like the child who informed her that the crayon she wanted for her drawing was not in the tin: "Tintintin." At one point she was asked by a little lad if we were together: 'Oo are tha wi', are tha wi' 'im?' She just stood and shrugged in that Gallic way they have. In another school, the teacher was describing the death of Admiral Nelson, how he was shot by a French sniper and lay dying in Captain Hardy's arms. One child piped up with the question: "And 'ow did 'ardy die?" She hadn't a chance, poor Mademoiselle de Marbot.'

'Never mind how she got on with the language,' said David. 'How on earth did she put up with you?'

'Actually,' said Sidney, 'we got on great guns, though I have to admit she did have a few difficulties appreciating my sense of humour.'

'Does anyone appreciate your sense of humour, Sidney?' asked David.

'Well, I certainty hope that Gervase does,' he replied.

'What do you mean?' I asked.

'Let me introduce you to someone, my dear friend and colleague,' he said. Then, in a strong American drawl, he continued. 'This is Brewster— John K. Brewster—and I'm with a delegation of Quakers from the States for the International Convention at York. I'd like to make you a proposition about the meeting house on your land.'

'Sidney!' I shouted, the truth dawning. 'You're a *monster!*'

CHAPTER TWENTY-FOUR

'Are you sure you'll be all right?' I asked.

It was the first night of *The Sound of Music*. Christine was intending to come with me but had been feeling rather tired and the thought of two and a half hours in the same position on a small seat in a stuffy theatre, listening to nuns climbing mountains, was not that appealing to her. She had told me, patting her very large stomach, that she had her very own mountain, without climbing any others.

'I'll be fine. Really,' she said. 'But I will be happier staying at home.'

'I don't suppose anybody would notice if I don't make an appearance,' I said. 'After all, I only have a couple of lines. I suppose Ray could fill in although he would rather swim in the uniform and, as I said before, I can't quite see him as an SS officer. Are you sure you don't want me to stay?'

'No!' she said firmly. 'From what you've told me of your producer, he would be in a real state if a member of the cast failed to turn up. I'm going to have a hot bath and go to bed with a cup of cocoa and a romantic novel.'

'If you're sure.'

'Do you want me to throw something at you?' she said. 'Go! I'll be fine.'

As it turned out, how wrong she was. The evening of the first performance of *The Sound of Music* would become a part of Phinn folklore.

* * *

Despite the fact that all the cast had arrived on time, the orchestra had its full complement and the Civic Theatre was beginning to fill up, Ray was in a panic, buzzing around like a jam-crazed wasp. The motif on his T-shirt seemed particularly apt for his state of mind: 'I used to have a handle on life— then it broke off.' That evening, he seemed to have a handle on very little, and he transmitted his twitchy nerves to some members of the cast.

When he saw my SS uniform, with a chest full of medals, hanging up in the dressing room, the shiny black boots and the frighteningly large Luger pistol in a leather holster, next to his shabby black suit and crumpled trilby hat, Mr Furnival felt quite aggrieved.

'I don't see why I can't have a uniform,' he told the producer. '*He's* got a uniform and he's got a lot smaller part than I have.' He sounded like a petulant child.

'That's because you're a Gauleiter and Gervase is an SS officer,' explained Ray. 'I told you that at

403

the dress rehearsal.'

'I think I would look a lot more threatening and sinister if I was in a black uniform,' persisted Mr Furnival.

'I think you look quite threatening and sinister enough in the black suit and hat,' said Ray.

'This is what I wear for funerals,' his vexed companion told him.

'Enough said,' remarked Ray.

'I thought I'd be in uniform,' complained Mr Furnival. 'I wear this black suit every day of my working life. I really do think I deserve a change.'

'You are not wearing a uniform,' said Raymond angrily, 'and that is that!'

'Well, what about the gun? Can I have the gun?'

'No, you can't.'

'Can I at least have a Tyrolean hat instead of the trilby?'

'Look, George!' snapped Ray. 'The directions say quite specifically that Herr Zeller wears a black suit with Nazi emblem on his lapel and not a uniform and he certainly wouldn't be wearing a Tyrolean hat. How threatening do you think he would look in a Tyrolean bloody hat?'

'Where's my Nazi emblem for my lapel, then? I haven't even got a Nazi emblem for my lapel,' moaned Mr Furnival, in no way mollified. He pointed to my uniform. 'He's got more medals on his chest than General Montgomery.'

'Well, improvise,' sighed Ray. 'Improvise. I'm sure in your line of work there's a lot of improvisation.'

'And what's that supposed to mean?' blustered Mr Furnival.

'Use your Rotary Club pin,' Ray told him.

Mr Furnival ballooned with anger. 'Use my Rotary Club pin! Use my Rotary Club pin! You must be mad. I'll have you know the Rotarians would have been the first to have been rounded up in this country if Hitler had won. We stand for Fellowship, Friendship and Service Above Self, not world domination. I'm not going on stage with my Rotary Club pin displayed for all to see. There's the District Governor in the audience. He'd have a seizure.'

'Stick a swastika over the top, then,' said Ray.

Before Mr Furnival could respond, a girl playing the part of a young nun arrived at the door of the dressing room with her costume over her arm. She was obviously very distressed.

'Come along, Bernice,' chivvied Ray, 'you should be in costume by now.'

'Mi mam says I can't be in it,' replied the girl sadly.

'Can't be in it!' exclaimed Ray. 'What does she mean, you can't be in it?'

'She says I can't be in it,' repeated the girl.

'She has left it a trifle late, hasn't she,' said Ray. 'It's opening night.'

'It's when I told her what I was playing,' said the girl, clearly very embarrassed. 'She said she didn't know there was any of *them* in *The Sound of Music* and she doesn't want me playing that sort of woman.'

'What sort of woman?' enquired the producer, mystified.

'That sort,' replied the girl, looking decidedly embarrassed.

'Bernice, darling,' said Raymond, trying to keep calm. 'I am not a mind-reader. I cannot read your thoughts. What does she mean, "that sort of woman"? She doesn't want you to play a nun? Has she some religious objection?'

'You said I was to be'—at this point the girl whispered theatrically—'a prostitute.'

'A prostitute!' gasped Ray. 'Has the world gone completely mad? Where in *The Sound of Music* is there a prostitute?'

'You said I was one.'

'Read my lips, Bernice. I said you were a postulant, a candidate for the religious life, a trainee nun, not a prostitute.'

'So I'm not a prostitute?' asked the girl.

'No, Bernice, you are not a prostitute,' said Ray. 'You are a postulant. Now, you ring your dear mother and tell her the good news and then get changed.' Ray flopped onto the chair beside me. 'Whatever next?' he asked. He did not have long to wait.

The rather spotty young man playing Rolf entered the fray. He waddled into the changing room slowly and carefully as if he had a ferret down his trousers.

'Ray, do I *have* to wear these leather shorts?' he asked, sucking in his breath as if he had acute indigestion. 'They're cutting off my circulation.'

The producer looked heavenwards and sighed heavily. 'Yes, you have to wear the shorts, Fraser.'

'They are incredibly tight. I can hardly move.'

'They're *lederhosen*. They're supposed to be tight.'

'It's like having two tourniquets around my legs. I have difficulty walking in these shorts, never mind dancing. They really are very constricting and as for going to the toilet—'

406

'They'll give,' replied Ray. 'They're made of leather. Just move about a bit and—' He stopped mid-sentence as Mrs Cleaver-Canning sailed past the door in her capacious black Mother Abbess costume, hung with a huge silver cross. She was like a galleon in full sail with the wind behind it. Ray smacked his hand to his forehead dramatically and looked as if he was about to swoon.

'Margot, darling, could I have a small word?' he shouted after her.

Mrs Cleaver-Canning retraced her steps and made a stately entrance. 'Yes, Raymond?' she asked. 'What is it?'

'Oh my!' Ray exclaimed. 'Whatever have you got on your face?'

'My make-up,' she replied simply. 'What do you imagine I've got on my face?'

'Don't you feel you've gone just a teensy-weensy bit overboard with the greasepaint?'

'Not at all.'

'You cannot go on stage with that face, Margot,' moaned Ray. 'You look like a Liverpool tart.'

'I beg your pardon, Raymond!' she replied, giving him a lemon-sucking grimace.

'Don't you feel, just a smidgen, that scarlet cupid-bow lips, bright blue eye-shadow and crimson rouge are a touch out of character for a nun? You're supposed to be the Mother Abbess, not a woman of ill-repute looking for sailors on the dockside.'

'I deeply resent that analogy, Raymond,' responded Mrs Cleaver-Canning. 'This, for your information, is my normal make-up, slightly exaggerated for dramatic purposes, and I have not the slightest intention of removing it. And another thing, there is no possibility, no possibility at all, of Winco trimming his moustache. It may look somewhat out of character, I have to admit, for a German admiral, but he has had that handlebar since he was a pilot officer in the RAF and I don't—'

'Of course, you don't! Why should you?' snapped Ray petulantly. 'Why should anyone listen to me? I'm just the producer after all. My opinion counts for nothing.' He then pushed past her and strutted off, complaining to himself. 'I've just about had enough.'

'He'll be fine, once the curtain rises,' Mrs Cleaver-Canning told me calmly, adjusting her wimple in the mirror. 'One has to make allowances. Opening night nerves, that's all. He was the same last year when we did *Carousel*. Nearly fainted with the stress. It's always the case with these creative people. They're terribly temperamental. Charles, in my flower-arranging club, is just the same. If his arrangement is not exactly right he nearly breaks a blood vessel. Now, come along, Mr Phinn. You must see Winco in his German admiral's uniform. He looks quite dashing.'

*   *   *

Although I say it myself, the Fettlesham Literary Players put on the performance of their lives. Of course, it was Mrs Cleaver-Canning who stole the show, filling the hall with her deep, resonant contralto voice. Following the first rendering of 'Climb Every Mountain', the wholly enthusiastic audience demanded a reprise to which she graciously acceded. Everyone joined the von

408

Trapps with 'Edelweiss', they applauded loudly when the children danced, cheered when the Nazis were foiled and, much to Mr Furnival's delight, loudly hissed the Gauleiter each time he made an appearance.

When the curtain fell Ray danced onto the stage, ecstatic. 'Wonderful! Marvellous! Magnificent! Superlative! Margot, you were a *tour de force!*' he cried, embracing Mrs Cleaver-Canning—not that his little arms reached round more than half her considerable size. 'Oh my dears, I think I'm going to cry. You were all so so good.'

All the players were milling around on the stage, re-living the performance, exchanging recollections, laughing, when the theatre manager, a tall man with a thick black moustache and dressed in a dinner jacket and bow tie, appeared from the wings, like the pantomime villain. 'Is there a Mr Pin here?' he called loudly.

'Who?' asked Ray.

'A Mr Pin? I was told there was a Mr Pin in the cast.'

'There's a Mr Phinn.' I said. 'That's me.'

'Is your wife having a baby?'

'Yes, she is,' I replied, my heart beginning to pound.

'There's been a phone call.'

'A phone call?' I repeated faintly.

'From your wife.'

'Oh Lord, what did she say?' I asked, my stomach churning.

'She's gone to the hospital.'

'What? When?' My stomach was doing kangaroo jumps.

Everyone on the stage was hushed, listening to

the little drama.

'She told me to tell you not to worry. She's all right but her waters have broken and would you get there as soon as you can.'

'When was this phone call?' asked Mrs Cleaver-Canning angrily, pushing her way through people to where I was standing with the theatre manager.

'About half an hour ago,' he told her casually.

'What!' she hissed.

The man seemed to quail in front of her vast presence. 'I . . . I . . . would have said s . . . s . . . something but I didn't want to interfere with the p . . . p . . . performance.'

'You silly man!' snapped Mrs Cleaver-Canning. 'Did it not enter your tiny little head that it was important? His wife's having a baby!'

'I must go at once,' I said, feeling all hot and flustered. Mrs Cleaver-Canning, resting a chubby hand on my arm, said calmly, 'Now, *calma*, Gervase, deep breaths, deep breaths. Women have had babies before. Your wife will be fine. Now, you are in no fit state to drive. Winco will take you to the hospital in the Mercedes. Winco!' she bellowed. Her husband appeared, as if on cue, from behind a piece of mountain scenery.

'Here,' he shouted back.

'Bring the car around. We are taking Mr Phinn to the hospital.'

'Oh dear, is he unwell?'

Mrs Cleaver-Canning sighed. 'Just fetch the car, Winco.'

'Righto,' he replied. 'I had better change out of this costume. I can't very well—'

'There's not enough time,' his wife interrupted. 'We leave at once. Come along Winco. Get a

410

move on.'

*   *   *

We had hardly crawled out of the theatre car park, held up by people going home after the performance, when Mrs Cleaver-Canning prodded Winco in the back.

'Put your foot down, for goodness sake, Winco,' she commanded. 'Chop chop!'

'But you're always telling me to slow down,' he growled.

'Well, this time I'm telling you to get a move on and don't spare the horses.'

'Righto,' he replied, slamming his foot down on the accelerator and screeching away in a cloud of exhaust smoke.

Anyone sharp-eyed enough to have caught sight of the occupants of the Mercedes that evening as it sped through the centre of Fettlesham in the direction of Fettlesham Royal Infirmary would have thought they were hallucinating: an ageing German admiral with a handlebar moustache was at the wheel of the car, a heavily bemedalled SS officer was in the passenger seat, and an overweight nun with crimson lips and sky-blue eye-shadow was sitting in the back gesticulating.

We hadn't long been on Infirmary Road before we heard the siren and saw the flashing blue light.

'Pull over, Winco,' ordered Mrs Cleaver-Canning. 'And let me do the talking.'

'Righto.'

Moments later, a police patrolman was at the driver's window.

'Good evening, officer,' said Mrs Cleaver-

Canning from the back seat.

'Ah! Good evening, Sister,' replied the policeman, transferring his official gaze into the back of the car. If he was surprised to see such an extraordinary trio in the car, he certainly didn't show it and maintained a perfectly straight face. He must, I supposed, have come across some pretty bizarre situations in his time.

'Mother Abbess, in fact. But we are in rather a hurry,' Mrs Cleaver-Canning explained.

'You are indeed, Mother,' said the policeman, with just a trace of a smirk on his face. He looked at Winco. 'Worried that you might miss the boat, Admiral?'

'Officer,' said Mrs Cleaver-Canning, a wide smile on her crimson lips, 'this gentleman in the front is about to become a father.'

'Congratulations,' said the policeman, taking a notebook from his pocket.

'Have you children, officer?' she asked.

'I'm sorry, Mother?' Each time he used the word, he accentuated it a trifle.

'I said, have you any children?'

'I have, yes. I have a little girl.'

'And were you present when she was born?'

'I was indeed, Mother, and a very happy occasion it was, too,' he replied good-humouredly.

'Well, the wife of the gentleman in the black uniform is about to give birth, imminently, in fact, and he would very much like to be there for the happy event.'

I was getting agitated by the time that was being wasted. Yet I dared not interrupt for fear of turning the policeman against us.

'I see,' said the policeman. He turned his

412

attention to Winco. 'Are you aware, sir, that the speed limit in this area of the town—'

'And that is why we were travelling at speed,' continued Mrs Cleaver-Canning, 'in order for him to get to the hospital on time. His wife has already gone into labour. The birth might be moments away. We were aware of the speed limit but, as a father yourself, I am sure you can understand, officer, the urgency of getting to the hospital.'

'I appreciate that, Mother, but—' he began.

'Actually, I'm not really a nun.'

'You don't say,' said the policeman.

'We are members of the cast of *The Sound of Music* which is being performed at the Civic Theatre all this week. We are in costume because we hadn't the time to change when the call came from the hospital.'

The policeman's face lit up. 'That's my favourite musical, *The Sound of Music*,' he said. 'I was a von Trapp when we did it at school.'

'Really,' said Winco suddenly. 'Who did you play?'

'Never mind that now, Winco,' his wife said. 'With this officer's permission, we really do need to be on our way to the hospital without further delay.'

'If you would like to follow me, sir,' said the policeman, 'I'll give you an escort.'

'Thank you so much,' said Mrs Cleaver-Canning. 'I am a personal friend of the Chief Constable, you know, and I shall most certainly mention to him how very helpful you have been.'

*　　*　　*

The maternity wing of Fettlesham Royal Infirmary appeared particularly busy when we arrived. There were men with flowers, women with fruit, over-excited children who should have been in bed ages before, porters wheeling trolleys, doctors with clipboards, nurses scurrying hither and thither. It seemed that the whole county was giving birth that night.

Mrs Cleaver-Canning had swept through the doors and into the mêlée in a queenly manner and headed for the reception desk, with me following closely behind, Winco bringing up the rear. It was clear she was in charge. All conversation ceased when the majestic figure in a nun's habit strode to the front of a small queue and announced, 'If you would be so kind, this is an emergency.'

'You go ahead, Sister,' said the elderly woman at the front of the queue. 'I think you do a marvellous job. I was taught by nuns.'

'Thank you so much,' said Mrs Cleaver-Canning. Then, facing the startled man behind the reception desk she asked, 'Could you tell us where Mrs Phinn is, please? She was brought in earlier this evening in labour.'

The receptionist ran his finger down a list of names. 'No Thinnis here,' he said shaking his head.

'No, no! Phinn. The name is Phinn!'

'There's no Phinn here either.'

'There's no "f" in Phinn,' Mrs Cleaver-Canning told him.

'I beg your pardon, Sister!' he spluttered. 'There's really no need for that sort of language.'

'When I said there is no letter "f" in Phinn,' she told him, 'I meant the name begins with a "ph" as in Philip. P-H-I-N-N.'

414

'Oh, oh, I see,' he said, looking greatly relieved. 'Phinn with a "ph". Yes, here it is. First name Christine. Christine Patricia Phinn. She came in earlier this evening. She's in Ward 6.'

'Has the baby arrived yet?' I asked, my heart in my mouth.

The man stared for a moment at the uniform.

'What?' he asked.

'The baby, has the baby arrived yet?'

'This is the worried father,' Mrs Cleaver-Canning informed him.

'I can't say,' the receptionist told me, still eyeing the uniform. 'You'd better go straight down there now. Ward 6.'

'You've been marvellous,' I told Mrs Cleaver-Canning and Winco. 'Thank you so much. You really don't need to wait.'

'Nonsense!' said Mrs Cleaver-Canning. 'We would like to have a progress report first. You hurry off to see your wife. Winco and I will wait.'

'Little Sisters of the Poor,' I heard the elderly woman inform Mrs Cleaver-Canning as I headed in the direction of the wards. 'I was taught by Little Sisters of the Poor.'

I just had time to hear the reply. 'My dear, I am not a nun but if I were to contemplate entering the religious life it would not be as a Little Sister of the Poor. I am neither little nor, thank God, poor.'

I was just in time. Christine was being wheeled to the delivery room when I rushed down the corridor in search of Ward 6. I was in such a panic, hot, flustered, out of breath, that I ran straight past her and only when I heard her voice did I stop and retrace my steps.

'I'm here!' she cried.

'Thank God!' I said, bending down and giving her a hug. 'Are you all right, darling?'

'She's fine,' said the nurse who was by the side of the trolley. 'This is the husband, I presume?'

'This is the husband,' Christine said.

My panic fled as I looked down at the smiling mother-to-be. She looked calm and serene. Her blue eyes shone, her blonde hair fell about her shoulders like a golden curtain. She looked rosy-cheeked and so beautiful. I squeezed her hand.

'Are you ready?' I asked.

'As ready as I'll ever be,' she replied softly.

'Typical man,' said the nurse. 'Leaves it to the last minute, when it's all over, bar the shouting. If only men had to have babies. I suppose you want to be in at the birth.'

'Of course,' I said.

'Well, if you faint, nobody will bother with you. I've got a far more important person to deal with.'

'I won't faint,' I said confidently.

'Aye, bigger men than you have said that.' She caught sight of the uniform. 'Didn't anyone tell you the war is over? What on earth are you wearing? No, don't tell me. I probably wouldn't believe you, anyway. Just cover yourself up or you'll frighten the nurses. You need to get a gown and mask before you come into the delivery room, and get those boots covered up. I'll show you where they are in a moment. And keep out of my way.'

'Yes nurse,' I said meekly.

At ten-thirty, Richard Leslie Phinn was born, weighing in at 7 lbs 1 oz. As I cradled him in the crook of my arm and stroked his little head, my eyes began to fill. He was so tiny and delicate, red as a radish, with a small round face, soft wisps of golden hair and great blue eyes. He was his mother's son all right.

'Richard Leslie?' said the nurse, giving me a wry smile. 'Is that what you're calling him?'

'That's right,' I told her. 'Richard after my father and Leslie after my wife's.'

'Oh,' she said, 'I thought you would call him Adolf.'

*　　　*　　　*

Because little Richard Leslie had arrived prematurely, Christine stayed in hospital for the next few days. I visited her and my son every day that week, usually in the early evening before I went down to the theatre for the evening performance. Harold had immediately told me to take some time off, but I was happy to work during the day while Christine was still in the Royal Infirmary, planning to be at home the week they returned. On the Friday, we sat together with our child between us, marvelling at his tiny fingers and toes, his head of soft silky blond hair and his great blue eyes. Although a little tired, Christine looked radiant. We were both so happy.

'Motherhood really suits you,' I told her. 'I'd like another five, please.'

'We'll talk about that when we get home,' she said. The baby stirred. 'He's a little tinker, this one,' she said, stroking the baby's cheek. 'He cries for his milk and then takes ages getting started. The nurses are being very kind, and helping as much as possible, but it is hard work.'

'I'll have a strong word with him,' I said. 'We should start as we mean to go on.' I stroked the baby's head gently. 'Are you listening to me, young man,' I said. 'You must drink plenty of milk. Then you'll grow to be big and strong.' The baby screwed up his little face and gave a great burp.

'There's your answer,' laughed Christine.

'I've already bought him a book,' I told her.

'A book!' she exclaimed.

'Well, we'll have to get him reading soon. Then he'll need some building blocks and a colouring book and a paintbox and a sand pit in the garden and—'

'So speaks the school inspector,' said Christine, smiling.

'I want our son to have the very best start in life,' I said. 'The very best.' As I looked down at our baby, snuggling up to his mother, I thought of little Matty and the other sad, fragile children whom I had come across on my travels as a school inspector; children who were neglected, disparaged, damaged and sometimes abused, children who would never know the warmth, encouragement and love of a good home.

'Penny for them,' said Christine.

'I'm just thinking how very lucky I am,' I said, and kissed her most tenderly.

'I see you've been demobbed,' said the ward sister, coming in at that moment.

'I'm sorry?'

'Out of uniform.'

'Oh, that. I'm in a play. I'm not really an SS officer, you know.'

'You do surprise me,' she said, examining the chart at the foot of the bed.

'I'm a school inspector actually.'

'Oh, is there a difference?' she said.

418

'I shan't respond to that,' I told her.

'The doctor's been and everything is fine,' said the sister. 'Mother and baby are doing very well, so you can take them home when you're ready. Now, do try and persevere with the breast-feeding, Mrs Phinn. Tricky Dickie will soon get a taste for it and then there'll be no stopping him.'

As Christine was packing the few things she had in her bedside cabinet, I picked the clipboard off the bottom of the bed. The sheet of paper attached to it read 'Fettlesham Royal Infirmary/Maternity Unit'. Below was 'BABY: Richard Leslie Phinn. WEIGHT: 7lbs 1oz.' Then, at the bottom was space for 'DOCTOR'S COMMENT'. I was removing the sheet of paper when the ward sister came in and caught me red-handed.

'What are you up to?' she asked.

'May I have this, please?'

'No, you may not. It's hospital property.'

'Oh please,' I begged.

'It's more than my job's worth.'

'Please.'

'Why do you want it, anyway?'

'I want to keep it until my son is twenty-one,' I told her seriously, 'and on that birthday I want to present it to him in a gilt frame, saying: "When I am dead and gone, Richard, perhaps you might sometimes look upon that scrap of paper in the golden frame and remember this very special day, your coming of age, and I hope you might remember a father and a mother who were so very proud of you and loved you more than any other parents loved a son. You see, it's the first thing anybody wrote about you." I shall tell him, "It is the doctor's comment written during your first

419

week of life." You see, sister, that is why I want to keep this sheet of paper.'

'Oh,' said the nurse, who had listened open-mouthed to my commentary. 'How lovely. You're making me cry. And what does the doctor say?'

Smiling, I passed over the piece of paper so she could read what the doctor had written: 'Poor sucker.'

A Parent's Prayer

Always believe in yourself.
Promise always to be compassionate.
Appreciate that you make mistakes.
Recognise that I do too.
Entrust me with your worries.
Never doubt that I will support you when you
    need me.
Talk to me about the things you find difficult.
Share your dreams.
Please understand that I can have moods just
    like you.
Receive a little advice now and again.
Accept that I sometimes get things wrong.
You need to help me to get things right.
Enjoy your life.
Realise that I love you without reservation.